# PSHE Education

## for Key Stage 4

Teacher's Resource Book

Lesley de Meza, Stephen De Silva
& Philip Ashton

DYNAMIC LEARNING

HODDER EDUCATION
AN HACHETTE UK COMPANY

The Publishers would like to thank the following for permission to reproduce copyright material:

**Acknowledgements**

Matching Grids to Key Stage 4 Programmes of Study (on the CD): Qualifications & Curriculum Development Agency (QCDA); p47: Activity adapted from *Risk-Taking* by Lesley de Meza and Paul Law (Me-and-Us, 2008); p67: Teen survey results, Palo Alto Medical Foundation, www.pamf.org/teen/life/stress/whatstress.html; pp197–8: adapted from information found on www.ecademy.com.

Crown copyright material is reproduced under Class Licence Number C02P0000060 with the permission of the Controller of HMSO.

Every effort has been made to trace all copyright holders, but if any have been inadvertently overlooked the Publishers will be pleased to make the necessary arrangements at the first opportunity.

Although every effort has been made to ensure that website addresses are correct at time of going to press, Hodder Education cannot be held responsible for the content of any website mentioned in this book. It is sometimes possible to find a relocated web page by typing in the address of the home page for a website in the URL window of your browser.

Hachette UK's policy is to use papers that are natural, renewable and recyclable products and made from wood grown in sustainable forests. The logging and manufacturing processes are expected to conform to the environmental regulations of the country of origin.

Orders: please contact Bookpoint Ltd, 130 Milton Park, Abingdon, Oxon OX14 4SB. Telephone: (44) 01235 827720. Fax: (44) 01235 400454. Lines are open 9.00–5.00, Monday to Saturday, with a 24-hour message answering service. Visit our website at www.hoddereducation.co.uk.

© Lesley de Meza, Stephen De Silva & Philip Ashton, 2011
First published in 2011 by
Hodder Education,
An Hachette UK Company
338 Euston Road
London NW1 3BH

Impression number    5    4    3    2    1
Year                         2015  2014  2013  2012  2011

Cover photo © Image Zoo Illustration/Veer
Typeset in Arial 10.5/12pt by Fakenham Prepress Solutions, Fakenham, Norfolk NR21 8NN
Printed in Great Britain by Hobbs the Printers, Totton, Hants

A catalogue record for this title is available from the British Library

ISBN: 978 1444 12072 1

# Contents

# Introduction

## About PSHE Education

Personal, Social, Health and Economic (PSHE) education is a planned programme of learning opportunities and experiences that help young people grow and develop as individuals and as members of families and of social and economic communities.

This resource is intended to support the provision of PSHE education in secondary schools. It should be used in the context of a whole-school approach to meeting the statutory aims of the curriculum to which PSHE education is essential. The aims are to enable all young people to become:

- successful learners who enjoy learning, make progress and achieve
- confident individuals who are able to live safe, healthy and fulfilling lives
- responsible citizens who make a positive contribution to society.

PSHE education is described in two interrelated Programmes of Study, one for personal well-being and one for economic well-being and financial capability.

The Programmes of Study should be used flexibly to ensure that PSHE education provision is appropriate to students' needs. It is important to provide opportunities to address real life and topical issues and show students that they can make a difference to their own and others' lives.

The Programmes of Study for PSHE education – as in all other subjects – have their main focus on key concepts and processes rather than content. Each programme of study includes:

- an importance statement that describes why the subject matters and how it can contribute to the aims
- key concepts that define the big ideas that underpin the subject
- key processes – the essential skills of the subject
- range and content, setting out the breadth of subject matter which teachers should draw on to develop the key concepts and skills
- curriculum opportunities that enhance and enrich learning, increasing its relevance and making links to the wider curriculum.

The key **concepts** for PSHE education in **personal well-being** are:

- personal identities
- healthy lifestyles
- risk

- relationships
- diversity.

The key **processes** for PSHE education in **personal well-being** are:

- critical reflection
- decision-making and managing risk
- developing relationships and working with others.

The key **concepts** for PSHE education in **economic well-being and financial capability** are:

- career
- capability

- risk
- economic understanding.

Introduction

The key **processes** for PSHE education in **economic well-being and financial capability** are:

- self-development
- exploration
- enterprise
- financial capability.

# About the course

The course is based on the two PSHE education Programmes of Study and includes the following resources:

- Student's Book
- Teacher's Resource Book
- Dynamic Learning online – this is a subscription service (see www.dynamic-learning.co.uk) which provides the Student's Book as an e-book with additional digital resources, such as video, images, interactive activities and weblinks, to further enhance the teaching and learning of the course.

The resources are organised into 11 chapters:

1  *The Media and Young People*
2  *Healthy Choices*
3  *Emotional and Mental Health*
4  *Relationships*
5  *Diversity*
6  *Values*
7  *Consumerism*
8  *Personal Finance*
9  *The Future*
10 *Employability*
11 *Business and Enterprise*

Each chapter is divided into a series of topics which include a range of issues for students to consider. The topics are organised into lessons which are designed to:

- help students focus on the main points they need to learn by providing learning objectives and structuring the activities around them
- give students the opportunity to develop the skills they need through a variety of activities
- encourage students to feel confident in sharing their thoughts and feelings in a supportive atmosphere.

The activities provide opportunities for students to explore the key concepts of PSHE education. They have been designed to be used as stand-alone activities as well as part of a structured sequence to form the longer lesson; so, depending on how PSHE education is organised in your institution, they can be used in more 'bite-sized' chunks if needed. They are designed to help students:

- recognise and manage risk
- take increasing personal responsibility in choices and behaviours
- make positive contributions to family, school and community
- begin to understand the nature of the world of work, the diversity and function of business and its contribution to national prosperity
- develop as a questioning and informed consumer
- learn to manage money and finances effectively.

The activities' active, student-centred nature ensures that students develop skills relevant to the subject. The approaches are compatible with the curriculum opportunities described in the two PSHE education Programmes of Study, ensuring that the learning is developed in varied and relevant ways and that young people make links with the world outside the classroom. Activities may also contribute to cross-curricular dimensions such as healthy lifestyles, identity and cultural diversity, and community participation.

In the Teacher's Resource Book each topic begins with a summary of the main learning points and how they link into the Programmes of Study. There are then advice and answers for the activities in the Student's Book. The topic ends with an opportunity for students to review and reflect on their learning. This essential requirement of PSHE education enables them to retain skills, knowledge and understanding, and helps them to transfer learning to real-life situations.

Each chapter in the Teacher's Resource Book ends with an extended assessment opportunity based on one of the activities from the chapter.

# Assessment

Assessment in PSHE education needs to be undertaken for a variety of reasons:

- As with any area of learning, students should have the entitlement to reflect on their progress and to set targets for future learning.
- Assessment can demonstrate that the subject makes a difference.
- It can show that students are achieving in PSHE in ways that can help them succeed in other areas of the curriculum.

Assessment for learning in PSHE education happens naturally. Many of the topics in this book begin with questions to prompt reflection on what students may already know about the topic before moving on to reflect on what else could help them understand it more fully.

Assessment of progress and achievement has been more challenging for PSHE Education. Because of the personal nature of much of the work, there can be the potential here to stray into the realm of making judgements about an individual's worth, personality or value. The authors would discourage such an approach which often equates assessment with grades or marks.

We would encourage schools to use assessment in its broadest sense – evidence can take many different forms (it doesn't have to be death by worksheet!).

All good PSHE assessment needs to reflect:

- a whole-school approach
- regular opportunities planned from the outset of the course
- assessment tasks that are inclusive of all students
- active involvement of students in their own assessments
- use of a variety of opportunities and evidence.

Assessment in PSHE naturally begins with self-reflection on progress. Its aim would be to identify how new or developing understanding, skills and values could be used to enhance personal statements.

# ASSESSMENT TASKS IN PSHE EDUCATION 4

Each topic within the Student's Book has a series of tasks which have the potential to be used for assessment opportunities. Notes in this Teacher's Resource Book provide guidance on how to manage feedback and reflection.

In addition there are a series of identifiable opportunities to carry out an optional and more in-depth assessment.

**Teachers will need to have planned and thought about the use of these optional assessment opportunities <u>before</u> they start a chapter**. This will enable them either to take more time with the task being performed – or alternatively to flag up with students a return to that task at some future point.

We have used the non-statutory PSHE End of Key Stage Statements (EKSS) to provide the criteria for reflection and assessment in each case. The grid below shows where these assessment opportunities arise in each chapter:

| Chapter | Topic | Activity | Page | End of Key Stage Statement |
|---|---|---|---|---|
| 1 The Media and Young People | Health | 6 & 7: Using positive language | 13–14 (TRB)*<br><br>13 (SB)** | **Healthy lifestyles**<br>Learners are able to:<br><br>■ describe the short- and long-term consequences of personal health choices, including choices relating to sexual activity and substance use and misuse, and make decisions based on this knowledge. |
| 2 Healthy Choices | Drugs | 5: Drugs – who is most responsible? | 38 (TRB)*<br>25 (SB)** | **Healthy lifestyles**<br>Learners are able to:<br><br>■ identify reasons why people might use illegal drugs and explain how drug use can impact on physical, mental and economic aspects of people's lives, relationships and the wider community. |
| 3 Emotional and Mental Health | Facing challenges | 3: Problem-solving | 74 (TRB)*<br>46 (SB)** | **Healthy lifestyles**<br>Learners are able to:<br><br>■ identify some of the causes and symptoms of mental and emotional ill health, and identify strategies for recognising, preventing and addressing these in themselves and others. |

*PSHE Education for Key Stage 4 Teacher's Resource Book © Hodder Education*

| Chapter | Topic | Activity | Page | End of Key Stage Statement |
|---|---|---|---|---|
| 4 Relationships | Where to turn for help and support | 2: Who can they speak to? | 98 (TRB)*<br><br>61 (SB)** | **Healthy lifestyles**<br>Learners are able to:<br><br>demonstrate confidence in finding professional health advice and help others to do so. |
| 5 Diversity | Challenging discrimination | 3: Children with HIV & 4: Point of view | 108–109 (TRB)*<br><br>67 (SB)** | **Diversity**<br>Learners are able to:<br><br>■ take the initiative in challenging or giving support in connection with offensive or abusive behaviour. |
| 6 Values | Diverse and conflicting values | 4: Different values | 122–123 (TRB)*<br><br>73 (SB)** | **Diversity**<br>Learners are able to:<br><br>■ explain how differing cultures, faiths and beliefs may influence lifestyle choices, and demonstrate respect for these differences. |
| 7 Consumerism | Ethical consumerism | 4: What else do you want to know? | 130–131 (TRB)*<br><br>78 (SB)** | **Financial capability**<br>Learners are able to:<br><br>■ critically evaluate a wide range of goods and services from the consumer's point of view. |
| 8 Personal finance | Budgeting | 5: The dream retirement | 141 (TRB)*<br><br>85 (SB)** | **Financial capability**<br>Learners are able to:<br><br>■ explain some of the financial products and services that will help them manage their current and future personal finances, identify a range of post-16 options and careers advice and support networks that they can use to plan and negotiate their career pathways. |

| Chapter | Topic | Activity | Page | End of Key Stage Statement |
|---|---|---|---|---|
| 9  The Future | Study or employment – what's out there? | 1: What are my options? | 162 (TRB)* <br><br> 95 (SB)** | **Economic well-being and financial capability** <br> Learners are able to: <br><br> ■ identify a range of post-16 options and careers advice and support networks that they can use to plan and negotiate their career pathways, relate their abilities, attributes and achievements to career plans, setting personal targets and evaluating choices. |
| 10  Employability | Creating a Curriculum Vitæ (CV) | 2 & 3: My CV | 171 (TRB)* <br><br> 101 (SB)** | **Career** <br> Learners are able to: <br><br> ■ complete application procedures, including CVs and personal statements, and prepare for interviews. |
| 11  Business and Enterprise | The world of business | 5: Marketing a product | 193–194 (TRB)* <br><br> 117 (SB)** | **Financial capability** <br> Learners are able to: <br><br> ■ demonstrate a range of enterprise skills when working independently and with others, and critically evaluate a wide range of goods and services from the consumer's point of view. |

\* TRB = Teacher's Resource Book
\*\* SB = Student's Book

# 1 The Media and Young People

## Topic: Body image

| | |
|---|---|
| **Notes** | It used to be said, 'beauty is in the eye of the beholder'. Nowadays that can be hard to believe since we're constantly bombarded with visual images of the 'perfect body' – slim, gym-toned bodies that for many of us are far removed from our natural shape and appearance.<br><br>This topic starts the investigation of the media by looking at what 'beautiful' means. It investigates the machinery of the media and the effect this has on our perceptions of body image and ultimately, our self-esteem. |
| **Learning outcomes** | **In this topic students will learn about:**<br>■ how the media influences the way we see ourselves<br>■ how issues of 'body image' in the media affect people's health.<br><br>**They will explore:**<br>■ whether males and females feel differently about body image<br>■ how the 'deficit model' is used to sell things to us. |
| **Links to Personal Well-being PoS** | **1.1 Personal identities**<br>**a** Understanding that identity is affected by a range of factors, including a positive sense of self.<br><br>**2.1 Critical reflection**<br>**d** Students should be able to reflect on feelings and identify positive ways of understanding, managing and expressing strong emotions and challenging behaviour, acting positively on them.<br><br>**3 Range and content**<br>**b** The study of personal well-being should include how the media portrays young people, body image and health issues.<br>**c** The study of personal well-being should include the characteristics of emotional and mental health, and the causes, symptoms and treatments of some mental and emotional health disorders. |
| **Links to Economic Well-being PoS** | **1.2 Capability**<br>**d** Becoming critical consumers of goods and services. |
| **Links to SEAL outcomes** | **Self-awareness**<br>Students know that they are unique individuals and can think about themselves on many different levels. |
| **Links to ECM outcomes** | Be healthy ■ Enjoy and achieve |
| **Assessment opportunity** | See Topic: Health; Activities 6 & 7: Using positive language (pages 13–14) |
| **Resources** | ■ Student's Book (pages 4–7)<br>■ Appendix (see the CD): Active Learning Methodologies<br>    □ Brainstorming (page 3)   □ Small group work (pages 6–7) |

# STARTER ACTIVITY

Carry out a brainstorm on what students think of when they hear the word 'BEAUTY'. See Appendix (on the CD): Active Learning Methodologies: Brainstorming (page 3). Use the following questions to process the brainstorm words:

- What do you notice about the kinds of words listed?
- Which are positive, which are negative?
- Did any words surprise you; if so, which ones and why?
- Did you disagree with any of the words which went up; if so, which and why?
- How is 'beauty' (other than in the cosmetics industry) used to sell products, goods and services?

# MAIN ACTIVITIES

### ACTIVITY: WHAT IS 'BODY IMAGE'? (Student's Book, page 4)

> 1. a) Do you agree with the definition of body image in Source 1? Why/Why not?
>    b) Come up with an alternative and perhaps better definition of body image.

Other possible definitions might include:

- the subjective inner picture of one's outward physical appearance
- how a person feels about how she or he looks
- what you believe about your physical appearance based on self-observation and the reactions of others
- the way a person thinks about his or her body and how it looks to others.

> 2. Do you think young people generally have a positive or negative body image? Give two examples to explain your answer.

An individual's perception of their body image will be affected by a range of things – self-esteem being a key factor. When researching this topic the authors found that most studies confirmed that young people did not have a positive image of their own bodies.

As an example, BBC Radio 1's Newsbeat and 1xtra's TXU in February 2007 asked 25,000 young people how they felt about their bodies:

- Some 51 per cent of young women would have surgery to improve their looks and a third of those who are a size 12 think they are overweight.
- Breast enlargement was the most popular operation for women, whilst liposuction was the next most popular. Liposuction and nose jobs were the most common choices for men.
- Almost half the women surveyed said they had skipped a meal to lose weight.
- More than half of girls aged 12 to 16 felt that their body image either stops them from getting a boyfriend or from relaxing in a relationship.
- Young men also appear to feel the pressure to look good. About 20 per cent said that they have taken protein supplements in a bid to help themselves bulk up.

> 3. What part do you think the media play in forming our body image?

The media have always influenced our ideas of the ideal body. Throughout history there have been changing fashions in clothes and in what people do to their bodies; for example, each generation of artists has painted to their ideal.

Encourage students to investigate and compare two different looks, such as Renoir's 'Dancing Girl with Castanets' from 1909: www.nationalgallery.org.uk/paintings/pierre-auguste-renoir-dancing-girl-with-castanets

… and only a decade later the flapper look of the 1920s: www.fashion-era.com/flapper_fashion_1920s.htm.

A key factor in the twenty-first century is that the pressure to conform to a particular body image has become more global and the means of conveying this message has become more powerful and more immediate.

Most images we see in the media portray perfection or an ideal that is influenced by the fashion industry. These images are not necessarily reliable – airbrushing and digital manipulation are common techniques.

The following give examples:

The body fat of models and actresses portrayed in the media is at least 10 per cent less than that of healthy women.

British Medical Association, 2000

'They have ads of how you should dress and what you should look like and this and that, and then they say, 'but respect people for what they choose to be like'. Okay, so which do we do first?'

Kelsey, 16, quoted in Girl Talk: www.media-awareness.ca/english/issues/stereotyping/women_and_girls/women_girls.cfm

Using the above material it should be possible to help students see that media portrayals are not necessarily an accurate picture. Often they are tweaked to provide a media ideal – which is rarely achievable.

**ACTIVITY: WHAT IS NORMAL? (Student's Book, page 5)**

> **4. In groups:**
>    **a) Choose one of the following different categories of celebrity:**
>      ■ **Actors/Actresses**   ■ **Sportsmen/Sportswomen**
>      ■ **TV personalities**   ■ **Musicians/Popstars**
>    **b) Brainstorm the names of as many people as you can think of who fit into your category.**
>    **c) Organise the names of your celebrities under the most appropriate heading below.**
>
> | Underweight | Normal | Overweight |
> | --- | --- | --- |
> | | | |
>
>    **d) Discuss the following:**
>      ■ **If a column has more names than all the others, why do you think this is?**
>      ■ **Can you name any other celebrities to fit into columns where few names appear?**
>      ■ **Are there any 'normal' celebrities?**

See Appendix (on the CD): Active Learning Methodologies: Small Group Work (pages 6–7).

■ Give each group several sticky notes and ask them to write on each the name of a different and well-known person from their category. Allow a few minutes to complete the task.

- Display the three columns for all the class to see – labelled 'Underweight', 'Normal' and 'Overweight'. Students then place their 'celebrities' under the most appropriate column heading.
- Use the following process questions to lead a discussion:
  - □ If a column has more names than all the others, why is this?
  - □ Can they name any other celebrities to fit into columns where few names appear?
  - □ Are there any 'normal' celebrities?
  - □ What is 'normal'?
  - □ Are there many overweight or disabled celebrities represented? If not, why not?
  - □ Are celebrities role models for the rest of us? If so, why?

### ACTIVITY: MEDIA INFLUENCE (Student's Book, page 5)

> **5. a) Read Source 2. Do you agree with it? Choose three different types of media from the definition in Source 1 and find two examples from each – one to support and one to disprove the findings of the article.**
>    **b) Which examples were easier to find? What does this tell you about media influence on body image?**

Once students have undertaken their research/investigation, invite them to share their results with the whole class and explain how these examples demonstrate an increasingly rigid and uniform standard of beauty.

### ACTIVITY: CAN WE EVER BE ATTRACTIVE ENOUGH? (Student's Book, page 6)

> **6. Read Source 3. In what ways do you think the media has had an influence on how men want to look?**

Possible responses can include:

- Many images of men are airbrushed to create 'perfection'.
- Images of semi-clad men with six-packs are rarely real; e.g. make-up will have been applied to create shadows and definition.
- Models may have had cosmetic enhancement; e.g. pectoral implants.

All of the above has started to create the same body image issues for men (as for women) who do not feel they can measure up to the perfection on display.

> **7. Do you think the media target men and women equally? Give reasons for your answers.**

The general view seems to be that women have been targeted more than men – but men are now also targets in their own right even if the volume of media attention is still uneven.

Styling programmes (for example, 'How to Look Good Naked' or 'The Clothes Roadshow') devote the majority of their episodes to makeovers for women, with the very occasional programme about men.

It is clear that there are far more women's magazines on the market which deal with fashion and beauty than there are men's magazines on these topics. As an example, Wikipedia lists 82 magazines of general interest to women and 27 of general interest to men.

Advertisements about appearance also seem more directed at women. As an example, ten times more advertisements and articles relating to weight loss appear in women's magazines as compared to men's magazines (Source: Food for thought: Substance Abuse and Eating Disorders: Columbia University, NY, 2003).

> **8. Read Source 4. How does the diet industry contribute to creating a 'deficit model'?**

The media is used by commercial organisations to sell their wares and increase their profits. Concerns about improving health and well-being are never purely altruistic – they ultimately want to say 'you are not yet good enough and you can be even better by using this product'.

Use the Student's Book: Source 4 The deficit model and the diet industry (page 7) to help aid discussion of this question.

The discussion could be extended further by asking students to work in groups to analyse how the deficit model works for a product of their choosing.

### ACTIVITY: HAPPY WITH WHO YOU ARE (Student's Book, page 7)

> **9. How can people learn to be happy with themselves without worrying whether they conform to a certain look or not?**

It will probably never be possible for most people to completely free themselves from the media's influence over us when it comes to the way we see our body image. However, it is possible to be more analytical and to question some of the messages we are being sold. In 2010 a major fashion retailer had to withdraw the sale of its range of padded bikini tops for girls as young as seven following criticism. This is an example of the public refusing to accept a product that had the potential to turn small girls into miniature women instead of children. The public rejected a particular type of body image being foisted on children.

Most people enjoy looking good to themselves and other people. However, self-esteem and personal happiness are likely to be longer-lasting when they are based on a view of yourself that goes deeper than the superficial and/or fleeting messages of the media.

The following may also be of use to teachers in selecting support materials or background reading on self-esteem and related issues:
www.thesite.org/healthandwellbeing/wellbeing/bodyimageandselfesteem/buildingself
esteem.

Other body image topics can also be found on www.thesite.org – however, do note that this website is aimed at 16–24-year-olds.

# REVIEW AND REFLECTION

'Beauty is only skin deep.'

Ask individuals to identify one person, one place and one thing that they consider beautiful and why they think this.

# Topic: The cult of celebrity

| | |
|---|---|
| **Notes** | This topic begins by looking at research which shows that in recent years many young people's thoughts about having traditional careers have been superseded by the craving for fame, stardom, celebrity and the overwhelming desire to have a personal, financial fortune. It then goes on to consider why this change in aspirations may have occurred, citing amongst other things the rise in reality television.<br>Students are also encouraged to think about:<br>– What is real and what is fantasy in terms of careers.<br>– If and how the media have a part to play in promoting future occupations by balancing reportage on celebrity with that of positive career role modelling.<br>– Ways to encourage peers towards tenacity and resilience when it comes to career pathways.<br><br>The topic closes by looking at how social networking and other media might affect career choice and progression. |
| **Learning outcomes** | **In this topic students will learn about:**<br>■ the effect of 'celebrity' on young people's career choices<br>■ the role the media plays in promoting celebrity lifestyles.<br><br>**They will explore:**<br>■ whether young people are overly influenced by glamour and the cult of celebrity<br>■ the connection between actions and consequences when seeking fame. |
| **Links to Personal Well-being PoS** | **2.1 Critical reflection**<br>a Students should be able to reflect critically on their own and others' values and change their behaviour accordingly.<br>**2.3 Developing relationships and working with others**<br>b Students should be able to use the social skill of negotiation within relationships, recognising their rights and responsibilities and that their actions have consequences. |
| **Links to Economic Well-being PoS** | **2.3 Enterprise**<br>a Students should be able to identify the main qualities and skills needed to enter and thrive in the working world.<br>**3 Range and content**<br>c The study of economic well-being and financial capability should include rights and responsibilities at work and attitudes and values in relation to work and enterprise. |
| **Links to SEAL outcomes** | **Social skills**<br>Students can communicate effectively with others, listening to what they say as well as expressing their own thoughts and feelings. |
| **Links to ECM outcomes** | Be healthy ■ Keep safe ■ Achieve economic well-being |
| **Assessment opportunity** | See Topic: Health; Activities 6 & 7: Using positive language (pages 13–14) |
| **Resources** | ■ Student's Book (pages 8–11)<br>■ Appendix (see the CD): Active Learning Methodologies<br>   □ Whole-class work (page 7)   □ Case study/scenario (page 3) |

# STARTER ACTIVITY

## ACTIVITY: CAREER OR FAME? (Student's Book, page 8)

> 1. Look at Source 1.
>    a) How have the ambitions for future careers changed over 25 years?
>    b) Why do you think they have changed?

Lead a discussion on why the current and previous top ten ambitions have changed. See Appendix (on the CD): Active Learning Methodologies: Whole-class work (page 7).
  The most common reasons are likely to be:

- Celebrity dominates newspapers and TV shows.
- We live in a media-saturated world where celebrity is a growing new power. It manipulates taste, fashion and advertising. It is all-pervasive.
- Celebrities are idolised. They seem to have become new gods and goddesses. They seem unreal and inaccessible and yet become the object of our wants and desires.
- Reality television programmes proliferate in the TV schedules. On 18 July 2000 the first series of *Big Brother* in the UK was shown on Channel 4 – a decade later the schedules are full of reality-type shows; e.g. *I'm a Celebrity – Get Me Out of Here*, *Strictly Come Dancing*, *Masterchef*.
- Reality programmes either give a 'fly-on-the-wall' look at the life of 'celebrities' or they catapult unknown/ordinary people into the public eye.
- The illusion of 'celebrity' is created by conferring instant fame on unknown/ordinary people; e.g. *X Factor*, *Pop Idol*, *Britain's Got Talent*, *Big Brother*, etc.
- A perception that appearing on TV equals 'fame' – and is a measure of success.
- Media headlines and stories about people in 'professions' such as teachers, bankers, doctors, etc, tend to be sensational and/or damning.
- Earning potential is influential. Professional footballers can earn millions of pounds.

# MAIN ACTIVITIES

## ACTIVITY: REALITY SHOW OR REALITY LIFE? (Student's Book, page 9)

> 2. Read the article in Source 2. Work in small groups to discuss the article and whether you think young people are losing the ability to differentiate between fantasy and reality. Which of the points of view do you agree with – Hannah Frankel or Nick Williams? Give reasons.

Students should work in small groups to discuss the article and the differing viewpoints. The differing viewpoints are shown in the table below:

| Hannah Frankel | Nick Williams |
|---|---|
| Odds of being picked for a reality show and going on to further fame are 30 million to one – worse odds than winning the lottery. | Most young people understand the difference between the fantasy life and reality. |
| About 16 per cent of teenagers believe they will be 'the one'. | We constantly stress that long-term success can only result from genuine talent and incredible hard work. |

| Hannah Frankel | Nick Williams |
|---|---|
| More than one in 10 young people would drop education to give fame a shot according to a Learning and Skills Council survey. | Celebrity only becomes a corrosive aspect when vulnerable people misunderstand the game. |

Students should note which they agree with and provide supporting reasons – by citing examples such as:

- Some people have left school before taking important public exams (A levels) to take part in reality TV shows like *Big Brother* because they thought it would bring them fame.
- People have argued with judging panels who have turned them down over their perceived ability to sing/dance/do stand-up.

### ACTIVITY: MEDIA AS ROLE MODEL (Student's Book, page 10)

**3. Read Source 3. Where do young people get their inspiration for future careers?**

Students should read the article about primary-school children and their aspirations and then work in small groups to answer the question.

Examples could include:

- the media –TV/internet/films/newspapers, etc.
- celebrities – e.g. Premier League footballers
- family and friends – role models with a career students aspire to
- people they know/meet within and outside their own communities
- school
- helping agencies – Health Service/Voluntary groups, etc.

**4. If the media had an obligation to balance its focus on celebrity with positive, everyday, career role models – what would these be?**

Examples could include:

- running positive headlines/stories that put successful people in a positive light
- praising/celebrating different professions on a regular basis
- providing a focus on positive role models with interviews, etc.
- running 'you can make a difference' stories about people in different careers
- for every negative headline connected to a career include two positive ones.

### ACTIVITY: POT OF GOLD OR OWN GOAL? (Student's Book, page 11)

**5. Read Source 4. Mike is thinking of leaving school without taking his GCSEs. What arguments would you use to convince him to think again?**

See Appendix (on the CD): Active Learning Methodologies: Case study/scenario (page 3).

Students should work in pairs to create a series of 'career' interview questions (and solutions/possibilities) to use with Mike. It should be as motivational as possible. They should use the case study as part of their preparation, creating a list of facts/possible avenues of progression/contingency plans as shown in the table below.

*PSHE Education for Key Stage 4 Teacher's Resource Book © Hodder Education*

| Current FACTS to present to Mike | Possible avenues of progression | Contingency plans |
|---|---|---|
| Mike is a bright student. | Use your abilities. | Value what you have got – look back over results and think about future. Don't chuck it all away. |
| School tests predict Mike should do well. | You've made it this far – might as well take the exams – can only help not harm. | If so bored with learning in school perhaps transfer to college and do exams there. |
| Mike recognises it is tough to make it in football. | Representing school/county/ local league. | Get some football qualifications – e.g. referee/coach. |
| Mike does not have a clear idea of how to turn professional. | See when/if professional clubs are 'scouting'. Try for a football academy. | Coach a local under 10s team. |
| Mike has been told to have a back-up plan. | Already spending one day a week at college, learning about bricklaying and other trades. | Learn something about accounting/finances – if you make it in football you're also going to need a business brain for future plans. Ditto – if you go ahead in trade. |

# REVIEW AND REFLECTION

**ACTIVITY: THE INTERNET – FAMOUS OR INFAMOUS FOREVER (Student's Book, page 11)**

6. Read the information about the internet and look at Source 5. Even knowing the pitfalls of the internet, why do some people still seek instant fame and celebrity via the web?

Run this as a pair or individual feedback activity.

If there is time, students could create their own social network page to dissuade others from following Sarah's example.

# Topic: Health

| | |
|---|---|
| **Notes** | This topic now takes a positive approach towards the media's engagement with young people by looking at its role in promoting health messages. Students are encouraged to look below the surface of health messages/campaigns to examine how they influence people to change behaviours. Students also have the opportunity to express their views about how campaigns might be made more positive and motivating. |
| **Learning outcomes** | **In this topic students will learn about:**<br>■ the media's role in promoting positive health<br>■ how social marketing is used in health campaigns.<br>**They will explore:**<br>■ techniques used in the social marketing of health<br>■ how health campaigns might be made more positive. |
| **Links to Personal Well-being PoS** | **1.2 Healthy lifestyles**<br>**a** Recognising that healthy lifestyles, and the well-being of self and others, depend on information and making responsible choices.<br><br>**1.3 Risk**<br>**b** Appreciating that pressure can be used positively or negatively to influence others in situations involving risk.<br><br>**2.2 Decision-making and managing risk**<br>**b** Students should be able to find and evaluate information, advice and support from a variety of sources and be able to support others in doing so.<br><br>**3 Range and content**<br>**b** The study of personal well-being should include how the media portrays young people, body image and health issues. |
| **Links to SEAL outcomes** | **Managing feelings**<br>Students understand that health can be affected by emotions. |
| **Links to ECM outcomes** | Be healthy ■ Stay safe |
| **Assessment opportunity** | Activities 6 & 7: Using positive language (see pages 13–14)<br>**End of Key Stage Statement – healthy lifestyles**<br>Learners are able to:<br>■ describe the short and long-term consequences of personal health choices, including choices relating to sexual activity and substance use and misuse, and make decisions based on this knowledge. |
| **Resources** | ■ Student's Book (pages 12–13)<br>■ Appendix (see the CD): Active Learning Methodologies<br>  □ Small group work (pages 6–7) |

# MAIN ACTIVITIES

**ACTIVITY: MEDIA HEALTH CAMPAIGNS (Student's Book, page 12)**

> **1. Look at Source 1. Why do you think the '5 A DAY' campaign was so successful in raising awareness about the need to eat more fruit and vegetables?**

Possible explanations might include:

- 5 A Day was a simple, catchy, memorable phrase.
- It seems achievable.
- It was a slogan that all cultural groups could accept in dietary rules.
- The NHS and other health organisations used lots of posters and advertising to reinforce the message.
- Schools were given money to support 'Free Fruit' for children in early years.
- Supermarkets quickly saw the potential for selling more – so they took it up.

> **2. What other government campaigns can you think of that have been targeted at improving people's health/safety? The photos in Source 2 might help you or you could visit the following website, which gives more examples: www.dh.gov.uk/en/MediaCentre/Currentcampaigns/index.htm.**

Examples could include the following campaigns:

- anti-smoking and giving up smoking – e.g. the 'dripping fat' advert run by the British Heart Foundation had 90 per cent of smokers recognising the image. Fat oozed out of a cigarette to suggest how the arteries of the human body are clogged up when you smoke
- road safety campaigns – e.g. 'Kill your speed not a child', aimed at reducing speed on the roads to improve safety
- anti-drink-driving campaigns – e.g. 'THINK! – Don't Drink and Drive' campaign
- anti-'illegal' drugs campaigns – e.g. the 'Pablo the Drug Mule Dog' campaign
- screening programmes campaigns – aimed at encouraging people to be screened for bowel cancer, breast cancer, testicular cancer; e.g. ' Everyman – Stamp Out Male Cancer' campaign
- seasonal campaigns – e.g. 'Catch it, Bin it, Kill it!', aimed at preventing the spread of swine 'flu
- information campaigns – e.g. 'Stroke: Act F.A.S.T.', aimed at informing people how to spot a stroke happening and to call for immediate help
- sexual health campaigns – e.g. 'Sex – Worth Talking About', aimed at helping young people to make more informed choices about contraception, look after their sexual health and avoid unwanted pregnancies
- teen partner violence campaign – e.g. 'If You Could See Yourself …', aimed at tackling attitudes to violence in teenage relationships.

> **3. Are there any that are targeted particularly at young people? If so, how?**

Some of the general campaigns mentioned above have young-people-specific materials or are specifically targeted at young people. Campaigns aimed directly at young people may be more ephemeral to ensure that they are kept current. Check to see what is around now by visiting www.dh.gov.uk/en/MediaCentre/Currentcampaigns/index.htm.

> **4. Imagine that the government makes a decision that there will only be ONE public health campaign per year aimed at young people of your age. What health message should that campaign convey in the twelve months starting today?**

Students could consider the following:

- What is your message to young people of your age?
- Why do you think your chosen message is more important than any other?
- How can your basic message be reinforced over the twelve-month period?

**ACTIVITY: ANALYSING SOCIAL MARKETING AND HEALTH (Student's Book, page 13)**

> **5. Using the images in Source 2 and the information in Source 3, answer the following questions for each image:**
> **a) What is the health issue?**
> **b) What is the message?**
> **c) What technique(s) are being used?**
> **d) How effective do you think this example is in getting people to change their behaviour?**

Possible explanations might include:

|  | IMAGE A | IMAGE B |
|---|---|---|
| 1. What is the health issue? | Littering | Condom usage/safer sex |
| 2. What is the message? | This is an environmental/public health hazard – which makes 'you' look uncouth/a slob/yobbish. Pigs are happy to live in excrement – the implication being that people who litter are similar to pigs. | Remembering to have condoms available and use them particularly (if there is a possibility of having sex) when planning social/celebratory events, e.g. partying. |
| 3. What technique(s) are being used? (See Source 3.) | It uses a combination of 6 and 7. | It draws on 3, 4 and 5. |
| 4. How effective do you think this example is in getting people to change their behaviour? | The imagery is intended to stay in the viewer's head and make them think twice before littering.<br><br>Littering is an on-going problem – which may need a societal change in addition to personal responsibility. | The images and messages are clear and sharp. An additional message follows up the impact by providing further information and the 'Ask Brook' confidential helpline. |

Discussion on the effectiveness of these adverts will hopefully be wide-ranging. More able students may reflect on the key factor that the adverts are just one approach to seeking change – there will be other important factors which will need addressing in alternative ways.

**ACTIVITY: USING POSITIVE LANGUAGE (Student's Book, page 13)**

> **6. Using the example of the Pig Boy campaign from Source 2 (or one of the campaigns you researched for Activity 2), how could you make the campaign positive rather than negative?**

- Encourage students to appreciate that people may respond better to being praised for what they do well.
- 'Telling people off' may de-motivate them.
- Scare and 'death' images generally have a short-lived impact.

> **7. Outline a health/safety campaign using a positive approach.**
> - **Decide what health topic you want to draw attention to.**
> - **Decide on the age group you are aiming to reach.**
> - **Decide what important information/message you need to put across.**
> - **Decide the positive features of your campaign and why you think they will work better than a negative approach.**

Use the Brook campaign as an example: it's seasonal, it's humorous and it encourages use of condoms, i.e. responsible behaviour – it doesn't dwell on negative consequences or preach at the audience.

Use small group work to enable students to undertake the task. See Appendix (on the CD): Active Learning Methodologies: Small group work (pages 6–7).

---

# End of Key Stage Statement – healthy lifestyles

Learners are able to:

- describe the short- and long-term consequences of personal health choices, including choices relating to sexual activity and substance use and misuse, and make decisions based on this knowledge.

**Assessment activity**

Activity 7 can be extended by the working groups taking their planning a stage further. Presentations can be designed so that each group:

- produces an overview of the campaign (see bullets above in the activity) explaining why the topic, etc. was chosen
- produces an explanation of how their campaign will encourage people to make positive personal health choices
- ensures their campaign includes sufficient information so that people make a decision based on what they have learned
- produces example materials; e.g. posters, postcards, PowerPoint® presentations, etc.
- produces an explanation of how the materials would be marketed (e.g. offered to others for consumption)
- produces a description of how the campaign would be evaluated to see if it had some success/impact.

---

**Assessment method – peer assessment**
Each group presents to the whole class. Following the presentation, peers are asked to stay in their working groups and identify:

- at least one thing they liked about the presentation content
- at least one thing they liked about the presentation style
- one thing they think could have improved the presentation content
- one thing they think could have improved the presentation style
- whether the campaign conveyed sufficient information to allow people to make a decision
- whether they think the campaign would be successful in motivating people to make positive, personal health choices.

---

# REVIEW AND REFLECTION

There is a lot of debate over whether health messages in the media should be negative (e.g. every cigarette you smoke shortens your life) or positive (e.g. regular exercise keeps you lively, happy and healthy). Do you think young people respond better to negative or positive health messages? Why?

# Topic: Reporting on young people

| | |
|---|---|
| **Notes** | This topic begins by referring to research undertaken by young people into how the media reports stories about them. The findings indicated that much reporting was negative. The topic then looks at a positive story on the theme of volunteering and caring. This provides an opportunity for students to go on to discuss their own qualities and skills. <br><br> The topic ends with the recommendation that young people should try and promote their own positive news stories. |
| **Learning outcomes** | **In this topic students will learn about:** <br> ■ how the media portrays young people <br> ■ positive media stories about young people. <br><br> **They will explore:** <br> ■ positive skills and qualities of themselves and others. |
| **Links to Personal Well-being PoS** | **3 Range and content** <br> **b** The study of personal well-being should include how the media portrays young people. |
| **Links to Economic Well-being PoS** | **2.1 Self-development** <br> **a** Students should be able to develop and maintain their self-esteem and envisage a positive future for themselves in work. <br><br> **3 Range and content** <br> **a** The study of economic well-being and financial capability should include different types of work, including employment, self-employment and voluntary work. |
| **Links to SEAL outcomes** | **Self-awareness** <br> Students can identify their strengths and feel happy about them. |
| **Links to ECM outcomes** | Make a positive contribution ▪ Enjoy and achieve |
| **Assessment opportunity** | See Topic: Health; Activities 6 & 7: Using positive language (pages 13–14) |
| **Resources** | ■ Student's Book (pages 14–15) <br> ■ Appendix (see the CD): Active Learning Methodologies <br>    □ Small group work (pages 6–7)    □ Case study/scenario (page 3) <br> ■ Internet access |

# STARTER ACTIVITY

Show the YouTube clip of the advertising campaign run by *The Guardian* newspaper called 'The Whole Picture': www.youtube.com/watch?v=M3bfO1rE7Yg&feature= player_embedded. You need to pause it about 16 seconds into the clip and lead a discussion about how it might be interpreted.

The most common interpretation is likely to be that the young man is mugging the older man for his briefcase. Explore the reasons why most people think this. You may be looking for stereotypes; for example:

- young man looks yobbish – see clothing
- businessmen are always respectable
- briefcase suggests professional man
- young man seems to be attacking so must be up to no good.

In reality the film goes on to reveal that the young man is pushing the businessman out of harm's way as a piece of scaffolding (out of shot) is about to fall on him.

The point of the advertising campaign was to encourage viewers to gain as much information as possible before making a judgement. Play the rest of the clip and relate it to not always taking stories and images about young people at face value.

# MAIN ACTIVITIES

### ACTIVITY: THE WHOLE PICTURE (Student's Book, page 14)

> 1. **Read Source 1. Discuss each bullet point with a partner – do you agree with the points made? Why/why not?**

Discuss each bullet from Source 1 in turn, taking feedback from students in the class.

> 2. **As part of the research into the media and young people, the researchers looked at stories about young people in newspapers over the course of a week and classified them. They found that in one week in 2007, 23 per cent of the stories were positive, 29 per cent were neutral or balanced and 48 per cent were negative.**
>
>    **In groups, each look at one newspaper every day of a week and cut out the stories on young people. Then classify them into positive, neutral/ balanced or negative. Do your findings mirror those in 2007, or is the situation different now?**

Teachers may wish to be prepared and have examples of newspaper stories on young people that have been recently published – making these as local as possible may be of help.

### ACTIVITY: POSITIVE PEOPLE (Student's Book, page 15)

> 3. a) **Read Source 2 and make a list of all the positive skills and qualities you can find about Tom Gallagher.**

Use small group work to undertake the task. See Appendix (on the CD): Active Learning Methodologies: Case study/scenario (page 3).

Some positive skills and qualities for Tom could include:

- team worker – e.g. part of team of eight
- visionary – e.g. saw a problem and found solution
- mentoring – e.g. supporting younger pupils
- organiser – e.g. setting up prefect rota
- public contributor – e.g. served on youth town council
- fundraising – e.g. charity events in local community.

> **b) Which of the qualities and skills do you recognise in yourself? What other positive skills and qualities would you add if the story had been written about you?**

Students work individually to compile their own list. If students are struggling to reflect on their personal attributes then ask them who else they could think of/write about – this may help those who find it hard to be objective.

> **4. To counter-balance negative reports about young people, prepare an article for the local media on a positive impact a particular young person, a school or a community group has made in your area.**

Use pairs or small group work. See Appendix (on the CD): Active Learning Methodologies: Small group work (pages 6–7).

Encourage students to use their IT skills for displaying their stories. Consider whether any stories have potential for actual publicity; for example, school newsletter/ magazine, local press/radio, etc.

# 2 Healthy Choices

## Topic: Taking responsibility for your health

| | |
|---|---|
| **Notes** | Health is an important topic for young people – and this topic emphasises that personal responsibility and choice need to be considered. It takes the approach that health is a holistic issue – and young people need to think about emotional and spiritual health as well as the physical aspect. |
| **Learning outcomes** | **In this topic students will learn about:**<br>■ factors that contribute to a healthy lifestyle.<br><br>**They will explore:**<br>■ individual priorities for keeping healthy<br>■ a self-assessment on healthy eating<br>■ realistic approaches to a healthy future. |
| **Links to Personal Well-being PoS** | **1.2 Healthy lifestyles**<br>a Recognising that healthy lifestyles, and the well-being of self and others, depend on information and making responsible choices.<br><br>**2.1 Critical reflection**<br>a Students should be able to reflect critically on their own and others' values and change their behaviour accordingly.<br><br>**2.2 Decision-making and managing risk**<br>a Students should be able to use knowledge and understanding to make informed choices about safety, health and well-being, evaluating personal choices and making changes if necessary.<br><br>**3 Range and content**<br>d The study of personal well-being should include the benefits and risks of health and lifestyle choices … |
| **Links to SEAL outcomes** | **Managing feelings**<br>Students understand that health can be affected by emotions. |
| **Links to ECM outcomes** | Be healthy ■ Enjoy and achieve |
| **Assessment opportunity** | See Topic: Drugs; Activity 5: Drugs – who is most responsible? (page 38) |
| **Resources** | ■ Student's Book (pages 16–17)<br>■ Appendix (see the CD): Active Learning Methodologies:<br>  ☐ Small group work (pages 6–7)  ☐ Brainstorming (page 3)<br>■ Internet access<br>■ Resource sheet 2.1 |

# STARTER ACTIVITY

**ACTIVITY: WHAT IS 'HEALTHY'? (Student's Book, page 16)**

> 1. Name three things you do that make you healthy and keep you healthy. Categorise them under 'body', 'mind' and 'spirit'.

This activity can be done in a brainstorm or in small group work. See Appendix (on the CD): Active Learning Methodologies: Brainstorming (page 3) and Small group work (pages 6–7).

The following may help the discussion:

| Body | Mind | Spirit |
|------|------|--------|
| Healthy eating | Good sleep patterns | Time to chill out/ meditate/pray |
| Regular physical activity | Read, do quizzes and puzzles | Music, poetry, art can all help lift the spirits |
| Drink water regularly | Talk through problems | Take a relaxing walk |
| Regular eye and dental checks | Exercise is known to also help mental health | Laughter is good for you |
| Use sunscreen/avoid sun (tanning) beds | Keep things in perspective – no one is 'perfect' | Spend time with people you care for and who care for you |

# MAIN ACTIVITIES

**ACTIVITY: VALUING YOUR HEALTH (Student's Book, page 17)**

> 2. Look at Source 2. Which of the three categories of mind, body and spirit would you place each of these under? Can some of them be placed in more than one category?

| MIND | BODY | SPIRIT |
|------|------|--------|
| (c) A good night's sleep | (a) 5-a-day fruit and vegetables | (c) A good night's sleep |
| (e) Being able to talk about loss and death | (b) Walking instead of driving/using the bus | (e) Being able to talk about loss and death |
| (f) Not bottling things up | (d) Using the stairs instead of the lift | (f) Not bottling things up |
| (g) Laughing when you can | (h) Access to local healthcare | (g) Laughing when you can |

| MIND | BODY | SPIRIT |
|---|---|---|
| (h) Access to local healthcare | (j) A balanced approach to eating | (m) Relaxation – time to chill |
| (i) Having interests, hobbies and pastimes | (k) Being alcohol aware – and drinking in moderation | (o) Feeling loved and loving others |
| (k) Being alcohol aware – and drinking in moderation | (l) 30 active minutes five times a week, e.g. swimming, rollerblading, active play, etc. | |
| (m) Relaxation – time to chill | (n) Going smoke free | |
| (o) Feeling loved and loving others | | |

> **3. Draw a health pyramid as shown. Put the different ways to good health listed in Source 2 into your health pyramid – making a decision on where each should go. Note that you have 15 ideas but only 10 spaces on your pyramid. Think carefully about which you will choose. Be ready to explain your choices.**

This activity encourages students to express their own views, consider which of their choices are the most important and to listen to other people.

This can be done by one of two methods:

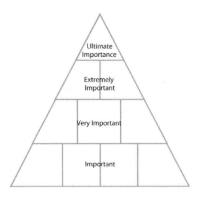

1. The building blocks in Source 2 can be produced as sets of cards which students can choose from to formulate their own pyramids in small groups. Resource sheet 2.1 (page 22) can be used to create the cards. A variation on using cards is that cards are placed upside down in a pile and students take turns in picking the top card and placing it on the pyramid explaining why they have chosen that position. They may need to negotiate with each other as new cards arise.

2. Each small group can draw a pyramid, discuss the options and then write in their choices.

After the activity discussion can be promoted by considering the following questions:

- Did anyone's choices surprise you?
- How did you feel when others clearly had different views from yours?
- Why do people have such different views of health?
- Does the pyramid reflect a realistic view of what teenagers do, or does it reflect an idealistic picture?

*PSHE Education for Key Stage 4 Teacher's Resource Book © Hodder Education*

> 4. Sometimes people say they cannot eat healthily because fresh and healthy food is more expensive and they don't have the time to cook it from scratch. So what is 'eating healthily' about? Use www.nhs.uk/Tools/Pages/HealthyEating.aspx to find out if you know what eating healthily means. Find out whether you're a healthy eater or could improve your eating patterns.

An alternative way of carrying out this activity would be to provide students with literature (leaflets, posters, books) that provides nutritional information. Much of this can be sourced from the British Nutrition Foundation (www.nutrition.org.uk).

Questions to aid feedback:

- How do take-away fast food, shop-bought ready meals and cooking from fresh ingredients compare on:
  - □ price
  - □ nutritional value
  - □ calorie count
  - □ flavour?
- What freshly made meals could be produced in 15–20 minutes?
- Why do most people say sitting down to enjoy a meal with others is healthier than 'eating on the run'?

# REVIEW AND REFLECTION

**ACTIVITY: DO IT NOW! (Student's Book, page 17)**

> 5. By now you'll appreciate that you are going through a stage in your life that will affect your future. This is especially true now while your intellectual and physical skills are still developing (see Source 3). What healthy habits can a teenager realistically develop now to help them optimise their future health?

Use the question to review how much has been digested from the learning in the previous activities.

Possible responses include:

- good sleep patterns
- making time to relax
- regular physical activity
- reading
- doing quizzes and puzzles
- drinking water regularly
- regular health checks
- walking instead of driving/using the bus
- using the stairs instead of the lift
- having interests, hobbies and pastimes
- a balanced approach to eating
- drinking in moderation
- going smoke free.

# RESOURCE SHEET 2.1

| | | |
|---|---|---|
| a) 5-a-day fruit and vegetables | b) Walking instead of driving/using the bus | c) A good night's sleep |
| d) Using the stairs instead of the lift | e) Being able to talk about loss and death | f) Not bottling things up |
| g) Laughing when you can | h) Access to local healthcare | i) Having interests, hobbies and pastimes |
| j) A balanced approach to eating | k) Being alcohol aware – and drinking in moderation | l) 30 active minutes five times a week, e.g. swimming, rollerblading, active play, etc. |
| m) Relaxation – time to chill | n) Going smoke free | o) Feeling loved and loving others |

# Topic: Sex and relationships

| Notes | The starting point here is the principle of a normative approach which does not assume underage/early sex. Research with young people (UK Youth Parliament) indicates that they want to discuss more than the biological aspects of sex. For this reason this topic includes an activity specifically focused on the feelings young people may have when faced with the possibility of a sexual relationship. Although not included in the Student's Book, there is in this Teacher's Resource Book on page 00 a substantial activity focusing on factors that contribute to 'safer sex', and this is explored both in terms of sexually transmitted infections (STIs) and contraception. The final activity moves away from the positive norm to look more critically at the choices faced by young people in situations of unplanned pregnancy. This provides the appropriate context to think about issues such as abortion, adoption, teenage parenthood, etc. |
|---|---|
| Learning outcomes | **In this topic students will learn about:**<br>■ the age of consent<br>■ contraception<br>■ sexually transmitted infections (STIs).<br>**They will explore:**<br>■ the need to think about relationships<br>■ factors that contribute to 'safer sex'<br>■ the choices faced by young people when they have an unplanned pregnancy. |
| Links to Personal Well-being PoS | **1.2 Healthy lifestyles**<br>b Understanding that our physical, mental, sexual and emotional health affect our ability to lead fulfilling lives and that there is help and support available when they are threatened.<br>**1.4 Relationships**<br>a Understanding that relationships affect everything we do in our lives and that relationship skills have to be learnt and practised.<br>c Understanding that relationships can cause strong feelings and emotions.<br>**2.2 Decision-making and managing risk**<br>c Students should be able to assess and manage risk in personal choices and situations, minimise harm in risky situations …<br>**3 Range and content**<br>d The study of personal well-being should include the benefits and risks of health and lifestyle choices, including choices relating to sexual activity …<br>e The study of personal well-being should include where and how to obtain health information, … ways of reducing risk and minimising harm in risky situations, how to find sources of emergency help … |
| Links to Economic Well-being PoS | **2.4 Financial capability**<br>d Students should be able to identify how finance will play an important part in their lives and in achieving their aspirations. |
| Links to SEAL outcomes | **Social skills**<br>Students can assess risk and consider the issues involved before making decisions about their personal relationships. |
| Links to ECM outcomes | Be healthy ■ Keep safe ■ Achieve economic well-being |
| Assessment opportunity | See Topic: Drugs; Activity 5: Drugs – who is most responsible? (page 38) |
| Resources | ■ Student's Book (pages 18–21)<br>■ Appendix (see the CD): Active Learning Methodologies:<br>   □ Continuum (page 4) □ Small group work (pages 6–7) □ Case study/scenario (page 3)<br>■ Resource sheet 2.2 (page 31) |

# BACKGROUND INFORMATION

*'It is vital that we remember always to talk about delaying early sex – not first sex ... this allows for the possibility of our working with young people who have had sex to take time out from doing this again until they feel it is right for them.*

*'When people are asked about their issues and concerns relating to young people and early sex, anxieties about the pressure on young people to have sex is often first and foremost in people's thoughts. These pressures are seen to come from peers and partners, the media and a generally over-sexualised culture and from the assumption – which is in fact inaccurate and a key misconception – that everyone over 12 is 'at it'!'*

*(Jo Adams. 2005. © Let's Leave It Till Later – A Manual for Training 'Delay' Trainers)*

- In the UK, the average age at first intercourse is 16 years for heterosexual men and women.
- For gay men, average age at first sexual experience with another man is 17.5 years.
- Almost one-third of men and one-quarter of women admit having sex under the age of legal consent but around 20 per cent of men and almost 50 per cent of women wish they had waited longer.
- The majority of teenagers report using a condom the first time they had sex; in Great Britain, fewer than 10 per cent of teenagers used no contraception at all.
- Young people feel under considerable peer pressure to have sex and report that drug and alcohol use are a significant factor in their sexual activity.

*'Sexual Health in Practice' – Healthcare A2Z in association with the RCN PNA:*
*www.in-practice.org/sexualhealth*

**Teenage fiction on the theme of sex and relationships**
*A further way of exploring issues surrounding relationships is through literature. Some teachers have recommended the following:*

*Rich and Mad by William Nicholson, published by Egmont. Maddy Fisher and Rich Ross both want to fall madly in love. This book is about first love and first sex and their whole relationship. The book has been well reviewed by teachers and teenagers – but it should be noted that there is some explicit content regarding their sexual relationship.*

*Dear Nobody by Berlie Doherty, published by Puffin. The story of 18-year-olds Chris and Helen and their unborn child. The book explores how it feels to be preparing to enter higher education and the difficulties of their relationships with their families.*

# STARTER ACTIVITY

**ACTIVITY: SEX – WHY ALL THE FUSS? (Student's Book, page 18)**

1. **Based on media reports, soap operas, music videos, etc. what do you think is the average age that young people in the UK have sexual intercourse for the first time? Is it:**

   - **14.5?**    - **15.5?**    - **16.5?**

The answer is 16.5 – use this information to help the students reflect on why both young people and adults assume that young people are having sex at an earlier age than that.

Do some students find 16.5 being the average age hard to believe? Why?

Use the information in the Student's Book about the age of consent and the background information above to extend the discussion.

# MAIN ACTIVITIES

**ACTIVITY: RIGHT PERSON; RIGHT TIME; RIGHT PLACE; RIGHT REASON (Student's Book, page 19)**

> 2. **Choose the three statements you most agree with in Source 1 and explain why you agree with them.**

Use the information in the Student's Book from the UK Youth Parliament Survey to lead into group work which uses the statements in Source 1. See Appendix (on the CD): Active Learning Methodologies: Small group work (pages 6–7).

When processing the group feedback from discussions the following may be helpful:

**Work on the concept of 'rights in relationships'**
The statements are all phrased as 'I' statements to emphasise the importance of personal choice. Young people may need to be supported in their right to say 'no' to something someone else wants. Supplementary questions about supporting each person's right to choose could include:

- What fears and anxieties may stop us from saying what we really want in a relationship?
- Which things might be difficult to say to another person in a relationship?
- What might help us in asking for what we want and refusing to do what we don't want?

**Work on the concept of 'anticipated regret'**
Work with young people on sexual health promotion has tended to identify the importance of helping them explore the idea of 'anticipated regret'. In other words, research tends to show that young people who have had early sex often express regrets. These focus on: lack of planning and a subsequent realisation that this wasn't 'The right person; right time; right place; right reason'.

Research in the *British Medical Journal* highlights the following significant issues:

- 'Reports from young people with recent experience of sexual intercourse showed higher levels of regret for boys than was previously thought.
- For both sexes pressure surrounding the event was associated with regret.
- For girls, lack of prior planning with their sexual partner was significant and regret was related to the feelings they had about lack of control.
- Health promotion should aim to help young people to develop relationship and negotiation skills.
- Prior planning is associated with contraceptive use.'

*BMJ* 2000; 320:1243–1244, 6 May

**ACTIVITY: HOW DO YOU KEEP SEXUALLY HEALTHY? (Student's Book, page 20)**

> **3. Read the statement of values and answer the following questions. To keep themselves safe what:**
> **a) does a young person need to know about sex?**

A biological understanding of how their sexual body parts work and how to reduce risks; for example, from sexually transmitted infections, unplanned pregnancy, etc.

> **b) does a young person need to know about relationships?**

How a relationship is formed and built; how some relationships can be mutual and positive; how some relationships can be controlling and negative – how to tell the difference between these.

> **c) skills does a young person need?**

- communication skills – to be able to discuss feelings, emotions and desires, likes/dislikes, etc. with potential partners
- assertion skills – to be able to make personal choices and stick to them – perhaps in the face of pressure to do something different
- decision-making and prioritising – to be able to reflect and make personal choices.

> **d) sources of help does a young person need to know about?**

Local and national services that offer help/support/guidance; e.g:

- sexual health and family planning (contraception) clinics
- young people's drop-in services/clinics
- Youth Connexions
- counselling services (including relationship counselling)
- reliable internet sites; e.g. Talk to Frank; Brook; The Site; nhsdirect.

**ACTIVITY: WHAT IS SAFER SEX? (Additional activity not in Student's Book)**

Teachers may wish to use this activity depending on the level of knowledge that the group may have. It is a continuum, structured so that initially students consider risks of pregnancy through different sexual behaviours. Then the next stage asks them to consider whether they need to reconsider their responses in the light of risks from Sexually Transmitted Infections.

> **If someone has decided to have sex what do they need to know to keep themselves as safe as possible?**

**Stage 1**
Carry out a continuum activity using Resource sheet 2.2. This has a list of statements you should read out or display in turn. Use Set A Continuum cards on the Resource sheet for this stage of the activity.

For advice on how to carry out a continuum activity see Appendix (on the CD): Active Learning Methodologies: Continuum (page 4).

If necessary direct students to Source 2 (contraception) in the Student's Book (page 20).

As you process where cards were placed use the answers below to inform your discussions.

| Activity | High risk of pregnancy | Low risk of pregnancy | Comment |
|---|---|---|---|
| Sexual intercourse – using a condom | | ✓ | See Student's Book, Source 2, page 20.<br><br>If the condom is used correctly it is a simple and very effective method of contraception and may help prevent transmission of many STIs.<br><br>The condom needs to be quality marked, within its use-by date and latex condoms should not be used with any oil-based products.<br><br>For how to use a condom correctly see: www.nhs.uk/Livewell/Sexandyoungpeople/Pages/Howtouseacondom.aspx.<br><br>A range of YouTube clips are also available – review them to choose one suitable for the age and experience of the group.<br><br>Femidoms (female condoms) have a very high failure rate when it comes to preventing pregnancy – therefore they are not recommended. |
| Sexual intercourse – using 'the pill' | | ✓ | See Student's Book, Source 2, page 20. |
| Sexual intercourse – using contraceptive injections | | ✓ | See Student's Book, Source 2, page 20. |
| Sexual intercourse – using contraceptive implants | | ✓ | See Student's Book, Source 2, page 20. |
| Sexual intercourse – using an IUS (Intra-Uterine System) | | ✓ | See Student's Book, Source 2, page 20. |
| Emergency contraception after sexual intercourse | | ✓ | See Student's Book, Source 2, page 20. |
| Sexual intercourse with no contraception | ✓ | | This is how to get pregnant! |
| First time sexual intercourse using no contraception | ✓ | | Contrary to myths, conception can happen the very first time a girl has sexual intercourse. |

| Activity | High risk of pregnancy | Low risk of pregnancy | Comment |
|---|---|---|---|
| Sexual intercourse when the male pulls out before he ejaculates | ✓ | | As soon as erection is achieved seminal fluid can be released – it contains sufficient sperm to result in conception. More fluid is released throughout intercourse though a man won't feel this happening until he reaches the point of ejaculation. |
| Sexual intercourse standing up | ✓ | | This is another myth about avoiding pregnancy – jumping up and down after sex doesn't work either. Sperm do not respect gravity! |
| Urinating immediately after sexual intercourse | ✓ | | This myth is based on the false idea of flushing out the sperm. Urine exits the bladder through the urethra, which lies above the vaginal opening. Sperm in the vagina won't even get wet when urinating. Some people believe that douching (showering or rinsing the vagina) could also flush out sperm. It does not. |
| Sexual intercourse without an orgasm | ✓ | | Women: do not need to experience an orgasm to get pregnant. Men: as soon as erection is achieved seminal fluid can be released – it contains sufficient sperm to result in conception. More fluid is released throughout intercourse though a man won't feel this happening. |

### Stage 2

Students often only focus on pregnancy when asked to consider risks involving safer or unsafe sex. This stage moves the activity on to considering safety in terms of Sexually Transmitted Infections (STIs).

Tell students to remove the two Set A Continuum cards and replace them with Set B Continuum cards (from Resource sheet 2.2) and replace the statements accordingly.

At this point there should now only be the statement card 'Sexual intercourse – using a condom' under the low-risk heading. A condom is the only method of contraception that may prevent transmission of STIs from one partner to another. The condom creates a barrier which can prevent infections being transferred. No other contraceptive method does this.

If the diaphragm or cap is mentioned: It only creates a barrier across the cervix that prevents sperm from entering the uterus/womb. It does not prevent infections going into the vagina.

Femidoms (female condoms) have a very high failure rate, therefore they are not recommended.

Use 'STIs – Did you know …' in the Student's Book (page 21) for further discussion.

## ACTIVITY: UNPLANNED PREGNANCY (Student's Book, page 21)

4. **Vikki and Joe are looking forward to October – one of them has a place at art college and the other at university. They don't live far apart and their families know each other well. Vikki and Joe have been together since Year 11 and six months ago their relationship became a sexual one. They thought they had their contraception sorted out. So, when Vikki missed a period she didn't panic. But when she missed the next one they were both shocked to find that she was pregnant.**

**In common with many other young couples in this situation they faced the following options:**

- **abortion**
- **adoption**
- **grandparents bring up baby**
- **care for the baby themselves.**

**Consider each option and decide:**
**a) What might they feel about this?**
**b) What do they need to think about?**
**c) What should they do?**

See Appendix (on the CD): Active Learning Methodologies: Small group work (pages 6–7) and Case study/scenario (page 3).

- Allocate each group one of the options.
- Groups should begin by having a few moments to brainstorm their gut reactions to the option they are considering – point (a). Take feedback immediately afterwards and compare some of the different feelings.
- Now groups should consider points (b) and (c).
- Work through each option in turn.

If the following points have not been raised, highlight them in relation to the option being discussed.

- **Education:**
  - continuing into higher education as planned, halting, possibility of returning to it
  - not taking any further qualifications and the possibility of restricting career and earnings as a result
  - how to study and care for a baby
  - cost of child care whilst studying
  - ability to repay student loan.

- **Finances:**
  Pregnancy is the time when you need to do some serious budgeting.
  - Even before your baby is born, researchers estimate that parents spend an average of £1,560. A third of this goes on things like maternity wear, health supplements, books and magazines, with the rest going on prams, car seats, changing and feeding equipment, baby monitors, toys and clothes.
  - According to research you will spend a minimum of £424 buying the basics for a new-born baby, based on the lowest prices available on the High Street.
  - Extra fruit and vegetables during pregnancy are estimated to cost £11.50 a week and nappies for the first 30 months will add up to £536 or more.
  - Whilst breast-feeding is free, baby milk will cost £285 in the first six months, £127 for the second six months and £129 a year for fresh milk after that.

□ Parents on a shoestring budget can raise a child from birth to the age of five on £20,315 if they buy only the bare necessities.

□ The average cost of raising a child from birth to the age of 21 has risen to a staggering £165,000. That works out at £657 a month and £22 a day.

*Pregnancy and Birth* magazine, 2001; *The Independent*, 6 March 2001; www.babyworld.co.uk, 2010

■ **Employment:**
□ how to work and care for a baby
□ cost of child care whilst working
□ no maternity/paternity leave as won't have been full-time employed for a year to gain entitlement to such leave.

■ **Emotional impact:**
□ abortion: religious feelings; ethical issues; guilt; 'what if' questions; relief; new beginning
□ adoption: guilt; 'what if' questions; loss of control about the child's future; regret; relief; hope for a better life for the child
□ grandparents bring up baby: loss of control; different opinions on up-bringing; resentment; how it will be explained to the child; which grandparents will take this role; trust; gratitude
□ become teen parents and care for baby themselves: 'what I might have done (with my life) if…'; worries about getting it right; loss of freedom; excitement; love and joy.

# REVIEW AND REFLECTION

Explain that you are not going to ask your students to answer this question out loud in class – but they should spend a few moments thinking about who they might turn to if they had a problem related to sex.

# RESOURCE SHEET 2.2

**STATEMENTS**

| | | | |
|---|---|---|---|
| Sexual intercourse – using a condom | Sexual intercourse – using 'the pill' | Sexual intercourse – using contraceptive injections | Sexual intercourse – using contraceptive implants |
| Sexual intercourse – using an IUS (Intra-Uterine System) | Emergency contraception after sexual intercourse | Sexual intercourse with no contraception | First time sexual intercourse using no contraception |
| Sexual intercourse when the male pulls out before he ejaculates | Sexual intercourse standing up | Urinating immediately after sexual intercourse | Sexual intercourse without an orgasm |

**SET A CONTINUUM CARDS**

| |
|---|
| High Risk of Pregnancy |
| Low Risk of Pregnancy |

**SET B CONTINUUM CARDS**

| |
|---|
| High Risk of STIs |
| Low Risk of STIs |

# Topic: Drugs

| | |
|---|---|
| **Notes** | Government guidance to schools recommends that the term 'drugs' refers to all drugs, including medicines, volatile substances, alcohol, tobacco and illegal drugs. Young people will have been progressively learning about reasons for not misusing a range of drugs since primary school. This unit begins with the premise that we live in a world where drugs are taken for all sorts of reasons and are widely accepted. The law as it relates to drugs and the other risks involved in drug use form activities for exploration in this unit. The moral and social issues surrounding the supply of drugs are explored through an examination of a supply chain. This asks students to look beyond a simplistic answer of 'blame the dealers'. |
| **Learning outcomes** | **In this topic students will learn about:**<br>■ drugs and the law ■ an example of a 'drugs' supply chain'.<br>**They will explore:**<br>■ what is meant by a 'drug-taking society' ■ drugs and risk. |
| **Links to Personal Well-being PoS** | **1.2 Healthy lifestyles**<br>**a** Recognising that healthy lifestyles, and the well-being of self and others, depend on information and making responsible choices.<br>**2.2 Decision-making and managing risk**<br>**a** Students should be able to use knowledge and understanding to make informed choices about safety, health and well-being, evaluating personal choices and making changes …<br>**3 Range and content**<br>**d** The study of personal well-being should include the benefits and risks of health and lifestyle choices, including choices relating to sexual activity and substance use and misuse, and the short- and long-term consequences for the health and mental and emotional well-being of individuals, families and communities.<br>**e** The study of personal well-being should include where and how to obtain health information, … ways of reducing risk and minimising harm in risky situations, how to find sources of emergency help … |
| **Links to Economic Well-being PoS** | **3 Range and content**<br>**k** The study of economic well-being and financial capability should include social and moral dilemmas about the use of money. |
| **Links to SEAL outcomes** | **Social skills**<br>Students can work and learn well in groups taking on different roles and co-operating with others to achieve a joint outcome.<br>**Motivation**<br>Students can take responsibility for their lives, believe that they can influence what happens to them and make wise choices. |
| **Links to ECM outcomes** | Stay safe ■ Keep healthy |
| **Assessment opportunity** | Activity 5: Drugs – who is most responsible? (page 38)<br>**End of Key Stage Statement – healthy lifestyles**<br>Learners are able to:<br>■ identify reasons why people might use illegal drugs and explain how drug use can impact on physical, mental and economic aspects of people's lives, relationships and the wider community. |
| **Resources** | ■ Student's Book (pages 22–25)<br>■ Appendix (see the CD): Active Learning Methodologies:<br>  □ Role play (page 10)  □ Small group work (pages 6–7) |

# STARTER ACTIVITY

**ACTIVITY: A DRUG-USING SOCIETY? (Student's Book, page 22)**

1. It has been said that we live in a drug-using society. Leaving out illegal drugs, discuss whether you think this is true. Use the following ideas to help your discussion:
   - complementary therapies (e.g. plants such as echinacea and arnica) draw on natural remedies to prevent or treat illnesses
   - alcohol and tobacco are widely used recreationally by large numbers of people – people can become dependent on them
   - using over-the-counter medicines (bought from pharmacies, supermarkets, etc.) is a standard way of dealing with feeling unwell
   - walk-in centres and GP practices can supply prescription medicines to treat a wide range of problems – some people become over-reliant and may develop dependency.

A reminder of definitions may be helpful to aid discussion:

- United Nations Office on Drugs and Crime: the word 'drug' is defined as a substance people take to change the way they feel, think or behave.
- Government guidance to schools reminds us that 'drugs' refer to all drugs, including medicines, volatile substances, alcohol, tobacco and illegal drugs.

2. **Have we created a 'pill-for-every-ill' culture?**

There are more and more prescribed medicines available to deal with illness as well as a range of over-the-counter medicines – the latter, for example, take up a fair bit of space in the average supermarket. Some people can be frustrated if they end up believing there will always be some remedy to solve their illness. Often a person won't benefit from medication – what they need to do is allow their body to recover naturally.

Recent campaigns have reminded the public that the common cold can't be cured by antibiotics – because it is caused by a virus, not an infection. Nevertheless many people visit their doctors and request antibiotics.

The 'pill-for-every-ill' mentality means we accept drugs as a normal part of life. Some people self-medicate using illegal drugs.

# MAIN ACTIVITIES

**DRUGS RISKS – TRUE OR FALSE? (Student's Book, page 23)**

3. Decide if the following statements are true or false.
   a) Possessing magic mushrooms is not against the law.

**FALSE:** Magic mushrooms grow wild in many parts of the country and they contain a hallucinogenic drug called 'psilocybin'. They are classed as illegal in every form: to gather or possess them and to prepare them in any way (for example, cooking, brewing or just drying them out); all are illegal. The main danger with 'mushies' is that users may pick the wrong species by mistake and some are highly poisonous.

**b) LSD is not addictive.**

**TRUE:** LSD isn't addictive, nor is it known to cause damaging effects on the body. However, the hallucinogenic effects may cause people to behave in ways that put them at risk or in danger.

**c) One of the main dangers of cannabis is the state of intoxication it produces.**

**TRUE:** Some users may experience temporary anxiety or mild hallucinations. The state of intoxication itself may impair the user's judgement, thus making it inadvisable to drive, cross roads or operate machinery. Other common effects of cannabis may be relaxation, talkativeness, a sense of well-being and a heightened perception of music and colour. People pre-disposed towards mental ill health are thought to be at greater risk of paranoia and schizophrenia.

**d) Injecting can be one of the most dangerous ways of taking drugs.**

**TRUE:** Injecting can be linked to a number of risks:

- infection of HIV or hepatitis because of using shared and/or unsterile equipment
- local and general infections from normal skin bacteria entering the bloodstream
- abscesses and thrombosis from injecting drugs that were designed to be swallowed
- gangrene as a result of injecting into an artery instead of a vein
- overdose when the dose of the drug is too high (it may be in a more pure form than the user was expecting).

**e) Solvent sniffing is not illegal.**

**TRUE:** The Intoxicating Substances Supply Act 1985 makes it an offence to supply to a young person under 18 a substance that the supplier knows, or has reason to believe, will be used for intoxication. Thus the law of supply extends beyond shopkeepers to anyone who gives a young person a 'sniffable' product. Solvent sniffing is extremely risky – sudden death from solvent abuse is widely recognised and little understood.

**f) It is illegal for a 16-year-old to smoke cigarettes.**

**FALSE:** It is illegal for a vendor to knowingly sell cigarettes to a child under 18 years of age. The 16-year-old is not breaking the law by smoking – however, the police have the authority to confiscate cigarettes/tobacco from those under 18.

**g) If a teacher knows a pupil has used illegal drugs they have to tell the police.**

**FALSE:** There is no legal obligation to do so – each school must have their own drugs policy which clearly sets out what will happen in that school.

**h) The police can enter a school and make a search without a warrant.**

**TRUE:** The police can enter without a warrant to arrest someone for a drug offence, to search following an arrest, to recapture someone unlawfully at large, to prevent a breach of the peace or where the school is in the vicinity of a drug supply incident.

**i) If a pupil tells a teacher that they have used illegal drugs the teacher is legally bound to tell their parents.**

**FALSE:** There is no strict legal responsibility to inform parents – each school must have their own drugs policy which clearly sets out what will happen in that school.

**j) If a person buys one ecstasy tablet for a friend with the friend's money – that person could be charged with supplying drugs.**

**TRUE:** Even if a person is not using their own money, the fact that they purchased (or even just gave) any illegal drug to another person, means they are breaking the law and can be charged with trafficking/supplying.

## ACTIVITY: WHAT'S THE RISK? (Student's Book, page 23)

**4. Look at Source 1 and answer the following questions:**
**a) Is anyone committing an illegal offence?**
**b) Are there any other risks being taken? What are they?**

Run this as a small group work activity. See Appendix (on the CD): Active Learning Methodologies: Small group work (pages 6–7).

| 1. **Hitesh** is growing cannabis plants in his greenhouse. He probably won't bother to harvest them. | 2. **Nancy**'s parents are really 'laid back' about cannabis. They used to smoke it themselves but don't anymore. They don't mind Nancy smoking cannabis in their house – on her own and/or along with her friends. |
|---|---|
| Why would he be growing something that is illegal if he did not intend to use it? Cultivating cannabis plants is illegal under the Misuse of Drugs Act – even if the plants are not processed or used in any way. Allowing one's home to be knowingly used for the cultivation, production or smoking of cannabis is against the law. How will other family members feel? Drug use is not risk free. Smoking cannabis can cause cancers, etc., just like tobacco. People who might have (undiagnosed) mental health issues may suffer from further related psychological problems. Other members of the family might be affected, particularly if Hitesh has mood swings or odd behaviour. | Nancy is breaking the law by smoking cannabis (and so would her friends be). Her parents could be prosecuted for allowing their house to be used for smoking cannabis. The law states that people have a responsibility to try to make sure that premises they own and run are not used for the use or supply of certain drugs – including cannabis. Nancy might be at risk of losing some friends if other parents get to hear about what is happening. See also comments for scenario 1. |

| 3. **Jermaine** is into athletics in a big way and takes steroids to improve his performance. He also gets steroids for **Chantal** but doesn't make any profit out of selling them to her. | 4. **Lee** bought what he thought was ecstasy from a dealer at a club. In fact it is ketamine. |
| --- | --- |
| Jermaine is breaking the law but Chantal is not. Anabolic steroids are controlled under the Misuse of Drugs Act as Class C drugs. It is always an offence to sell or supply steroids to another person. People can also be prosecuted for possession with intent to supply if they have large quantities of steroids without a prescription for them.

Those using steroids may be banned from competitive sports.

Physical effects include stunted growth in young people. Changes in the male reproductive system can also occur. Some men have experienced over-development of their breast tissue.

Women run the risk of menstrual problems, developing 'male' features such as growth of facial and body hair, deepening of the voice and decreased breast size.

Aggressive behaviours have been associated with steroid use. | It is illegal to possess or use ecstasy. It is classified as a Class A drug under the Misuse of Drugs Act – like heroin and cocaine. Ketamine is a Class C drug under the Misuse of Drugs Act – it is therefore illegal to possess or use it.

Ketamine has its own particular risks: Accidents from lack of co-ordination may be more likely and large doses could lead to loss of consciousness.

Ketamine use can also be particularly dangerous if used at the same time as depressant drugs such as alcohol, heroin or tranquillisers as it can shut the body down to such an effect that the lungs or heart stop functioning. |
| 5. **Tony** and **Lorraine** are 17. They go into their local pub and order a pint of beer and a pint of lager at the bar. A police officer walks in. | 6. **Damian** is 14 and regularly buys poppers (nitrite) from a local shop. |
| Under-age drinking is an offence that can lead to a summons but not to being arrested. Police do have the right to take names and addresses. If those involved do not co-operate in providing them with this information they could be arrested for obstruction. Also the publican (licensee) could be prosecuted for serving if s/he had good reason to think they were under 18.

Misuse of alcohol is associated with aggressive or violent behaviour, lack of judgement, etc.

At 17 they could be drivers – and if they drove a vehicle whilst under the influence of alcohol (or any illegal drug) they would be committing a serious offence. | Most nitrites are not illegal to manufacture, supply or be in possession of. European law suggests the seller might risk prosecution.

Health risks can include a pounding headache, dizziness, nausea, a slowed down sense of time and a flushed face and neck.

Users can lose consciousness especially if they are engaged in vigorous physical activity such as dancing or running. Regular use can result in people experiencing skin problems around the nose and lips. |

**ACTIVITY: DRUGS – WHO IS MOST RESPONSIBLE? (Student's Book, page 25)**

5. a) Split into five groups. Each group should take one of the characters in Source 2 and do the following:

- Prepare a case for your character in order to justify their place in the drugs trade and argue that they are not responsible for the drugs problem. You can go beyond the information above to give the character more appeal; for example, you can bring in details of families or friends ... or anything that will make the character more sympathetic.
- Choose someone who will take the role of the character and present their case for two minutes, as if in court.

b) After each character has spoken, take a class vote on whether they can see the point of view of your character and whether they sympathise with you.

c) After each character has spoken and been voted on, discuss who is the most responsible for keeping the drugs trade going.

If time is short this activity can be undertaken as a class discussion after reading Source 2.

Alternatively and more usefully in terms of participation in active learning, the following format could be used which is based on an activity originally published in DrugWise – 1986 ISDD/SCODA/Tacade.

See Appendix (on the CD): Active Learning Methodologies: Role play (page 10).

**A trial**

Ask for volunteers to represent each one of the following characters:

- a hill farmer in Afghanistan
- a drug producer
- a drug smuggler (mule)
- a drug supplier (dealer)
- a drug user.

Wherever possible find those who will be best at presenting a case for what they do. They should use Source 2 to prepare their case, with help from a small group of other participants. Their task in 'court' will be to try and persuade others that their place in the drugs supply chain is justified. They can go beyond the information they have to give the character more appeal; for example, they can bring in details of families or friends ... or anything that will make the character more sympathetic.

They will also have to understand that for the purposes of this activity, none of them is to feel guilty about what their character does.

**The hearing**

- Set up a hearing in which each of the characters has up to two minutes to make a case for what they do. They are to try and get support from the group for what they are doing.
- After each of the characters has spoken, other participants supporting that character may make additional points on their behalf. Then invite anybody unsympathetic in the class to speak against them. Move on to the next character and repeat the process.
- After every character has spoken, check sympathy levels for each character by taking a vote for each, one at a time. Ask, 'Who can see the point of view of this character and sympathise with them?' Move on to the next character and repeat the process.
- Review the 'sympathy' outcome with the whole group.

**End of the role play**
De-role the people playing the characters. Ask for comments on:

- Who is the most responsible for keeping the drug trade going? (Growers, suppliers, users?)
- Are the tobacco companies and the breweries in the same 'business' as the suppliers of illegal drugs (e.g. heroin)? Should they bear responsibility for the damage done by tobacco or alcohol? Or are the users of those substances to blame?

---

### End of Key Stage Statement – healthy lifestyles

Learners are able to:

- identify reasons why people might use illegal drugs and explain how drug use can impact on physical, mental and economic aspects of people's lives, relationships and the wider community.

**Assessment activity**
This activity can be extended to individual work by briefing students beforehand that they will be asked to undertake a 'personal diary entry'. This need only be seen by themselves and the teacher. Many teachers like to use a logbook or reflection diary/journal so that the learning from PSHE is captured and students keep track of their learning and progress.

**Assessment method – private reflection**
Imagining that they have spent the day in the public gallery of the courtroom, their responses are now sought to a series of questions based on what they have heard. These might include:

- What reasons can you identify that explain why people use illegal drugs?
- Describe the different effects that the drug trade can have on individuals and the wider community (you will need to think about the physical, emotional and financial impact on people's lives).
- Think back to the class discussion about which character was seen as most deserving of sympathy – do you agree with the way the class voted? Why? Or did you have a different opinion – what was it? Why?

You should collect in the diary/logbook work so that you can give feedback (written or verbal) to each student. Ensure that students receive comments on the quality of their answers.

---

# REVIEW AND REFLECTION

### ACTIVITY: A PIECE OF ADVICE (Student's Book, page 25)

6. Imagine you have the opportunity to offer the government one piece of advice to help reduce the negative effects of drugs. What would it be and why did you choose it?

Invite students to think back over the learning in this topic before deciding what advice they would choose.

# Topic: Alcohol

| | |
|---|---|
| **Notes** | This topic begins by looking at recommended daily and weekly alcohol consumption limits. It then moves on to take a wider view of the risks faced by people who misuse/abuse alcohol.<br><br>An opportunity is provided to discuss boundaries around alcohol from a parental viewpoint and sources of help and support services for those with alcohol issues are included as a small research idea.<br><br>Existing legislation is flagged up and students are asked to consider whether or not more legislation is required to change drinking behaviours. They are also asked to find pragmatic and possibly creative solutions outside legislative practices. |
| **Learning outcomes** | **In this topic students will learn about:**<br>■ minimising risks from alcohol use<br>■ legislation on alcohol use.<br><br>**They will explore:**<br>■ different views about young people's alcohol use<br>■ sources of local help and support. |
| **Links to Personal Well-being PoS** | **1.2 Healthy lifestyles**<br>**b** Understanding that our physical, mental, sexual and emotional health affect our ability to lead fulfilling lives and that there is help and support available when they are threatened.<br><br>**2.2 Decision-making and managing risk**<br>**c** Students should be able to assess and manage risk in personal choices and situations, minimise harm in risky situations and demonstrate how to help others do so.<br><br>**3 Range and content**<br>**d** The study of personal well-being should include the benefits and risks of health and lifestyle choices, including choices relating to sexual activity and substance use and misuse, and the short- and long-term consequences for the health and mental and emotional well-being of individuals, families and communities.<br>**e** The study of personal well-being should include where and how to obtain health information, ways of reducing risk and minimising harm in risky situations, how to find sources of emergency help ... |
| **Links to Economic Well-being PoS** | **3 Range and content**<br>**k** The study of economic well-being and financial capability should include social and moral dilemmas about the use of money. |
| **Links to SEAL outcomes** | **Social skills**<br>Students can communicate effectively with others, listening to what others say as well as expressing their own thoughts and feelings. |
| **Links to ECM outcomes** | Be healthy ■ Stay safe ■ Achieve economic well-being |
| **Assessment opportunity** | See Topic: Drugs; Activity 5: Drugs – who is most responsible? (page 38) |
| **Resources** | ■ Student's Book (pages 26–29)<br>■ Appendix (see the CD): Active Learning Methodologies:<br>  □ Small group work (pages 6–7)   □ Pairs work (pages 6–7) |

# STARTER ACTIVITY

**ACTIVITY: OVER THE LIMIT? (Student's Book, page 26)**

> **1. Using the illustration in Source 1, what could the following groups drink in a week and still stay within the recommended maximum?**
> **a) men**

21 to 28 units across the week – not all consumed at once nor at weekends only.

> **b) women**

14 to 21 units across the week – not all consumed at once nor at weekends only.

> **c) teenagers**

Under 15 years – none; over 15 years – infrequently.

The picture in the Student's Book of the alcohol units according to drink type could be used to illustrate what these limits actually mean in terms of drinks consumed.

# MAIN ACTIVITIES

**ACTIVITY: PARTY, PARTY! (Student's Book, page 27)**

> **2. Look at Source 2. Which of the responses do you:**
> **a) most agree with?**
> **b) least agree with?**
> **Give reasons to explain your answers.**
> **c) Try writing a response that reflects your views.**

- Use pairs work. See Appendix: Active Learning Methodologies: Pairs work (pages 6–7).
- Invite different students to read different responses out loud so that the whole range of responses can be heard.
- Then ask pairs to discuss and answer a) and b).
- Process the answers as a whole-class activity – some of the following may help the discussion:
  - ☐ Were you surprised at the range of parental responses?
  - ☐ What do you think parents of students in your year group would have said?
  - ☐ What would you like to hear a parent say about this?

**ACTIVITY: MORE THAN HEALTH RISKS (Student's Book, page 27)**

> **3. Most people think of the risks associated with misusing alcohol as health risks; for example, liver disease and mental health problems. However, it poses risks for other things as well. Give examples of negative effects alcohol has for each of the following:**
> **a) family**
> **b) the law**
> **c) employment**
> **d) finance**
> **e) social relationships.**

Use small group work and allocate one issue per group. See Appendix (on the CD): Active Learning Methodologies: Small group work (pages 6–7).

The following may be useful in processing feedback: Professor Sir Liam Donaldson, the Chief Medical Officer for England, said: 'The science is clear. Drinking particularly at a young age, a lack of parental supervision, exposing children to drink-fuelled events and failing to engage with them as they grow up are the root causes from which our country's serious alcohol problem has developed.'

Source: www.direct.gov.uk/en/NI1/Newsroom/DG_183393

| | Negative effects of alcohol misuse |
| --- | --- |
| **Family** | <ul><li>tension through erratic behaviour and irrational mood swings</li><li>violence towards other family members</li><li>alcohol user can become physically/mentally ill and need care</li><li>family loss of income if user isn't working</li><li>marriages/partnerships may break down.</li></ul> |
| **The Law** | <ul><li>drunken behaviour in public can lead to arrest and charges</li><li>drunken brawls (fights) can lead to violence and therefore arrest</li><li>driving under the influence of alcohol is dangerous to self and others – treated seriously by the courts.</li></ul> |
| **Employment** | <ul><li>sick days, apathy and loss of concentration at work can lead to poor performance and loss of job</li><li>work colleagues may see the user as unreliable.</li></ul> |
| **Finance** | <ul><li>cost of alcohol coupled with dependency may create problems as more income is used up (see employment issues above)</li><li>extreme cases may see user resorting to theft (including from family), begging, dishonesty.</li></ul> |
| **Social relationships** | <ul><li>user may become unreliable, seen as untrustworthy and lose friendships</li><li>mood swings will affect relationships</li><li>user may be seen as an embarrassment through their behaviour.</li></ul> |

## ACTIVITY: DRINK PROBLEMS (Student's Book, page 27)

4. Most areas have local organisations that people can turn to if they need help and support with alcohol-related problems.
   a) Find out what local support groups exist in your area, what they do and how they can be accessed. The NHS has a directory that lists local alcohol addiction support groups (www.nhs.uk/servicedirectories).
   b) Use the information you find to produce a poster for your school's PSHE notice board about local alcohol support groups and the service they provide.

This activity can be run as in-class research using ICT facilities and any local service literature available.

National services include:

- www.alcoholconcern.org.uk/concerned-about-alcohol/alcohol-services
- www.nhs.uk/livewell/alcohol/Pages/Alcoholsupport.aspx
- www.adfam.org.uk
- www.alcoholics-anonymous.org.uk

**ACTIVITY: MORE LAWS? (Student's Book, page 28)**

> 5. **What problems do you think brought about the need for the laws in the timeline in Source 3? In groups, choose one law and discuss reasons why you think this law was passed. Feed back your reasons to the class.**

These laws are about people living together in a safer society where not everyone can do exactly what they want. Problems that brought about these laws may have included:

1872 Licensing Act: danger to self and others – as Victorian towns grew in population and public transport was more easily accessible, people needed to know they would be kept safe.

1898 Inebriates Act: disorderly behaviour – with social problems such as poverty, abuse, etc.

1930 Road Traffic Act: increasing traffic needed clearer rules about how to behave.

1967 Road Safety Act: technology made it possible to have more accurate measures to ascertain when somebody might lose control through intoxication.

1974 Health and Safety at Work Act: danger to self and others – improving incomes meant more money was available and sometimes this was spent on alcohol, so people might be drunk during the working day.

Football Matches: acts in 1980 and 1985 created offences because increasing violence at and around football matches was often made worse by alcohol (this is still true today).

1988 Cyclists: The Road Traffic Act: realisation that the law needed to cover all road users.

1991 Road Traffic Act: increasing problems called for an extension of the 1930 and 1967 legislation.

1997 Confiscation of Alcohol (Young Persons) Act: alcohol has become cheaper and more easily available and the age of consumption has become younger – and cultural attitudes have made it the norm in some groups of young people.

2001 Criminal Justice and Police Act: this aimed to give powers to the police to deal with issues as and when they happened.

2003 Licensing Act: the wide availability of alcohol (for example, in corner shops) meant it was more easily accessible to young people, so laws tried to limit the negative effects.

> 6. **Alcohol consumption and problems associated with it still appear to be increasing. Do we need more legislation? The ideas in speech bubbles on page 29 of the Student's Book are all possible areas for new legislation about alcohol. Give an example of an argument for and against each.**

|  | For | Against |
|---|---|---|
| a) Set a minimum price for alcohol to reduce sales to young people. | Stops the sale of cheap alcohol | Young people can acquire alcohol from other sources (parents, friends, etc.) |
| b) Supermarkets to stop multi-buy/bargain deals of cheap alcohol. | Stops bulk-buying | People should be free to choose how they spend their money |
| c) Reduce hours that pubs and clubs can open and sell alcohol. | Hours of drinking can be limited and reduced | People can consume elsewhere |
| d) Total ban on consuming alcohol on the street/in public places/on public transport. | It may feel less threatening if people are not drinking in public | People may drink before they go out |
| e) Restrict happy hours or irresponsible price-based promotions; for example, women 'drink for free' promotions are still all too common. | Reduces the availability at certain times | It may encourage more consumption in the limited times |
| f) Restrict the way alcohol is sold, such as offering drinks in small as well as large glasses or measures; for example, too often only one size is offered or a large is automatically given. | Allows choice about how people consume their alcohol | People may not limit the amount – they simply buy more drinks |
| g) Display alcohol in designated and separate areas; for example, no more displays by the checkout. | Can reduce 'impulse' buying of alcohol | Alcohol may not often be an impulse buy |

> **7. Are there any other realistic and more workable solutions (other than more legislation) to reduce the problems associated with alcohol consumption?**

The following may help in discussion about providing alternative solutions:

- A 'cultural shift' may be more effective than legislation, e.g. using social marketing techniques to encourage behaviour change, such as using messages like the one below:

  'Did you know that if you regularly exceed your recommended daily alcohol intake amount you increase the risk of having a stroke through high blood pressure?'

  Department of Health's Alcohol Social Marketing Strategy, May 2007

- Point out the positive benefits of drinking less. You will:
  - ☐ lose weight
  - ☐ sleep better
  - ☐ have more energy
  - ☐ improve your memory
  - ☐ have no more hangovers
  - ☐ be in better physical shape
  - ☐ save money
  - ☐ improve your mood
  - ☐ improve your relationships.
- TV soaps and other programmes need to shift their main action/meeting points away from pubs/clubs – these suggest the norm is to drink more than is in fact the case.
- As with smoking, ban alcohol advertising completely, especially when associated with sport.
- Find celebrity role models who are positive examples of not misusing alcohol. The article below gives some examples:

  'For every pie-eyed party animal pictured leaving Chinawhite at 3a.m, there's someone who is sober – e.g. Chris Martin (Coldplay) and his wife actor Gwyneth Paltrow, Natasha Kaplinsky (Newsreader), Catherine Tate (comedian/actor). Little Britain's David Walliams never has anything other than mineral water in hand. Former Blue Peter presenter Konnie Huq may frequently be seen out and about and in full control of her faculties. Note, too, the clear skin and bright eyes of the 'alcohol intolerant' newsreader Kaplinsky, or Simon Amstell, presenter of TV quiz show Never Mind the Buzzcocks, who also eschew alcohol.

  'Tate says she hates the 'loss of control' she experiences when drinking. The X-Factor's successful songstress Leona Lewis is also a noted abstainer. And sobriety isn't just a celebrity-specific trend. Members of high society and politics alike are clean livers. Prince Andrew, French president Nicolas Sarkozy and even George W Bush have joined the club. And then there are the sports stars. All-nighters aren't conducive to being on top of your game, which probably explains why tennis ace Andy Murray is teetotal. Boxer Ricky Hatton abstains for most of the year before a fight, letting down his guard only for a brief, post-fight celebration. In Hollywood, Jim Carrey, Tobey Maguire, Natalie Portman, Bruce Willis and Samuel L Jackson are all noted alcohol abstainers.'

  The *Irish Tribune*, 3 August 2008: www.tribune.ie/article/2008/aug/03/the-end-of-the-bender-stars-embrace-sobriety

# REVIEW AND REFLECTION

### ACTIVITY: THE WISDOM OF HOMER SIMPSON (Student's Book, page 29)

> 8. Many people have made up witty sayings about alcohol – what's the message behind Homer's words: *'Beer. Now there's a temporary solution.'*?

Allow a few moments for thought and then invite volunteers to share their responses with the whole group.

# Topic: Weighing up the pros and cons

| Notes | Learning how to keep safe and healthy involves young people thinking about risk-taking. This topic provides a view of risk which acknowledges that there can be positive benefits as well as negative outcomes. Discussion on the topic of risk can sometimes lead to unintended disclosures. The importance of referring to and using the group agreement is noted in one particular activity and teachers are advised to take account of this. If you have not created one before, see Appendix (on the CD): Active Learning Methodologies. Students are encouraged to reflect on their own propensity for risk-taking and to identify what positive risks they might want to take in the future. There is evidence to show that those who engage in positive risk-taking are more likely to protect themselves from negative consequences. Students are encouraged to see that decision-making and managing risk is affected by how they manage their emotions and feelings. |
|---|---|
| Learning outcomes | **In this topic students will learn about:**<br>■ definitions of positive and negative risks<br>■ 'heart' and 'head' responses to risk.<br><br>**They will explore:**<br>■ their personal responses to risk and risk-taking<br>■ how different people perceive risk. |
| Links to Personal Well-being PoS | **1.3 Risk**<br>a Understanding risk in both positive and negative terms and understanding that individuals need to manage risk to themselves and others in a range of personal and social situations.<br><br>**2.2 Decision-making and managing risk**<br>e Students should be able to identify how managing feelings and emotions effectively supports decision-making and risk management. |
| Links to SEAL outcomes | **Self-awareness**<br>Students can reflect on their actions and identify lessons to be learned from them.<br><br>**Managing feeling**<br>Students have a range of strategies for managing impulses and strong emotions so that they do not lead them to behave in ways that would have negative consequences for them or for other people.<br><br>**Motivation**<br>Students can take responsibility for their lives, believe that they can influence what happens to them and make wise choices. |
| Links to ECM outcomes | Stay safe ■ Achieve economic well-being |
| Assessment opportunity | See Topic: Drugs; Activity 5: Drugs – who is most responsible? (page 38) |
| Resources | ■ Student's Book (pages 30–31)<br>■ Appendix (on the CD): Active Learning Methodologies:<br>□ Brainstorming (page 3)  □ Continuum (page 4)  □ Group agreement (page 2)<br>■ Resource sheet 2.3 (page 50) |

# BACKGROUND INFORMATION

*There is **no clear definition of gambling but** it is generally about:*

- *two or more people, usually an operator and an individual*
- *risking a stake, usually money, on the outcome of a future event*
- *the stake is paid by the loser to the winner.*

*In simple terms, gambling is any behaviour that involves risking money or valuables on the outcome of a game, contest or other event. This event or game may be totally or in part dependent on chance.*

*What is the law?*

- *National Lottery (NL): young people can buy, play and sell NL tickets and scratch cards from the age of 16.*
- *Football pools: anyone from the age of 16 may bet on the pools.*
- *Bingo: anyone can enter a bingo club but you must be 18 to take part in the gambling activity.*
- *Betting shop: no one under the age of 18 can enter a betting shop or place a bet.*
- *Casinos: no one under the age of 18 can enter the gaming area of a casino.*
- *Gaming machines: other than playing 'low stake – low pay out' machines in arcades or theme parks, it is illegal for anyone under 18.*

*Tacade – Just Another Game? and RIGT (Responsibility In Gambling Trust)*

# STARTER ACTIVITY

**ACTIVITY: WHAT'S THE BUZZ? (Student's Book, page 30)**

> 1. Look at Source 1. A young man is playing a game of chance. Discuss the following questions:
>    a) Look at the expression on the young man's face. What words would you use to describe the 'buzz' he might be feeling?

Use pairs discussion: See Appendix (on the CD): Active Learning Methodologies: Pairs work (pages 6–7).
   Answers could include:

- excited
- thrilled

- high
- happy

- on a roll
- spaced out.

> **b) Why are games like this so mesmerising?**

People often get caught up in the 'adventure' of the game:

- They can't wait to see what happens next.
- They challenge themselves against the clock to get to the next level.
- It becomes a real world to them.

It can also become a means of escape from their real world. In the final level the machine can become the player's 'best friend' – you can talk to it, shout at it and laugh at it – it never answers back.

c) **Are there any risks or dangers associated with 'gaming'?**

Some of the risks/dangers are listed in answer to question b) above. Others include:

- debt and money problems; in extreme cases, being in debt could lead to criminal activity
- social health costs – losing friends and human contact and forgetting how to 'be' with people.

# MAIN ACTIVITIES

## ACTIVITY: GAMBLING IS ... (Student's Book, page 31)

2. **In Source 2 there are some questions about gambling. What are your thoughts? Discuss the questions in groups.**

Before discussing the questions you may find it helpful to run a class brainstorm to identify what 'gambling' might include. See Appendix (on the CD): Active Learning Methodologies: Brainstorming (page 3).

Encourage students to think widely. The following list isn't exhaustive:

- arcade games
- bingo
- card games
- casino
- currency speculation
- dice games
- dog racing
- event betting
- football pools
- free draws and prize competitions
- gaming machines
- hedge funds
- horse racing
- illegal gambling; e.g. dog fighting
- inflation speculation; e.g. mortgages
- internet gambling
- lotteries including raffles
- phone-in competitions
- scratch cards
- stocks and shares.

Put students into small groups. See Appendix (on the CD): Active Learning Methodologies: Small group work (pages 6–7) and allocate one statement from Source 2 to each group. Their task is to decide whether they agree or disagree and to supplement their answer with three comments. After a few minutes bring the group back together and hear the feedback.

Sum up the activity by asking one or more of the following:

- Did any group find it difficult to reach agreement?
- Did any of the responses surprise you?
- Is it possible to reduce the risks of people getting into difficulties with gambling?

This activity was adapted from *Risk-Taking* by Lesley de Meza and Paul Law (Me-and-Us, 2008).

## ACTIVITY: PUSHING YOUR LUCK (Student's Book, page 31)

3. **You can be the world's greatest poker player, bingo babe or placer of bets – but if you can't manage your money you'll end up broke. What advice would you give to someone who was addicted to gambling?**

Invite feedback from volunteers. The following information may aid discussion:
  In many respects support for problem gamblers is under-resourced when compared with other forms of addiction. Students could be encouraged to find more information at:

- www.gamcare.org.uk
- www.gamblersanonymous.org.uk

Tacade have produced a teaching pack on gambling called 'Just Another Game', available free of charge when downloaded from Tacade's website. For further information visit www.tacade.com – click on the Gambling page. Amongst other ideas, Session 4 'In the Money' on pages 22–26 includes a dice game which provides another learning methodology; this is particularly useful for illustrating how games of (supposed) chance are weighted against the player.

### ACTIVITY: RATE THE RISK (Student's Book, page 31)

> **4. Rank the following activities from 'totally safe' to 'extremely risky':**
> - **bungee jumping**
> - **carrying a knife for protection**
> - **drinking a bottle of spirits**
> - **having unprotected sex**
> - **playing fruit machines**
> - **smoking cigarettes**
> - **speaking in front of a group**
> - **talking in internet chat rooms.**

See Appendix (on the CD): Active Learning Methodologies: Continuum (page 4).

1. This activity takes the form of a 'ladder of risk' where the bottom rung is 'totally safe' and the top rung 'extremely risky'.
2. Place the 'totally safe' and 'extremely risky' cards (Resource sheet 2.3, page 50) on an imaginary ladder stretching from one side of the room to the other.
3. Ask volunteers to each pick one of the 'rate the risk' cards (Resource sheet 2.3, page 50). In turn each takes up a position on the 'ladder'. They hold up their card and say why they chose that position on the ladder; e.g. 'I think this is extremely risky because …' or 'I think this is less risky than the last card so I'm going to stand here because …'.
4. When all the volunteers are standing, invite other members of the class to re-arrange the order of the 'rate the risk' cards and explain why they are doing so.

Whilst students are taking part in the risk ladder activity listen out for any words or phrases they use that indicate a 'heart' (feeling) response rather than a 'head' (thinking) response.
  Invite them to say whether they felt they were making 'heart' or 'head' responses when they were thinking about risk.

- Did some people make only one kind of response?
- Did some people use a mixture of 'head' and 'heart' responses?

There is now a natural flow into the next activity which invites students to reflect on their own personal responses to risk-taking.

**ACTIVITY: THINKING ABOUT YOU (Student's Book, page 31)**

> 5. a) **What is the biggest negative risk you've ever taken?**
>    b) **Did you do anything to limit the potential for harm?**
>
> 6. a) **What's the biggest positive risk you've ever taken?**
>    b) **What did you gain from taking it?**
>
> 7. **Looking to the future, what positive risk would you most like to take?**
>    a) **What might stop you from taking that risk?**
>    b) **What would you gain from taking that risk?**
>
> 8. **On a scale of 1–10, how big a risk-taker would you say you are (with 1 as mega safe!)?**

Before undertaking this activity, remind all students of the group agreement. See Appendix (on the CD): Active Learning Methodologies: Group agreement (page 2). Tell them that they should talk only about examples with which they are comfortable.

This activity is best started with individual students personally reflecting on how they would answer the questions. Students are invited to compare their answers with another person. The activity will work best if students are allowed to work in friendship pairs as far as possible.

In taking feedback ask for volunteers.

# REVIEW AND REFLECTION

**ACTIVITY: OBSESSED? (Student's Book, page 31)**

> 9. **Look at the young man in Source 1. If you are experiencing strong emotions (pleasure, fear, a 'buzz', etc.), does that make it harder or easier to weigh up the risks in any situation? Explain your answer.**

For some people strong emotional feelings change their perceptions and they are less able to make logical, reasonable decisions about risks.

# RESOURCE SHEET 2.3

**CONTINUUM CARDS**
**Scale cards**

| Totally safe |
|---|

| Extremely risky |
|---|

**Rate the risk cards**

| Bungee jumping | Playing fruit machines |
|---|---|
| Carrying a knife for protection | Smoking cigarettes |
| Drinking a bottle of spirits | Speaking in front of a group |
| Having unprotected sex | Talking in internet chat rooms |

*PSHE Education for Key Stage 4 Teacher's Resource Book © Hodder Education*

# 3 Emotional and Mental Health

## Topic: Recognising and balancing emotions

| | |
|---|---|
| **Notes** | The topic begins with a recap on emotional health and helps students review a range of emotions. They are asked to investigate and possibly model some typical emotions.<br><br>It then moves to two particular elements of emotional health: considering their personal support networks and identifying good friendship-building skills. These have been chosen to help young people rebalance a sometimes remote version of friendship and relationships, i.e. via technology (web/text) rather than real life. The emphasis is on getting out and about, meeting people and doing things together. |
| **Learning outcomes** | **In this topic students will learn about:**<br>■ emotional health and how to recognise it<br>■ the usefulness of personal support networks.<br><br>**They will explore:**<br>■ the eight main types of emotions<br>■ ways to expand social life and friendships. |
| **Links to Personal Well-being PoS** | **1.2 Healthy lifestyles**<br>**b** Understanding that our physical, mental, sexual and emotional health affect our ability to lead fulfilling lives and that there is help and support available when they are threatened.<br><br>**2.3 Developing relationships and working with others**<br>**a** Students should be able to use social skills to build and maintain a range of positive relationships, reflect upon what makes these successful and apply this to new situations.<br><br>**3 Range and content**<br>**d** The study of personal well-being should include the benefits and risks of health and lifestyle choices including … mental and emotional well-being of individuals, families and communities. |
| **Links to SEAL outcomes** | **Managing feelings**<br>Students understand how health can be affected by emotions.<br><br>**Empathy**<br>Students can work out how people are feeling through their words, body language, gestures and tone.<br><br>**Social skills**<br>Students can make ... friendships. |
| **Links to ECM outcomes** | Be healthy ■ Stay safe ■ Enjoy and achieve |
| **Assessment opportunity** | See Topic: Facing challenges; Activity 3: Problem-solving (page 74) |
| **Resources** | ■ Student's Book (pages 32–34)<br>■ Appendix (on the CD): Active Learning Methodologies:<br>  □ Brainstorming (page 3)  □ Pairs work (pages 6–7)  □ Small group work (pages 6–7) |

# STARTER ACTIVITY

### ACTIVITY: EMOTIONALLY HEALTHY? (Student's Book, page 32)

> **1. If you were asked to describe a physically healthy person you could probably provide a good list of features; for example, eats a balanced diet, has good energy levels, etc. If you were asked to describe an emotionally healthy person, what would that list of features include?**

This activity lends itself to a brainstorm. See Appendix (on the CD): Active Learning Methodologies: Brainstorming (page 3). Possible answers could include:

People with good emotional health:

- are in control of their thoughts and behaviours
- feel positive about themselves and have good relationships
- can keep their problems in perspective
- have both self-awareness and self-control
- are compassionate and empathetic
- appear 'bright eyed' and alert
- have good/positive posture
- have a sense of contentment (at peace with themselves)
- enjoy their life
- have a positive attitude (to life)
- are resilient when things go wrong or they are feeling low.

# MAIN ACTIVITIES

### ACTIVITY: HOW DO YOU KNOW? (Student's Book, page 33)

> **2. Look at Source 1, which identifies the eight main emotions.**
> **a) What characteristics in each facial expression represent the emotion?**

- **Anger:** Brow furrowed; 'hard' look in the eyes; hands reaching out as if to grab.

- **Fear:** Wide-eyed; raised eyebrows; open-mouthed; hair standing on end; tendons tense and stretched.

- **Sadness:** Corners of mouth turned down; eyes down turned and staring into the distance; posture closed and slumped.

- **Enjoyment:** Smiling mouth and eyes; laughing/grinning; very relaxed posture.

- **Love:** Dreamy look; far-away smile; relaxed posture.

- **Disgust:** Face screwed up in displeasure; tongue stuck out as if expressing 'ugh!'.

- **Shame:** Eyes red-rimmed; hand covering mouth as if sorry/embarrassed to have said something; looks as if she wishes she could hide/disappear.

- **Surprise:** Very wide-eyed; mouth open in an 'ooh' but speechless; jaw has dropped open.

The following facial features will give us clues to a person's emotions/how they are feeling:

**Mouth:** Is it tight-lipped or open? Is it closed tightly? Does it look pinched or pursed? Is it turned up at the corners – as if in a smile? Or turned down in a sad way?

**Eyes:** Are they screwed up or tight and rather pinched looking? Are they wide open or staring? Do they look warm and inviting, cold and disinterested, or shocked, or frightened? Are they looking at you or away from you?

**Eyebrows:** Are they raised, frowning, or relaxed? Is one up and one down – as if questioning something?

**Forehead:** Is it furrowed and wrinkled (not by age but by what's happening on the rest of the face)? Or is it relaxed?

**Nose/nostrils:** Are they flared, or pinched or relaxed?

**Chin:** Does it look a bit 'wobbly' or does it look firm and determined?

> **b) Can you identify a word that describes the degree of feeling being shown?**

Some of the other words to describe degrees of feeling of the main emotion are listed below Activity 3.

> **c) Compare your answers with someone else – did you see similar degrees of feeling?**

Two people may read the same facial expression differently: one may see worry where another person sees panic. Why do you think this happens? This may be because what they see reminds them of their own experiences – so they may relate their personal feelings to someone else.

> **3. a) Choose one or two of the eight main emotions and create a collage of examples from photos, film or art that illustrate it. You could use the internet, magazines, books and films in your research.**
> **b) On your collage explain which emotion is represented by using evidence from the facial expression, tone of voice, body language, etc. In your explanation try and use different words to describe the degree of emotion being used. It may help to brainstorm these first.**

It is suggested students work in pairs to complete this activity. See Appendix (on the CD): Active Learning Methodologies: Pairs work (pages 6–7).
  Words to describe degrees of emotion/feeling might include:

- anger: fury, annoyance, hostility, angst, rage
- fear: anxiety, worry, apprehension, dread, terror, panic
- sadness: depression, despair, disappointment, grief, misery, regret
- enjoyment: ecstasy, euphoria, happiness, interest
- love: desire, gratitude, hope, lust, affection
- disgust: hatred, horror, loathing, revulsion, repulsion
- shame: self-contempt, embarrassment, guilt, remorse
- surprise: hysteria, shock, wonder, amazement.

Alternatively, or if time allows, volunteers could work in pairs to create body sculptures or 'snap-shots' of emotions (without words being used). The rest of the class then have to guess what emotion is being represented and explain how the body language and expressions portrayed this.

**ACTIVITY: WHO WOULD I INCLUDE? (Student's Book page 33)**

> 4. **Look at Source 2. Not everyone will have eight types of support on their personal network. What would be the two or three key strands that you would include on yours and why? Discuss your answer in pairs or small groups.**

The supportive nature of this activity means that students should work in pairs or small friendship groups. See Appendix (on the CD): Active Learning Methodologies: Small group work (pages 6–7).

Care should be taken so that no individual is personally asked to reveal their 'support network' if they don't want to.

**ACTIVITY: STEPPING STONES (Student's Book page 34)**

> 5. **Discuss why each of the points in Source 3 is an important part of making and keeping friends.**
>
> 6. **If you knew someone who wanted to make more friends, or expand their social life, what steps other than those mentioned in Source 3 would you suggest they could take?**

Small group work is appropriate for this activity. See Appendix (on the CD): Active Learning Methodologies: Small group work (pages 6–7).

Some ideas include:

**Spend more time around people.** If you want to make friends, you first need to put yourself out there somehow in order to meet people. Friends seldom come knocking on your door whilst you sit at home playing computer games. Social networking on the web – or by texting – is no substitute for spending time with real live people!

**Join an organisation with people who have common interests.** You don't necessarily have to have a lot of common interests with people in order to make friends with them, but if you have something in common with people it can make it a lot easier to start a conversation and plan activities together.

**Join a sports team.** A common misconception about this is that you have to be really good at playing a particular sport. As long as you enjoy the sport and support your teammates, joining a local team with a laid-back attitude could be a great way to make new friends.

**Volunteer.** This is a great way for people of all ages to meet others. By working together you build bonds with people, and you might meet others who have a passion for changing things the way you do – a common cause.

**Make eye contact and smile.** If you have an unfriendly countenance, people are less likely to be receptive to you. Be approachable – frowning or appearing blankly deadpan may make you look troubled or disinterested.

**Introduce yourself** at the beginning of the conversation. It can be as simple as saying 'Oh, by the way, my name is ...'. Once you introduce yourself, the other person will typically do the same. Remember his or her name! If you show that you remembered things from your past conversation(s) with the person he or she will see that you were paying attention and are interested.

**Ask them to join you for a drink or coffee.** Sharing food and drink can be sociable activities so this will give you a better opportunity to talk and get to know each other a little bit better. A good way to extend yourself is to say: 'Hey, if you ever want to get together for coffee or something, let me give you my mobile number.' This gives the person the opportunity to contact you; they may or may not give you their information in return, but that's fine. Remember simple rules about personal safety when meeting people you don't know well.

**Be a good friend.** Once you've started spending time with potential friends, remember to do your part (i.e. initiating some of the activities or asking how the other person is feeling) or else the friendship will become unbalanced and an uneasiness or distance is likely to arise.

**Be reliable.** If you and your friend agree to meet somewhere, don't be late, and do not stand them up. If you're not going to make it on time or make it at all, call them as soon as you realise it. Apologise and ask to reschedule.

**Be a good listener.** Many people think that in order to be seen as 'friend material' they have to appear very interesting. Far more important than this, however, is the ability to show that you're interested in others.

**'Friends of a friend.'** If you have a friend who knows some good people that you aren't acquainted with, ask them to invite those people to hang out with the two of you. It is a great way to make some friends who have common interests. But remember – don't use a friend to get something you want and then dump them.

# REVIEW AND REFLECTION

**ACTIVITY: EMOTIONAL IDOL (Student's Book, page 34)**

> 7. Who is the most emotionally healthy person you know and what makes them so?

Students who may struggle with this could choose a character from a book, TV programme or film and describe what it is about them that makes them emotionally healthy.

# Topic: Stresses, pressures and exams

| | |
|---|---|
| **Notes** | The topic begins by helping students identify warning signs in relation to stress, pressures and anxiety. They then reflect on helpful stress-busting ideas to pass on to friends.<br><br>Amongst young people there can be a denial about the need for sufficient sleep. The importance of getting into good sleep habits is identified and students are encouraged to create a realistic routine for themselves and others to follow.<br><br>A range of suggestions are provided for dealing with exam worries and students are encouraged to consider these and identify alternatives where appropriate. |
| **Learning outcomes** | **In this topic students will learn about:**<br>■ common physical and emotional signs of stress<br>■ why good sleep habits are essential to managing pressures.<br><br>**They will explore:**<br>■ ways of managing stress and anxiety<br>■ recommended routines for dealing with exam pressures. |
| **Links to Personal Well-being PoS** | **1.2 Healthy lifestyles**<br>a  Recognising that healthy lifestyles, and the well-being of self and others, depend on information and making responsible choices.<br><br>**2.1 Critical reflection**<br>c  Students should be able to identify and use strategies for setting and meeting personal targets and challenges in order to increase motivation, reflect on their effectiveness and implement and monitor strategies for achieving goals.<br><br>**3 Range and content**<br>d  The study of personal well-being should include the benefits and risks of health and lifestyle choices including … mental and emotional well-being of individuals, families and communities. |
| **Links to SEAL outcomes** | **Self-awareness**<br>Students know and accept what they are feeling, and can label their feelings.<br><br>**Managing feelings**<br>Students understand how health can be affected by emotions and know a range of ways to keep themselves well and happy.<br><br>**Motivation**<br>Students can anticipate and plan to work around or overcome potential obstacles. |
| **Links to ECM outcomes** | Be healthy ■ Stay safe ■ Enjoy and achieve |
| **Assessment opportunity** | See Topic: Facing challenges; Activity 3: Problem-solving (page 74) |
| **Resources** | ■ Student's Book (pages 35–37)<br>■ Appendix (see the CD): Active Learning Methodologies:<br>   □ Brainstorming (page 3)   □ Small group work (pages 6–7)   □ Pairs work (pages 6–7) |

# STARTER ACTIVITY

**ACTIVITY: COMING TO GET YOU! (Student's Book, page 35)**

> 1. Imagine a scene from a science fiction film where a monster is chasing one of the characters. The character is unarmed and defenceless against the unremitting onslaught.
>    a) How would they feel?
>    b) What physical and emotional signs might signify that something scary was happening?

Run this as a brainstorm. See Appendix (on the CD): Active Learning Methodologies: Brainstorming (page 3).

Physical symptoms of anxiety include:

- finding it difficult to breathe
- a tight chest
- shaking
- palpitations
- a dry mouth
- blurred vision
- feeling sick
- loose bowels
- urinating frequently
- muscle tension
- extreme tiredness
- hot and cold flushes.

Emotional symptoms include feelings of:

- fear and worry of something like having a heart attack
- loss of control
- unable to cope
- state of panic.

You could extend the discussion to talk about other examples of how someone might show they are anxious about something such as:

- avoiding everyday situations or activities because they cause anxiety
- nervousness
- being tense, or on edge
- being unable to go to work or school or deal with family responsibilities
- believing that something bad will happen if certain things aren't done a certain way
- the belief that danger and catastrophe are around every corner.

# MAIN ACTIVITIES

**ACTIVITY: IF ONLY THERE'D BEEN MORE TIME (Student's Book, page 35)**

> 2. Most young people have different tips or techniques they use to reduce stress. What three methods to beat stress and anxiety would you pass on to a friend?

Run this as small group work. See Appendix (on the CD): Active Learning Methodologies: Small group work (pages 6–7).

Possible responses might include:

- Try to take one day at a time. Don't be too hard on yourself. Learning to deal with your anxiety can be extremely difficult and may take some time.

- Try to face the things or situations that make you anxious, and build confidence about being able to cope with your anxiety.
- Find ways of motivating yourself, such as setting small and achievable goals.
- Make a list of particular problems or difficult situations that you would like to overcome and attempt them step-by-step.
- Learn to relax by thinking about things that make you feel calm such as listening to music or reading.
- Use specific relaxation techniques such as meditation, yoga or pre-recorded relaxation tapes.
- Do some form of exercise on a regular basis. Physical exercise can trigger brain chemicals that will improve your mood. Feeling better about your body can make you feel more positive about yourself.

**ACTIVITY: ZZZZZZZZZZZ (Student's Book, page 36)**

> **3. Most sleep advisers recommend that in order to get a good night's sleep you should follow a routine of winding down before bedtime, and that bedtime should be calm without too much stimulation. Use the outline below to create a plan that will lead to a good night's sleep and help combat some of the problems outlined in Source 1.**
>
> | TIME | ACTIVITY |
> | --- | --- |
> | Arrive home from school | |
> | Two hours before sleep time | |
> | One hour before sleep time | |
> | Sleep time | Get into bed and go to sleep! |

This can be run as pairs work. See Appendix (on the CD): Active Learning Methodologies: Pairs work (pages 6–7).

During feedback, compare and contrast the suggested plans. The following is not the only way of answering but includes the steps recommended by most sleep advisors. They also recommend keeping to a routine as far as possible, especially on week nights: have a set time for the evening meal, bed and getting up in the morning.

| TIME | ACTIVITY |
| --- | --- |
| Arrive home from school | Get homework done, have a snack, get exercise and chores done now – energy levels need to be high now and then wind down later. |
| Two hours before sleep time | Avoid chocolate, caffeine, additives, alcohol and nicotine in the two hours before bedtime. Replace with a warm milky drink. |
| One hour before sleep time | Wind down – you need to practise this: switch off the computer, mobile phone and TV – instead have a bath, listen to music or the radio or read a book. |
| Sleep time | Ensure the bedroom is quiet and dark. It should be a 'media-free' zone. Get into bed and go to sleep! |

**ACTIVITY: PULLING IT ALL TOGETHER (Student's Book, page 37)**

> **4. Look at Source 2. What do you think of the suggestions for preparing for exams and keeping stresses at bay? Score each suggestion out of 10, with 10 being 'yes, that really works' and 1 being 'not much use'.**

Run this as small group work. See Appendix (on the CD): Active Learning Methodologies: Small group work (pages 6–7).

After taking feedback, invite students to return to their scorecards and to suggest a replacement piece of advice for any item on the original list that initially scored less than 5.

# REVIEW AND REFLECTION

**ACTIVITY: TOP TIP (Student's Book, page 37)**

> **5. What is your top tip for facing stresses and pressures in the weeks leading up to examinations?**

Invite volunteers to share their top tips. If appropriate, use some of the feedback to hold a vote on a whole-class top tip.

# Topic: Money stresses and pressures

| | |
|---|---|
| **Notes** | This unit begins with a short review of typical financial transactions that young people may have experienced by the time they reach Years 10 and 11. It focuses on three case studies illustrating how people have drifted into financial difficulties, and identified successful solutions. It aims to enable young people to set into context the relevance of financial education to their personal development and their increasing independence and responsibility. It may be that teacher-led discussion will help young people to reach a greater depth of understanding regarding what is financially possible for their parents and carers within the budget they have. It is important that young people understand the links between financial capability and health and well-being. Financial worries and uncertainty can lead to a physical decline in health and can have far-reaching consequences. |
| **Learning outcomes** | **In this topic students will learn about:**<br>■ money – borrowing and interest<br>■ risks attached to buying on credit.<br>**They will explore:**<br>■ emotional and financial costs of misusing money<br>■ solutions to financial problems. |
| **Links to Personal Well-being PoS** | **1.1 Personal identities**<br>c Understanding that self-esteem can change with personal circumstances, such as those associated with family and friendships, achievement and employment.<br><br>**1.2 Healthy lifestyles**<br>b Understanding that our physical, mental, sexual and emotional health affect our ability to lead fulfilling lives and that there is help and support available when they are threatened.<br><br>**2.2 Decision-making and managing risk**<br>e Students should be able to identify how managing feelings and emotions effectively supports decision-making and risk management. |
| **Links to Economic Well-being PoS** | **1.2 Capability**<br>b Learning how to manage money and personal finances.<br><br>**1.4 Economic understanding**<br>b Understanding the functions and uses of money.<br><br>**2.4 Financial capability**<br>b Students should be able to understand financial risk and reward.<br><br>**3 Range and content**<br>k Social and moral dilemmas about the use of money. |
| **Links to SEAL outcomes** | **Empathy**<br>Students recognise and take account of their feelings of empathy and act on them by considering the needs and feelings of others. |
| **Links to ECM outcomes** | Achieve economic well-being ■ Be healthy |
| **Assessment opportunity** | See Topic: Facing challenges; Activity 3: Problem-solving (page 74) |
| **Resources** | ■ Student's Book (pages 38–41)<br>■ Appendix (see the CD): Active Learning Methodologies:<br>  □ Pairs work (pages 6–7)   □ Small group work (pages 6–7) |

# STARTER ACTIVITY

**ACTIVITY: MONEY, MONEY, MONEY (Student's Book, page 38)**

> 1. Everyone needs money in some shape or form. Using money can be a positive experience but misusing money has risks attached. Look at Source 1. Of all these different ways that a teenager might use money, which one might cause the biggest problems and why?

Run this as a pairs activity. See Appendix (on the CD): Active Learning Methodologies: Pairs work (pages 6–7).

| Ways of using money | Possible problems |
|---|---|
| Using a savings account | Temptation to dip into savings and not have money left when needed. |
| Managing an allowance and gift income | Spending it all before the next instalment of income is due. |
| Mobile phone tariffs | Not reading the small print; e.g. hidden charges.<br><br>Getting tied in to a long contract which isn't best value. |
| Opening a bank account | Not understanding bank charges.<br><br>Going into overdraft and incurring interest. |
| Using a debit card or pre-payment card | On a debit card you may not realise you have gone into overdraft.<br><br>Possible hidden charges if you don't read the card agreement. |
| Use of e-commerce | Internet spending can be so easy that you spend more than you planned for.<br><br>Some financial transactions may not be on safe and secure sites. |
| Earnings from part-time employment | Not being paid a fair wage |
| Independent travel | Not making best use of card insurance scheme for losing your card. |
| Buying clothing, small gifts, etc. | Going into debt/not staying within budget. |
| Selling goods | Allowing others to defraud you.<br><br>Not being aware of scams. |

# MAIN ACTIVITIES

### ACTIVITY: THE COST OF MONEY (Student's Book, page 38)

> **2. Read the three case studies on pages 39–40 of the Student's Book and answer the questions that follow them.**

Run this as a small group activity. See Appendix (on the CD): Active Learning Methodologies: Small group work (pages 6–7).

### Case Study 1: Sheila, Sam and Kirsty
### Questions

> **a) What kind of things might Sheila have bought using credit cards?**

Possible items:

- televisions
- iPod
- gaming consoles
- laptops and PCs
- clothing and bedding
- kitchen equipment.

> **b) Sheila feels that she has lost control – why is this the case?**

Possible factors:

- Generosity towards her children and indulging herself to feel good may have got out of hand.
- The children now have an expectation of her and she fears the guilt if she can't fulfil that so she keeps on buying.
- She has only been paying the minimum on her credit cards so the interest has built up – and she keeps on spending.
- She has nothing left at the end of the month from her job earnings so she uses her cards – she is in a vicious circle of spending and paying huge amounts of interest.
- Now that redundancy might happen she may not even be able to pay the minimum, household utilities, etc. – what will happen then?

> **c) How do you think Sam and Kirsty will react to the news their mother is going to give them? What will they be most worried about?**

Possible reactions can include a mixture of:

- feeling angry that they might not be able to have what they want, when they want it
- fear over their mother losing her job and what might happen as a result of that
- sadness at losing out on being able to keep up with friends
- worry about their mum and her problems.

> **d) Sheila decides she must talk about 'needs versus wants' with Sam and Kirsty. What does this mean?**

If you look at all your expenditure there will be some things that are essentials – these are your 'needs'; for example, food, shelter, utilities, clothing. On top of that people will have their 'wants' – they are not necessarily luxuries but things that make life easier or more enjoyable; for example, entertainment, treats, holidays, pets. Achieving the right balance of needs and wants will depend on your financial circumstances.

### e) What could each member of the family do to improve the situation?

Possible suggestions:

- Sam could get a part-time job and Kirsty could ask neighbours for a small reward for chores.
- Both could economise on travel and social lives and personal expenditure.
- Sheila can look for another job, with a better salary.
- Sheila can stop using her credit cards and approach her bank manager to see if she can find a cheaper way of paying them off.
- Sheila can look for other help; e.g. a credit union, free financial advice.
- All the family can take part in shopping more carefully, looking out for 'special offers', etc.
- All the family can check they are not wasting electricity or other utilities, in order to reduce bills.

## Case Study 2: Rafik
## Questions

### a) What kind of shops offer store cards?

Retail stores; for example, Debenhams. Store cards are specific to that shop or the group that shops belongs to. Some have a high APR, so may not be good value – you may be paying back much more than the goods originally cost if you don't pay the bill off at once.

### b) How big a factor in building up his debt was the need to keep up with others?

Possible points to raise:

- For some people it can be important to 'keep up' with their friends.
- Some people see themselves as leaders of trends and feel obliged to have the latest of everything.
- It looks as if Rafik has been influenced in his spending habits – he lives at home so his general living expenses shouldn't be that high.

### c) How might huge debts impact on Rafik's emotional health?

Possible points to raise:

- People can feel so overwhelmed by their debts (student loan, card debts, etc.) that sometimes they bury their heads in the sand. This doesn't solve the problem – and they carry on worrying but not addressing the real issue.
- Others may become depressed and this will increase if the problem isn't tackled.
- Emotional problems may impact on a person's ability to work, which exacerbates the problem.
- If someone loses their job, their self-esteem goes down and they may spend more of the money they haven't got – it's a type of 'vicious circle'.

> **d) What suggestions for improving his situation would Rafik have received when he used the free financial advice service?**

Possible solutions/advice:

- get rid of his store cards
- amalgamate his debts into one manageable debt – but see below about choosing an appropriate loan/lender with a fair interest rate
- agree a monthly repayment sum and stick to it – this will mean living within his means.

> **e) How does someone judge between what is promoted as a 'good deal' and what they can really afford? What pros and cons do they have to consider?**

Possible points to raise:

- If a deal seems too good to be true, it probably is!
- If something is offered cheaply/good value and can be paid off immediately (no interest accruing) then it may be a good deal.

Key questions are always:

- Do you really need this or has advertising convinced you?
- Will you still love it when you get it home? Retailers are not obliged to give you a refund if you have changed your mind.
- How often will you wear/use the item? Divide the number of times into the cost – and work out the cost per use – does it still seem a 'good deal'?

**Case Study 3: Summer**
**Questions**

> **a) Summer saw an advert offering to consolidate all her loans into one. She thought it seemed too good to be true. Was it?**

Points to consider:

- Anything that looks too good to be true probably is – if you don't understand all the details of the agreement, ask a friend or seek other impartial advice before you sign up to it.
- Ask for a 'payment schedule' that will show you the actual payments over a period of time – it should show how interest builds up.
- If you miss a payment, the interest will increase – you are paying interest on the interest.
- Companies that consolidate loans (other than banks) will often have extremely high interest rates.

> **b) Spending to cheer yourself up (retail therapy) is not unusual. In Summer's case it cost more than she had bargained for. How might spending beyond her means affect her emotions and relationships with others?**

Possible points to raise:

- Summer will have to change the way she runs her social life and her lifestyle. If she no longer has the money to do the things she has enjoyed with her friends, it will impact on her social life; e.g. not being able to eat out.
- She has lost her home, which will be devastating to most people. Losing something that was your own can reduce your sense of independence and confidence.
- People can feel so overwhelmed by their debts (mortgage, utility bills, card debts, etc.) that sometimes they bury their heads in the sand. This doesn't solve the problem – and they carry on worrying but not addressing the real issue.
- Emotional problems may impact on a person's ability to work, which exacerbates the problem.

**c) Summer responded to a TV advert offering what looked like a good loan. Why might shopping around for the most appropriate financial products and services be a more sensible solution?**

Points to raise:

- It is always a good idea to compare one financial product against at least one other – some people get several quotes. Look at comparison websites.
- Going to a reputable financial service; e.g. a bank, rather than a money-lender, is sensible.
- A reputable financial service will provide clear terms which should be easy to understand and will not pressure you into accepting their offer.
- Use Citizens Advice or Trading Standards to check out a company to see if it is a reasonable lender.

**d) If you don't understand the financial implications of living independently (without parental support) where would you go for help and advice?**

Possible answers:

- Look out for courses or information through Student Services and Connexions.
- Citizens Advice Bureaux may also have ideas and suggestions.
- Talk to personal advisors at your bank.
- Some companies; e.g. utilities, will help you calculate approximate monthly payments.
- For more ideas or practical advice on budgeting see www.direct.gov.uk/en/YoungPeople/Money/ManagingYourMoney/DG_10027616.

# REVIEW AND REFLECTION

**ACTIVITY: MONEY CAN'T BUY YOU HAPPINESS (Student's Book, page 41)**

**3. Look at Source 2. What costs nothing and brings *you* happiness?**

Take volunteer responses from around the class – as with all personal values, try not to undermine or disbelieve the different ideas students may have.

# Topic: Work–life balance

| | |
|---|---|
| **Notes** | 'Work–life balance' can be a challenging concept for students who are not yet in full-time employment. This topic encourages them initially to think about work–life in terms of study and personal/social fulfilment. Time management for students is briefly considered.<br><br>It moves on to ask them to reflect more directly on the work environment by seeking out the views and experiences of adults they know who are currently employed. This activity demands more planning and time in setting up and receiving feedback – however, it can prove a fruitful way of considering real-life experiences and what this might mean for the students themselves in the future. |
| **Learning outcomes** | **In this topic students will learn about:**<br>■ common stresses experienced by teenagers<br>■ strategies for time management.<br><br>**They will explore:**<br>■ the concept of a work–life balance<br>■ other people's attitudes to work and personal happiness. |
| **Links to Personal Well-being PoS** | **1.2 Healthy lifestyles**<br>**b** Understanding that our physical, mental, sexual and emotional health affect our ability to lead fulfilling lives and that there is help and support available when they are threatened.<br><br>**2.1 Critical reflection**<br>**c** Students should be able to identify and use strategies for setting and meeting personal targets and challenges in order to increase motivation, reflect on their effectiveness and implement and monitor strategies for achieving goals. |
| **Links to Economic Well-being PoS** | **1.1 Career**<br>**c** Understanding the qualities, attitudes and skills needed for employability.<br><br>**2.1 Self-development**<br>**a** Students should be able to develop and maintain their self-esteem and envisage a positive future for themselves in work.<br>**b** Students should be able to identify major life roles and ways of managing the relationships between them.<br><br>**3 Range and content**<br>**c** The study of economic well-being and financial capability should include rights and responsibilities at work and attitudes and values in relation to work and enterprise. |
| **Links to SEAL outcomes** | **Motivation**<br>Students have a range of strategies for helping them to feel and remain optimistic, approaching new tasks in a positive way. |
| **Links to ECM outcomes** | Be healthy ■ Achieve economic well-being |
| **Assessment opportunity** | See Topic: Facing challenges; Activity 3: Problem-solving (page 74) |
| **Resources** | ■ Student's Book (pages 42–43)<br>■ Appendix (see the CD): Active Learning Methodologies:<br>  □ Pairs work (pages 6–7)  □ Small group work (pages 6–7)  □ Interviews (page 8) |

# STARTER ACTIVITY

### ACTIVITY: IT'S SUCH A HASSLE! (Student's Book, page 42)

1. **124 teenagers were asked in a survey to talk about what stressed them the most. The topics they came up with (in alphabetical order) were:**

   - **family/parents**
   - **managing time**
   - **school/homework**
   - **social life**
   - **sports.**

   **Which of these do you think was mentioned most and which least? Put the five in the order you think they occurred – from most to least mentioned as the main source of stress.**

This activity can be undertaken as pairs work. See Appendix (on the CD): Active Learning Methodologies: Pairs work (pages 6–7).

Answers for feedback in order of stress caused:

| Issue | Number of times students mentioned this | Percentage % |
|---|---|---|
| School/homework:<br>■ grades<br>■ tests<br>■ thinking about the future<br>■ final exams | 138 | 55% |
| Family/parents:<br>■ expectations<br>■ pressure to do well<br>■ not achieving/blowing it | 37 | 15% |
| Social life:<br>■ friends<br>■ boyfriends/girlfriends<br>■ relationships<br>■ extra-curricular clubs, activities, etc.<br>■ sex | 22 | 9% |
| Managing time<br>■ no time<br>■ deadlines<br>■ keeping up<br>■ lack of sleep<br>■ doing two things at once<br>■ too much going on<br>■ unprepared | 20 | 8% |
| Sports – team and competitive:<br>■ competing for a place on a team<br>■ making enough time for practice<br>■ pressure of competition | 10 | 4% |

Palo Alto Medical Foundation, http://pamf.org/teen/life/stress/whatstress.html

# MAIN ACTIVITIES

## ACTIVITY: WORK–LIFE BALANCE (Student's Book, page 42)

> 2. What strategies would you recommend to a friend who felt stressed or overwhelmed when trying to manage their time and commitments? Use Source 1 to help you.

Put pairs from last activity together to form small groups. See Appendix (on the CD): Active Learning Methodologies: Small group work (pages 6–7).

If the following are not raised in feedback it will be useful to offer them to the students for reflection. Do they think these are important strategies that would help someone?

**Talk it through**
Speak with the adults in your life. They may not realise how much pressure you are feeling if you manage to 'get everything done'. Talk to a parent, teacher or other trusted adult and ask for help in dealing with stress.

**Set priorities**

- Decide what is most important and what needs to be done first. You do not need to do everything in one night.
- Prioritise what needs to be done early in the week, and what can be done later.
- If you are focusing on a few projects a night (rather than worrying about all of them every night) you will do a better job on each assignment.

**Do not be an over-achiever**
Being well-rounded is important. However, you do not need to be the captain of the football team, the lead in the school play and employee of the month. Choose one or two activities that you can enjoy whilst also getting your school work done and having time to relax or visit friends.

**Set realistic goals**
Set goals that you can see yourself achieving within a week, two weeks or maybe a month. Setting goals that are too high can make you feel more stressed if you cannot realistically achieve them.

**Acknowledge your feelings**
It is normal to feel overwhelmed when things get busy, assignments are due and an extra practice or rehearsal is scheduled. If you are feeling especially stressed or depressed, you may want to look at everything you are involved in and see if there are one or two things you can cut out until you feel better.

**Take care of yourself**

- Eat a balanced and healthy diet, exercise regularly and get enough sleep.
- Do not sacrifice your health because you feel you are too busy to take care of yourself.
- A combination of a healthy diet, regular exercise and plenty of sleep helps relieve stress.

**Schedule time for you**

- Set aside half an hour a day to do something that just makes you feel good.
- Read a book or a favourite magazine, take a walk or ride your bike.
- The time that you take for yourself will help you focus when you sit down to finish your homework or practice lines for the school play.

NB Source 1 in the Student's Book also provides a useful opportunity to read and reflect on time management.

**ACTIVITY: FINDING OUT MORE (Student's Book, page 43)**

3. Some people spend so much time working that they don't notice that they're missing out on time for themselves and the people who matter to them.
   a) Use the quiz in Source 2 to interview three people who are working. It will help them identify how healthy their work–life balance is.
   b) Feed back your findings to the class and then discuss the following questions:

   - The British workforce has a reputation for not taking a lunch break that gives them an opportunity to rest and refresh. Did your results confirm this?
   - Did you spot any common factors or experiences amongst people who felt they had a good work–life balance?
   - People can get very excited, passionate and involved in work – but can this be detrimental to the rest of their lives?
   - Should one live to work, or work to live?

Interviewing adults about their experience of work is a useful way for students to begin to project their own lives forward and reflect on what would be, for them, a good work–life balance. See Appendix (on the CD): Active Learning Methodologies: Interviews (page 8).

# REVIEW AND REFLECTION

**ACTIVITY: DIVIDING MY TIME (Student's Book, page 43)**

4. Here are five things that can compete for your time:
   - family
   - education/school
   - friends/social life
   - physical recreation
   - me-time.

Do you have an even balance of the time you spend on them?

Take volunteer responses from around the class. Encourage students to reflect on the issues but not to be too self-critical.

# Topic: Facing challenges

| | |
|---|---|
| **Notes** | This topic encourages students to take a positive outlook as they approach a time of significant change in their lives. It provides examples of three strategies which could be used as an approach to problem-solving.<br><br>Stories are provided as case studies to enable students to look at significant and at first glance overwhelming issues facing other young people who could be their peers. The ideas underpinning this are to help others solve problems and reflect on how this experience may be useful to them at a future time. It also provides an opportunity to empathise with the situations of others.<br><br>This empathy approach continues in looking at people older than themselves – both their own parents and senior citizens – and the financial demands on them. |
| **Learning outcomes** | **In this topic students will learn about**<br>■ strategies that can be used when facing new challenges<br>■ the meaning of 'empathy'.<br>**They will explore:**<br>■ how to take an empathetic approach to problem-solving<br>■ how they can apply problem-solving approaches to their own situations. |
| **Links to Personal Well-being PoS** | **1.3 Risk**<br>c Developing the confidence to try new ideas and face challenges safely, individually and in groups.<br><br>**2.2 Decision-making and managing risk**<br>e Students should be able to identify how managing feelings and emotions effectively supports decision-making and risk management. |
| **Links to SEAL** | **Empathy**<br>Students recognise and take account of their feelings of empathy and act on them by considering the needs and feelings of others. |
| **Links to ECM outcomes** | Enjoy and achieve ■ Make a positive contribution |
| **Assessment opportunity** | Activity 3: Problem-solving (page 74)<br><br>**End of Key Stage Statement – healthy lifestyles**<br><br>Learners are able to:<br>■ identify some of the causes and symptoms of mental and emotional ill health, and identify strategies for recognising, preventing and addressing these in themselves and others. |
| **Resources** | ■ Student's Book (pages 44–47)<br>■ Appendix (see the CD): Active Learning Methodologies:<br>  □ Small group work (pages 6–7)   □ Pairs work (pages 6–7)   □ Diamond nine (page 6) |

# STARTER ACTIVITY

## ACTIVITY: YES OR NO? (Student's Book, page 44)

> 1. Are you feeling confident about the challenges you will be facing in the next two years?

This activity can be undertaken either as a whole-class 'taking the temperature' activity – or as individual reflection. In either case the aim is to enable students to begin to reflect on the changes that they face in the transition through the KS4 public exam phase of their lives.

**Whole-class**
Various options include:

- Have two different colours of marbles – green for confident, yellow for not confident. Students pick a marble and place in one of two jars – a 'confident' or 'not confident' jar.
- Invite students to place a tick or a cross on a whiteboard or flipchart.

Both the above allow everyone to see the overall feeling of the class without any one individual explaining their stance or reason for choosing.

**Individual**
Students can reflect on this and can either make a note for sharing later with tutor or pastoral staff. Alternatively they could do this by sharing their feelings with one other classmate.

# MAIN ACTIVITIES

## ACTIVITY: WILL THESE WORK? (Student's Book, page 45)

> 2. Look at Sources 1 to 3 and discuss whether these approaches to facing challenges would be useful. What are the advantages and disadvantages of the different approaches?

Run this as small group work. See Appendix (on the CD): Active Learning Methodologies: Small group work (pages 6–7).

**Source 1 My view, your view, their view**
Advantages:

- This allows a person to see more than their own point of view.
- This method is suitable when one-to-one disagreements arise.
- Taking different points of view allows time to consider how to respond.
- This method focuses on feelings and allows recognition of individual feelings – unless feelings are addressed the individual may not be able to move on to solutions.
- The time taken to consider may help to diffuse a volatile situation or disagreement.

Disadvantages:

- Some may find it difficult to immediately see anything from another person's perspective (not being 'me, me, me').

- Different life experiences may make it difficult for individuals to participate in an equal way.
- This takes time – and one or other of the parties involved may not have the patience to work this through.

### Source 2 The Four Cs
Advantages:

- This is a clear, step-by-step approach.
- It can provide a starting point when someone doesn't know where to begin to work on their problem.
- It builds in time to think through the situation.
- It invites a look at the consequences – not just the 'what happens now'.
- The four words implied in the title are alliterative and memorable for easy recall.

Disadvantages:

- It sees only one perspective and is therefore most useful for only personal choices.
- It doesn't allow an opportunity to work through several problems simultaneously – it needs to be one at a time.
- It suggests there may be only one best option, where there may be several solutions.

### Source 3 SUMO
Advantages:

- It starts from a positive point of view, particularly when the user recognises the choice is theirs.
- It is most useful when the person needs to move out of a negative or 'victim' stance.
- It is strongly motivational and encourages movement beyond the problem by envisaging positive actions.
- It has a memorable set of phrases which use quirky humour.
- It encourages users to take care of themselves whilst acknowledging other people's views and feelings.

Disadvantages:

- It's a lot to remember – although each phrase will work on its own.
- It is not a one-off response to a particular problem but needs to be practised as an approach to problem-solving.
- It may take some time for an individual to move away from negative thought habits if that has been their pattern for a while.

More information can be found at www.thesumoguy.com.

### ACTIVITY: PROBLEM-SOLVING (Student's Book, page 46)

> 3. Read Sources 4–7 and consider the different challenges each person is facing. Which of the three approaches in Sources 1–3 (pages 44–45) would help them to manage the situation and their feelings surrounding it? Explain your reasons for each.

Continue working in the small groups from the previous activity. Depending on time available, each group could work on one or more of the stories shown in Sources 4–7 in the Student's Book.

*PSHE Education for Key Stage 4 Teacher's Resource Book © Hodder Education*

The strongly emotive nature of the activity is chosen so that students are encouraged to consider how managing feelings and emotions effectively supports decision-making and risk management.

The stories are all particularly challenging and present what may seem overwhelming problems. However, they are not exaggerations and are all based on recent interviews with young people (*The Guardian*, 15 April 2009). The aim is to help students reflect on a number of clearly difficult situations and begin to apply some way of helping the characters to move on. This distancing technique is particularly useful so that students don't have to talk about any issues of their own. It is important that both teacher and students acknowledge that these situations will not be solved by simply applying a one-off remedy or simplistic approach. Each of the stories will need the help and support of outside agencies – and young people should never feel they have to have all the solutions within their own resources.

### Robert, 17

Robert is facing a set of complicated issues and says himself that he doesn't know where to begin. The Four Cs approach can begin to give him a place to start. He may find it helpful to separate out the issues confronting him so he can deal with them one at a time. Robert does appear to have a lot on his plate and this is an unrealistic burden for a teenager to manage alone. The problems faced by young carers are often unseen by school and other agencies. For more information see www.youngcarer.com and www.youngcarers.net.

### Chanelle, 16

Chanelle could use the approach in Source 1 My View, Your View, Their View. She and her parents each have a particular way of looking at the problem. Each is entitled to their point of view – Chanelle is not the only one facing major choices and difficulties. It will help her be more realistic about the situation if she is able to see what others in her family have to face. There are a number of agencies that specialise in working with pregnant teenagers – they may be able to mediate in a situation like Chanelle's.

### Mac, 22

Source 3 SUMO could possibly provide Mac with the impetus he needs to help him overcome his very real problems. Ex-offenders do find it difficult to find trust and acceptance. This is particularly so when it comes to employment. Mac will need to find a positive attitude within himself to give him the resilience he will require in the face of prejudice and discrimination. He should not feel embarrassed about asking for support from specialist agencies who work to support ex-offenders. The following can provide more information: www.thesite.org/homelawandmoney/law/introuble/breakingfree and www.nacro.org.uk.

### Rachel, 15

All of the three approaches from Sources 1–3 could be helpful here. However, they are not sufficient on their own; there is clearly a need for Rachel to access external assistance. There is a Safeguarding Children issue involved and Rachel will need help to support her through this. See the following for further advice and information: www.nspcc.org.uk/what-we-do/the-work-we-do/the-work-we-do_wdh71772.html.

## End of Key Stage Statement – healthy lifestyles

Learners are able to:

- identify some of the causes and symptoms of mental and emotional ill health, and identify strategies for recognising, preventing and addressing these in themselves and others.

### Assessment activity

The activity can be extended by using the sources in the Student's Book.

The aim of the activity is to encourage students to review some of the causes and symptoms of mental and emotional ill health. They then examine the strategies they feel might help in each situation.

Students will reflect on a number of clearly difficult situations and begin to apply some way of helping the characters to move on. This distancing technique is particularly useful so that students don't have to talk about any issues of their own. It is important that both teacher and students acknowledge that these situations will not be solved by simply applying a one-off remedy or simplistic approach. Each of the stories will need the help and support of outside agencies – and young people should never feel they have to have all the solutions within their own resources.

### Assessment method – small group work

Allocate one of Sources 4–7 (the situations assigned to Robert, Chanelle, Mac and Rachel) to each small group.

Each group reads their assigned situation. They then remind themselves of the three strategies for facing challenges described in Sources 1–3; these are:

- My view, your view, their view
- The Four Cs
- SUMO.

The first response is to list some of the pressures and circumstances that may impact on their character's mental and emotional health.

Each group then goes on to identify which of Sources 1–3 they think is the most appropriate to help with the problems faced by their character.

The teacher writes up the names of the four characters. As each group responds, the pressures/circumstances are listed as well as their identified approach – these are shown under each character's name.

When all groups have fed back, identify when/if different solutions are suggested for a character. Draw out the understanding that different solutions may work equally well in each situation – there is no right answer. Does this help us understand that different issues affect people in different ways and that they may benefit from a variety of approaches?

See above for possible best practice answers to each character's situation.

In the final feedback, use some of the examples given by students to credit wide-ranging thinking and an empathetic understanding of their character's situation.

**ACTIVITY: IN THEIR SHOES (Student's Book, page 47)**

> **4. a) Sheila has a limited income and is living off her state pension. She can't afford all of these so which do you think Sheila should spend her money on?**
>
> **Afternoon at the pool with friends**
> **Birthday present for her grandchild**
> **Council Tax (a legal requirement)**
> **Food for the weekend**
> **Overdue electricity bill**
> **Packet of cigarettes**
> **Pet food**
> **Repair cost of broken TV**
> **Soap, shampoo**

The previous activity invited students to think of challenges faced by those of a similar age to themselves. Explain to students that this activity encourages them to consider a particular kind of challenge faced by a senior citizen – that of living on a limited income. It will be useful for them to know what a single person's state pension amounts to. See www.direct.gov.uk/en/Pensionsandretirementplanning for an up-to-date calculation of how much this would be.

Run this as pairs work. See Appendix: Active Learning Methodologies: Pairs work (pages 6–7).

The options for undertaking this activity include:

- a diamond nine – See Appendix (on the CD): Active Learning Methodologies: Diamond nine (page 6)
- dividing the list into three categories: necessities/desirables/luxuries.

> **b) Now reflect on this activity:**
>
> - **Was it easy to make decisions for Sheila?**
> - **What were the difficulties in prioritising her wants and needs?**

Take feedback as a whole-class discussion. In taking feedback when reflecting on the activity, recognise and praise empathetic rather than judgemental approaches; for example:

- cigarettes – a lifetime's use of tobacco will have fostered a deep dependence
- pet food – pets provide companionship for older people who live on their own
- TV – would young people think of this as a luxury in their lives?

> **c) Use your empathy skills to rewrite the expenses in a), imagining it is a list of nine financial demands on the parents of teenagers.**

Continue working in the same pairs as in question 4a. Ask students to brainstorm all the financial demands on the parents of teenagers that they can think of.

Now invite them to imagine that they are rewriting the list of financial demands to create a new diamond nine activity. What nine things do they think parents would include – and what order of priority would parents choose?

# REVIEW AND REFLECTION

**ACTIVITY: FACING FUTURE CHALLENGES (Student's Book, page 47)**

> 5. **Reflect back to when you chose options in Year 9 – or forward to what you will do after your GCSEs. These were and will be big challenges and opportunities. In the next few months you are likely to face a challenge or two. What might these be and which of the strategies you have learned about would you use and why?**

It may help students to visualise this task as setting out on a road – they may look back on where they have come from and how they overcame obstacles on the way. They may also look forward to the journey ahead, mapping any challenges they can see on their route.

Take feedback from volunteers and create a list of challenges and the suggested strategies to overcome them.

# Topic: Bereavement

| Notes | This topic *does* need to be addressed – although many teachers may be concerned about doing this. In writing this topic the authors have tried to ensure that both teachers and students are not put in a position where vulnerable emotions come to the surface. If a teacher or student has been recently bereaved it would be justifiable to absent themselves from the lesson – this raises issues of planning for both running the lesson and providing students with alternative support. |
|---|---|
| | The topic starts by exploring rituals associated with bereavement (initially through the death of a pet) and moves on to providing a model which helps to understand the feelings often experienced with a bereavement. |
| | An activity called 'Expressing feelings' moves closer to the emotional impact that death can bring. The suggested trigger for this is the song 'Tears in Heaven' by Eric Clapton; however, alternative poems and songs are also suggested. |
| | The main activity uses a technique which allows students to explore issues of support – but rather than invite them to do this directly for a bereaved person they are being asked to 'help the helpers'. |
| | A useful website and resource for teachers who may wish to understand more about supporting bereaved students (and more about the issue in general) is www.rd4u.org.uk and in particular the pdf of the leaflet called 'After Someone Dies'. |
| | www.griefencounter.org.uk is a charity set up to support children and young people who are bereaved – the material they produce is another excellent resource. |
| Learning outcomes | **In this topic students will learn about:**<br>■ numbers of people affected by bereavement<br>■ a model to explain the feelings experienced in bereavement.<br>**They will explore:**<br>■ a lyrical response to bereavement<br>■ ways to support a bereaved person. |
| Links to Personal Well-being PoS | **1.2 Healthy lifestyles**<br>c Dealing with growth and change as normal parts of growing up.<br>**2.3 Developing relationships and working with others**<br>e Students should be able to explore feelings and emotions related to changing relationships and develop skills to cope with loss and bereavement.<br>**3 Range and content**<br>i The study of personal well-being should include the impact of separation, divorce and bereavement on families and the need to adapt to changing circumstances. |
| Links to SEAL | **Empathy**<br>Students understand that people can all feel the same range of emotions … and that different people may express their feelings in different ways. |
| Links to ECM outcomes | Be healthy ■ Make a positive contribution |
| Assessment opportunity | See Topic: Facing challenges; Activity 3: Problem-solving (page 74) |
| Resources | ■ Student's Book (pages 48–49)<br>■ Appendix (see the CD): Active Learning Methodologies:<br>  □ Brainstorming (page 3)   □ Small group work (pages 6–7)<br>  □ Pairs work (pages 6–7)   □ Resource development (page 9) |

# BACKGROUND INFORMATION

*Before running this lesson you will find it helpful to consider the following:*

- *Up to 70 per cent of schools have a bereaved student on their role at any given time. One study found that 92 per cent of young people will experience a 'significant' bereavement before the age of 16 years. With the right help and support, most of these children will not need professional help. What they do need is the understanding of familiar and trusted adults. Schools are well placed to provide this.*
- *Check with pastoral staff to identify if any students participating in this session have been recently affected by bereavement. You may wish to consider alternative arrangements for them – this can include asking them whether they wish to remain in the session or not.*
- *The struggle for independence may cause bereaved teenagers to challenge the beliefs and expectations of others as to how they should be feeling or behaving. Death increases anxieties about the future, and they may question the meaning of life and experience depression. They may be having difficulty coming to terms with their own mortality and that of those close to them and cope by refusing to contemplate the possibility of death by experimenting with risk-taking behaviour.*
- *Teenagers may find it easier to discuss their feelings with a sympathetic friend or adult than with a close family member.*

*These points have been adapted from materials provided by www.childbereavement.org.uk.*

# STARTER ACTIVITY

**ACTIVITY: EARLY EXPERIENCES (Student's Book, page 48)**

1. **Most children's first experience of death is usually when a pet dies. They will often ask their parents to bury the dead pet in the garden and give it a 'funeral' service. What are the typical things a child might want to do at the pet's funeral?**

Run this as a brainstorm. See Appendix (on the CD): Active Learning Methodologies: Brainstorming (page 3). If the following ideas are not offered these suggestions may aid discussion:

- digging the grave together
- using shoebox/matchbox as a coffin for burial
- putting a pet toy in the grave
- making a cross or marker (often using lolly sticks!)
- walking in procession to the gravesite
- painting a large stone with the pet's name to mark the burial
- laying a small posy of flowers
- singing a song/hymn
- saying some nice words about the pet
- saying a prayer
- small children might want other pets there or bring teddy bears/dolls out to form a congregation.

# MAIN ACTIVITIES

### ACTIVITY: MARKING A BEREAVEMENT (Student's Book, page 48)

> 2. The photos in Source 1 show different funeral rituals. Discuss why people feel the need to have such rituals around the death of someone or something they love.

Look at Source 1 with the students and then extend the discussion by asking why children and also adults feel the need to have such rituals around the death of someone or something they love.

Points to raise:

- A ceremony marks the value or importance of the dead pet/person.
- Actions, words, etc. help the bereaved to move through sadness and give them some sort of voice when they are not sure what to say.
- A funeral is the beginning of the period of adjustment that the bereaved go through.
- People with religious beliefs will want to seek spiritual help; the words/hymns/songs can be a part of asking god for help.
- If particular class members want to talk about the funeral rituals in their own culture or faith this could be encouraged – you may want to seek support from the RE teacher to extend this activity.

### ACTIVITY: ADJUSTMENT (Student's Book, page 49)

> 3. 'Life will never be the same. It's different. And that's OK.' These are the words of someone who has experienced bereavement. Look at Source 2. How does it help to explain the feelings this person is going through?

Run this as a pairs activity. See Appendix (on the CD): Active Learning Methodologies: Pairs work (pages 6–7).

When taking feedback, if the following points are not made introduce them into the discussion:

- The drawing shows how a bereaved person starts in a very 'dark' place – feeling very low and often lost as to what to do and how to cope.
- There is no logic to the feelings a bereaved person may feel – the model shows this by going round and round a series of different feelings.
- One type of feeling does not necessarily always come after another.
- There will be 'good' days and 'bad' days.
- Sometimes something as simple as a piece of music will trigger sadness – at other times something which wouldn't necessarily seem funny may be the cause of great hilarity.
- The 'firsts' are often really difficult; e.g. the first Christmas or birthday they are not there, the first time you no longer have someone to buy a Father or Mother's Day card for, etc.
- Sometimes the bereaved person thinks they are 'over' things but feelings come back at unexpected times and places.
- The drawing shows two lines right through the whole grief spiral which are marked as 'confusion' – this is often what the person is feeling.

**ACTIVITY: EXPRESSING FEELINGS (Student's Book, page 49)**

> 4. **Look up the lyrics of 'Tears in Heaven', especially lines 5–8. How do you interpret what Eric Clapton was trying to say?**

Keep students in the same pairs as the previous activity. You may wish to play the song and encourage students to follow the words. There will be different interpretations to the words – and these should be explored.

The theme of the song is the bereaved person wondering what it would be like if he were to visit heaven and see the dead person again – would the dead person recognise him? Would the dead person be able to help him cope with the emotional and physical pains and strains of grief?

The last four lines of each verse particularly focus on:

- the bereaved person wanting so much to be with the person who has died but knowing that their own life continues
- the words 'time is a healer' and hoping this turns out to be true
- recognising that although his heart feels as if it is breaking now he has to be strong enough to cope until he eventually finds peace again.

In summary the message might be seen as 'Heaven and here (where I am) are different places and the two of us cannot continue to be together as we once were' – i.e. the period of adjustment continues.

Other material that may help students explore thoughts and feelings about bereavement include:

**Poems**

- 'Funeral Blues' or 'Stop All the Clocks' – WH Auden
- 'Remember' – Christina Rosetti
- 'Turn Again to Life' – Mary Lee Hall

**Songs**

- 'Paint It Black' – Rolling Stones
- 'Dance With My Father' – Luther Vandross
- 'Abraham, Martin & John' – Marvin Gaye
- 'Stairway to Heaven' – Led Zeppelin.

**ACTIVITY: HELPING OTHERS TO COPE WITH BEREAVEMENT (Student's Book, page 49)**

> 5. **Some people find it difficult to know what to say when someone dies. They might be unintentionally thoughtless or unkind. Perhaps they just don't understand, are frightened or unaware. In groups, produce a small resource designed to help someone support a friend who is bereaved.**
> a) **Choose the format of the resource (leaflet, pamphlet, webpage, etc.).**
> b) **Research and decide what you would include to help the supportive friend. Use the websites listed below as a starting point:**
> **www.griefencounter.org.uk**
> **www.childhoodbereavementnetwork.org.uk/haad.htm**
> **www.helpguide.org/mental/helping_grieving.htm**
> c) **Create your resource.**

Run this as a resource development activity – working in groups of about four. See Appendix (on the CD): Active Learning Methodologies: Resource development (page 9).

The activity has been designed to distance the discussion of bereavement issues to one step removed from the bereaved person; i.e. the resource is to help others to help the bereaved. The sensitivity of this area may be better handled by not inviting students or teachers to empathise directly with the bereaved person but rather with those around them.

Students can use the sites listed in the activity as a starting point. The following can provide guidance on resource content:

- sensitivity throughout towards the bereaved
- providing a definition of bereavement
- identifying ways to help someone else cope
- describing the feelings someone else might experience (see Source 2)
- providing a list of useful key contacts.

# REVIEW AND REFLECTION

**ACTIVITY: HERE AND NOW (Student's Book, page 49)**

> 6. Sometimes when a loved one has died people say, 'I wish I'd told them how much they meant to me'. Choose someone alive now of whom you think a great deal. Create a one-line appreciation message to give them.

This activity is designed to end on a positive note after having explored the deeper issues of bereavement.

Invite volunteers to share their responses. If no one wants to do this then suggest they take their appreciations and share them with the person for whom they were written.

# 4 Relationships

## Topic: Relating to others

| | |
|---|---|
| **Notes** | There could be students for whom participating in this topic may be uncomfortable – if they have few relationships themselves, find relationships difficult or have been recently bereaved. Be alert to this possibility, ensure that the climate feels safe and allow the opportunity for opt-out.<br><br>This topic introduces the concept of relationships by exploring different types and levels of relationships. It goes on to discuss why most people want close relationships and considers what may be good about relationships and what is sometimes difficult in relationships. The difference between 'friendships', 'non-intimate' and 'intimate' relationships is a focus for discussion. Building relationships and working at maintaining them is examined.<br><br>The final activity in the unit provides an opportunity for students to reflect on and think about their learning in relation to their future 'working' lives. |
| **Learning outcomes** | **In this topic students will learn about:**<br>■ different types and levels of relationships.<br>**They will explore:**<br>■ the varied roles within their relationships<br>■ the factors that make relationships successful or difficult<br>■ the place of rights, responsibilities and respect in relationships. |
| **Links to Personal Well-being PoS** | **1.4 Relationships**<br>**b** Understanding that people have multiple roles and responsibilities in society and that making positive relationships and contributing to groups, teams and communities is important.<br><br>**2.3 Developing relationships and working with others**<br>**a** Students should be able to use social skills to build and maintain a range of positive relationships, reflect upon what makes these successful and apply this to new situations. |
| **Links to Economic Well-being PoS** | **2.3 Enterprise**<br>**a** Students should be able to identify the main qualities and skills needed to enter and thrive in the working world. |
| **Links to SEAL outcomes** | **Social skills**<br>Students understand their rights and responsibilities as individuals who belong to many different social groups. |
| **Links to ECM outcomes** | Be healthy ■ Enjoy and achieve ■ Make a positive contribution |
| **Assessment opportunity** | See Topic: Where to turn for help and support; Activity 2: Who can they speak to? (page 98) |
| **Resources** | ■ Student's Book (pages 50–51)<br>■ Appendix (see the CD): Active Learning Methodologies:<br>  □ Brainstorming (page 3)   □ Small group work (pages 6–7) |

*PSHE Education for Key Stage 4 Teacher's Resource Book © Hodder Education*

# STARTER ACTIVITY

**ACTIVITY: WHO'S WHO IN THEIR LIVES? (Student's Book, page 50)**

> 1.  List all the different relationships you have seen in films, TV, books and advertising. Use the photographs on these two pages (Student's Book pages 50–51) to start you thinking about different types of relationships.

Use small group discussion. See Appendix (on the CD): Active Learning Methodologies: Small group work (pages 6–7). Allocate one setting (e.g. soap operas) per group.

Typical examples might include:

- married couples
- boyfriends/girlfriends
- same-sex relationships
- faith communities
- working relationships
- neighbours
- service relationships; e.g. shops or medical
- armed forces comrades
- fantasy figures
- families: parents, siblings, etc.

# MAIN ACTIVITIES

**ACTIVITY: WHAT ABOUT YOU? (Student's Book, page 50)**

> 2.  a) Now thinking about yourself, what different types of relationships do you experience in your life? Using Source 1 as a guide, create your own relationship rainbow.
>
>       - Start with yourself in the middle and represent some of your relationships, with little drawings and/or names or initials, using distance from yourself to indicate the significance of the relationship.
>       - Put up to ten people in the diagram, and include both close and distant relationships, and good as well as difficult relationships.

Run the first part of this as a class brainstorm. See Appendix (on the CD): Active Learning Methodologies: Brainstorming (page 3). Students should come up with a list of different relationships and write up their suggestions; for example:friends

- parents
- brothers and sisters
- neighbours

- teachers
- shopkeepers
- other service providers.

If students raise the idea of pets, this should be accepted too. For some people pets play a very significant part in their lives and are important in helping them learn about reliability, trust, care and responsibility.

Discuss the range of relationships that have emerged from this and the previous activity. Then ask students to complete their relationship rainbow.

---

**b) Choose one person from your rainbow with whom you have a significant relationship and answer the following questions:**

- **What type of relationship is it (friend/family/work, etc.)?**
- **Why is it significant?**
- **What makes it a good relationship or what makes it difficult?**

---

After students have completed their relationship rainbows ask everyone to choose one person from their rainbow with whom they have a **significant** relationship. Make it clear that they will be asked to share something of the nature of this relationship with others in their small group. Then ask them to reflect alone on this relationship and note their responses to the questions.

Now divide them into self-selected groups of three or four. Have individuals share with their group what they choose from what they have written down, taking no more than a couple of minutes each.

When all the groups are ready, bring them back together, draw out and discuss the questions in part c).

---

**c) As a class discuss:**

- **Why are close relationships important?**
- **Are close relationships important to everyone?**

---

Explore the different ways in which we use the term 'relationship' – pull out the differences between friendships, non-intimate relationships and intimate relationships. NB 'Intimate' does not have to mean physically intimate but rather close and personal.

**ACTIVITY: RELATIONSHIPS NEED WORK (Student's Book, page 51)**

Have students continue to work in the same small groups to discuss the questions.
Draw out the following when taking feedback:

---

**a) What makes for a good relationship?**

---

- open, honest communication
- negotiation and compromise
- shared humour/values/background/experiences/social groups
- kindness, caring and courtesy
- trust and reliability.

---

**b) What might make a relationship difficult?**

---

- imbalance of power
- lack of trust
- lack of communication
- taking the other for granted
- not showing respect or courtesy
- bullying and demanding behaviours.

> **c) How important are 'rights and responsibilities' in a relationship? Can you give a similar example to the passenger and bus driver on page 51 of the Student's Book?**

These two concepts go together. At some level **every** relationship involves both rights and responsibilities; for example, I have a right to expect the bus driver to stop, sell me a fare and look after my safety. I have a responsibility to pay my fare and behave safely and appropriately towards the driver and other passengers.

Ask students to give similar comparisons for other relationships.

> **d) A lot of young people say one of the most important elements of a relationship is 'respect'. What does that mean to you?**

There are many views on this. Here are some thoughts to promote discussion:

- 'Give respect, get respect' – but what on earth does it mean? Can we really define respect?
- Tony Blair: 'What lies at the heart of [anti-social] behaviour is a lack of respect for values that almost everyone in this country shares – consideration for others, a recognition that we all have responsibilities as well as rights, civility and good manners.'
- The logo of two arrows circling each other represents the idea that what goes around, comes around and 'do unto others as you would have others do unto you'. Another view is to see respect as a two-way street; if you don't see it that way then you create something called 'asymmetric relationships' and even asymmetric citizenship.

# REVIEW AND REFLECTION

### ACTIVITY: RELATIONSHIPS AT WORK (Student's Book, page 51)

> **4. People often overlook the fact that when they are at work they need good relationships. The people at work don't have to be your best friends, so why do you need to build good relationships with them?**

In preparing students for the world of work (and further study) it is important that they appreciate the maxim 'You do not have to like everyone but you need to be able to work with everyone'. Good working relationships will enable:

- an organisation to function at its best – increasing efficiency and work satisfaction
- people to enjoy coming to and contributing to the workplace
- a good working atmosphere which is conducive to creativity and productivity
- a good working atmosphere/ethos which communicates itself to customers/consumers.

# Topic: Parenting skills and family life

| | |
|---|---|
| **Notes** | This topic covers all kinds of families and the skills needed in family life. In approaching this topic the authors have chosen not to focus on the structural make-up of families (e.g. number of parents, are there any step-parents, etc.). Instead, students are invited to reflect on the dynamics of family life – i.e. what makes for a successful working relationship between different family members. In adolescence teenagers begin to realise that their parents are not perfect and that the way their home runs is not the only way a home can be run. By reflecting on this they can begin to develop their own belief systems and start to build strategies for their own future family life. An activity on parenting skills encourages the students to look at this in the broadest possible way – not just practical skills but also emotional and caring skills. Social pressure and trends indicate that parents need to work harder and longer to earn sufficient money to bring up a family. Bearing this in mind, an activity is included which asks students to consider (some perhaps for the first time) the overall budgeting problems that the average family faces. NB Care needs to be taken with 'looked after' children who may have had very negative family experiences or who have no current context in which to base their discussions. Pastoral staff will be a good source of advice. |
| **Learning outcomes** | **In this topic students will learn about:**<br>■ the different ways that families operate<br>■ the challenges of bringing up a family<br>■ family budgeting.<br>**They will explore:**<br>■ how different people interpret the word 'family'<br>■ the skills needed to be a good parent<br>■ ways that families can work together to manage money. |
| **Links to Personal Well-being PoS** | **1.4 Relationships**<br>**b** Understanding that people have multiple roles and responsibilities in society and that … contributing to groups, teams and communities is important.<br>**2.1 Critical reflection**<br>**e** Students should be able to develop self-awareness by …<br>**2.3. Developing relationships and working with others**<br>**b** Students should be able to use the social skill of negotiation within relationships…<br>**3 Range and content**<br>**g** The study of personal well-being should include the roles … of … family members.<br>**h** The study of personal well-being should include parenting skills … |
| **Links to Economic Well-being PoS** | **1.2 Capability**<br>**b** Learning how to manage money and personal finances.<br>**2.4 Financial capability**<br>**a** Students should be able to manage their money. |
| **Links to SEAL** | **Social skills**<br>Students can take others' thoughts and feelings into account … |
| **Links to ECM outcomes** | ■ Achieving economic well-being    ■ Making a positive contribution |
| **Assessment opportunity** | See Topic: Where to turn for help and support; Activity 2: Who can they speak to? (page 98) |
| **Resources** | ■ Student's Book (pages 52–55)<br>■ Appendix (see the CD): Active Learning Methodologies:<br>  □ Brainstorming (page 3)  □ Small group work (pages 6–7)<br>  □ Pairs work (pages 6–7)  □ Continuum (page 4)  □ Diamond nine (page 6)<br>■ Resource sheet 4.1 (page 91) |

# STARTER ACTIVITY

**ACTIVITY: WHAT CAN I SAY ABOUT FAMILY? (Student's Book, page 52)**

> 1. Each of the writers above (Student's Book, page 52) has different feelings about 'family' – some funny, some cynical, some realistic. Write a couple of lines to express what you feel about 'family'.

Encourage students to give feedback but be sensitive that for some of them this may not be a positive or easy task.

# MAIN ACTIVITIES

**ACTIVITY: WHAT IS FAMILY? (Student's Book, page 53)**

> 2. What do people mean when they call a social group they belong to their family?

Run this activity as a brainstorm. See Appendix (on the CD): Active Learning Methodologies: Brainstorming (page 3).
   Responses may include:

- an interesting point here is that in belonging to a social group one has usually exercised choice – which one can't do with one's own family
- a sense of belonging and having shared experiences/interests
- there can be great trust in a group who regard themselves as family
- a feeling of family based on loyalty in a group
- a group of people you could turn to (with a problem/if something was wrong).

NB Some people associate with 'gangs' with whom they experience a sense of family – not all gangs are bad! You could draw comparisons with the Sharks and the Jets in *West Side Story* if you wanted to talk about a 'bad' gang experience.

> 3. How do the photos in Source 1 show characteristics of a family?

Sometimes people talk about a group that they feel really close to as their 'family' even if they are not related by blood or upbringing. People in the photos in Source 1 may experience these and other family qualities:

- Shared interests and experiences
- Shared 'history' from the time they spend together
- Customs and traditions that the group share
- A bond of relationships
- Knowing the others will support/look out for/help them
- And that in turn they will feel the commitment to support/look out/help others.

**ACTIVITY: TYPES OF FAMILY (Student's Book, page 53)**

> 4. Different family groups have different ways of behaving together:
>
> - **authoritarian** – there are clear, fixed rules about what is and what is not allowed
> - **inconsistent** – sometimes there are strict rules but at other times none
> - **negotiating** – there is dialogue between adults (parents) and teenagers, with the young people gradually gaining more autonomy.
>
> Name one advantage and one disadvantage for each of these.

Run this activity as pairs work. See Appendix (on the CD): Active Learning Methodologies: Pairs work (pages 6–7). Students will have very individual perspectives on this depending on their own family situations. The following may help them develop self-awareness by reflecting critically on others:

- **Authoritarian**
  Advantage: knowing exactly what is expected of you
  Disadvantage: no flexibility when something/someone changes.
- **Inconsistent**
  Advantage: it can feel very flexible and as if you have choice
  Disadvantage: confusion – you never know if something is OK or not.
- **Negotiating**
  Advantage: allows you to gradually take on more independence
  Disadvantage: sometimes it can feel easier to do what you're told.

### ACTIVITY: PARENTING SKILLS (Student's Book, page 53)

> 5. The list of parenting skills in Source 2 is in alphabetical order. Which would be your priorities? Use a diamond nine format as shown below and place the nine skills using position 1 for the most important. Remember that position 9 doesn't mean that skill has no importance.
>
> ```
>             1
>         2       3
>     4       5       6
>         7       8
>             9
> ```

Run this as a diamond nine (prioritising) activity. See Appendix (on the CD): Active Learning Methodologies: Diamond nine (page 6).

A set of cards suitable for photocopying to use in this activity can be found on Resource sheet 4.1 (page 91).

It is important to remind students before they start that all these parenting skills are valuable and placing any towards the bottom of the diamond does not mean that they can be omitted from the skills of being a parent. Remind them that you are asking them to reflect on their priorities.

After processing the diamond nine you may wish to introduce the concept of 'good enough' parenting. In other words no parent can do all of this perfectly all of the time. Every parent/child relationship involves give and take, good days and bad days, etc. The issue here is: Are there **enough** of each of these skills being used?

### ACTIVITY: WHAT IS GOOD PARENTING? (Student's Book, page 54)

> 6. a) Read Source 3. In light of what you have learned about key parenting skills, do you think these are examples of good parenting? Give reasons why/why not for each.
>    b) Now write a list of statements like those in Source 3 that describe a good child (teenager).

- This could be run as group discussion work. See Appendix (on the CD): Active Learning Methodologies: Small group work (pages 6–7).
- Alternatively for a more dynamic active learning experience run this activity as a Continuum. See Appendix (on the CD): Active Learning Methodologies: Continuum (page 4). Use 'AGREE' and 'DISAGREE' cards at either end of the spectrum. Offer each statement with the prefix 'A GOOD PARENT WOULD ...'

□ always buy the latest gadgets/trainers/fashions for their children
□ be very strict about what time their children have to be back at home
□ check out their children's friends
□ give their children an allowance to spend each week – no strings attached
□ not allow their child to drink alcohol until they are 18
□ expect to know where their children are going to be when they are out
□ allow their children lots of freedom to make mistakes
□ permit their children to use illegal drugs at home, because it's safer than elsewhere.

## ACTIVITY: BORN NOT MADE? (Student's Book, page 55)

**7. Why do you think organisations such as Positive Parents (see Source 4) might appeal to some parents?**

Points to consider:

- Parents may feel that they need guidance and support because not everyone feels they instinctively know how to raise children.
- Some people may have had negative experiences in how they were brought up but do not know how they can begin to be more positive in raising their own children.
- It can be good to share points of view and hear other people's experiences.

**8. There are different points of view about whether there should be some sort of parenting qualification. In order to drive a car you need a licence – should something similar be introduced before you can become a parent? Discuss reasons for and against it being introduced.**

Run this as pairs work. See Appendix (on the CD): Active Learning Methodologies: Pairs work (pages 6–7).
  The following points may add to discussion:

| For | Against |
|-----|---------|
| Some people base their parenting on how their parents brought them up – and have no other experience. If their experience of being parented wasn't good they may benefit from some outside help/coaching. | Attending a course might raise some useful points but won't necessarily change what you do – i.e. if you don't want to take on what is being taught. |
| Children are wonderfully precious and can't ever be replaced – so it's worth trying to learn to get it right the first time. | If only one parent (of a two parent family) attends – would they both be working in the same way and setting the same routines? |
| Classes are shared with other parents who are facing the same problems. This can be a great form of support helping each other through the issues. It is nice to know that you are not alone. | Raising a family is a fundamental personal freedom and outside bodies; e.g. government, social workers, etc. should not interfere unless there is a real problem. |

**ACTIVITY: FAMILY BUDGETING SKILLS (Student's Book, page 55)**

> 9. Look at Source 5, which shows a typical family budget planner. The areas listed are those that the family regularly spend on; and right now they're having difficulties managing. Offer some suggestions for where and how the family – including the children – could make savings.

Run this as a small group activity. See Appendix (on the CD): Active Learning Methodologies: Small group work (pages 6–7).

Typical budgeting ideas for the whole family include:

- checking their mortgage payment plan and comparing it to other mortgage offers
- using comparison websites to get the best deal on household utilities, insurances, phone packages, etc.
- talking with bank manager or independent financial advisor regarding consolidating loans into one place with the lowest interest rate possible
- they can all try to economise in various ways; e.g. taking a packed lunch to work/school
- saving on gym/outside entertainment by finding 'free' things to do together – look online
- they could all agree between them to do without some 'luxuries'.

The young people, in particular, could contribute by:

- helping with the household chores – no need for a cleaner
- older children (over the NSPCC recommended age of 16) babysitting free of charge
- those who are old enough getting weekend/after-school jobs and therefore giving up having pocket money. They could also then buy their own non-essential clothing.

# REVIEW AND REFLECTION

**ACTIVITY: IMPACTING ON OTHERS (Student's Book, page 55)**

> 10. Most people could change one thing about their own behaviour to make life at home easier and happier with others. Assuming you're not perfect, what one thing would you change about yourself?

Ask volunteers for feedback – don't force examples in this instance.

> 11. Imagine you had to write a postcard of appreciation to your parent/carer. What one thing would you most value them for?

Take feedback from volunteers and encourage everyone to consider actually taking their message back to their own parent(s)/carer(s). Everyone enjoys being appreciated.

# RESOURCE SHEET 4.1

**DIAMOND NINE CARDS**

| | |
|---|---|
| **ASPIRING** | **CONTROL AND DISCIPLINE** |
| **LOVE AND AFFECTION** | **MANAGING THE HOME** |
| **PRAISE** | **RIGHT AND WRONG** |
| **SAFETY** | **TEMPER** |
| **TIME AND INTEREST** | |

# Topic: When relationships go wrong

| | |
|---|---|
| **Notes** | The Student's Book contains information for this topic on two key areas where young people may be vulnerable in their relationships: grooming and domestic violence. Forced marriage is another area where they might be vulnerable and is covered in the Teacher's Resource Book (Resource sheet 4.2, page 9). There is no specific activity focused around this material but the teacher is encouraged to engage the students in discussing these matters. They may seem controversial but research is showing that they are relevant to significant numbers of young people. In any case, all young people need to be aware of these social issues.<br><br>The topic also focuses on internet safety and respect in relationships as these have also been highlighted as areas of concern in young people's lives.<br><br>There is an activity which invites young people to reflect on the place of PSHE education in addressing social ills. The approach of expecting the school curriculum to sort out the world's problems is taken for granted especially by people outside education. The activity provides an opportunity for a more critical approach to be taken. |
| **Learning outcomes** | **In this topic students will learn about:**<br>■ things that can make relationships unhealthy or damaging<br>■ laws that support people in unhealthy relationship situations.<br><br>**They will explore:**<br>■ how respect can be an important part of a relationship<br>■ whether the PSHE curriculum should teach about current social problems. |
| **Links to Personal Well-being PoS** | **1.3 Risk**<br>a Understanding risk in both positive and negative terms and understanding that individuals need to manage risk to themselves and others in a range of personal and social situations.<br><br>**1.4 Relationships**<br>c Understanding that relationships can cause strong feelings and emotions.<br><br>**2.1 Critical reflection**<br>d Students should be able to reflect on feelings and identify positive ways of understanding, managing and expressing strong emotions and challenging behaviour, acting positively on them.<br><br>**2.3 Developing relationships and working with others**<br>d Students should be able to demonstrate respect for and acceptance of the differences between people, and challenge offensive behaviour, prejudice and discrimination assertively and safely. |
| **Links to SEAL outcomes** | **Social skills**<br>Students can assess risks and consider the issues involved before making decisions about their personal relationships. |
| **Links to ECM outcomes** | Stay safe ■ Enjoy and achieve ■ Make a positive contribution |
| **Assessment opportunity** | See Topic: Where to turn for help and support; Activity 2: Who can they speak to? (page 98) |
| **Resources** | ■ Student's Book (pages 56–59)<br>■ Appendix (see the CD): Active Learning Methodologies:<br>  □ Pairs work (pages 6–7)   □ Small group work (pages 6–7)<br>■ Resource sheet 4.2 (page 95) |

# STARTER ACTIVITY

## ACTIVITY: GOOD ADVICE (Student's Book, page 57)

> 1. Look at Source 1 and think back to other work you have done on internet safety. If you had to offer a younger sibling advice on this topic, what two do's and two don'ts would you suggest?

Run this as pairs work. See Appendix (on the CD): Active Learning Methodologies: Pairs work (pages 6–7).

In addition to the points in Source 1 the following points are also relevant.

| Do | Don't |
|---|---|
| think carefully about any personal information and photos you put online | let anyone persuade you to post inappropriate content online |
| remember to use the CEOP button to report anything that worries you | ever put anything online that could identify you; e.g. phone number, address, school, etc. |
| switch off if someone says/does something that upsets or worries you | ever worry about getting into trouble – if something has gone wrong or you are worried talk to a trusted adult |
| remember that social networking sites e.g. Facebook have a minimum age – stick to it | shut yourself away when using the computer – there should be nothing to hide |
| remember the safest option is to ignore 'free prize' pop-ups; if it sounds too good to be true it usually is – there'll be a catch! | agree to meet someone from a chat room – it would only be safe if you took along a parent/carer and the meeting was in a public place. |

# MAIN ACTIVITIES

## ACTIVITY: EXPECT RESPECT (Student's Book, page 59)

> 2. Read about problems in teenage relationships in Source 2. Now turn this on its head and answer this question: In a teenage relationship, what things would show the couple respected each other?

Run this as small group work. See Appendix (on the CD): Active Learning Methodologies: Small group work (pages 6–7).

When taking feedback the following points may help to extend the discussion.
Respect can mean many things. It might be seen in the following ways:

- The people listen to each other and negotiate what to do and where to go.
- They don't want to force their point of view on the other person.
- They will value each other and treat each other with care and consideration.
- They won't pressurise the other person to do something that they don't want to do.
- They will enjoy the fact that the other person has friends.
- They won't mind if the other person wants to spend time with friends.

**ACTIVITY: PSHE TOPICS (Student's Book, page 59)**

> 3. **Read Source 3.**
>    a) **What reasons would you add for or against lessons about domestic violence in PSHE?**
>    b) **What are your views?**

Be sensitive to the individual experiences of students and do not force answers from those who may not wish to offer a point of view.

Remind students that everyone has different experiences and home lives.

> 4. **Whenever something is a social problem someone usually suggests there should be lessons about it in school – and that often means in PSHE. Do you think PSHE lessons are the place to put the world to rights? Offer arguments for and against.**

Working in the same small groups as for the previous activity, allow time for students to list their arguments. If the following do not emerge, draw attention to them.

| For | Against |
| --- | --- |
| PSHE lessons can provide a place where everyone can have a rational and informed discussion about current issues – not just hearing media hype or personal prejudices. | The PSHE curriculum already has a great many topics in it. It can be difficult to find more time to do justice to everything that might come up. |
| PSHE lessons won't solve the issue – but if everyone has a better understanding then they will be more informed and able to make decisions; e.g. students will be able to vote (politics) and lobby in the future. | It's difficult for teachers to research and prepare new materials all the time. Teachers don't have to be experts on everything – nor should students expect them to be. |
| Young people can be influential – the UK Youth Parliament has had an effect as a direct result of talking about PSHE-related issues (SRE). | Societal problems are not just caused by young people – so targeting them in lessons has a limited effect. Problems are a nationwide issue and often need a cultural shift in attitudes for things to change. |
| Good PSHE lessons will provide 'signposting' towards appropriate sources of help and support – which students might not hear about elsewhere. | Some students will be affected by different social issues being discussed – unless the issues are handled with sensitivity and sufficient support services are in place, it may be better not to try and tackle everything. |

> 5. **What topic would you:**
>    a) **add to PSHE**
>    b) **remove from PSHE?**

This is a review and reflection task that you could treat as a mini-evaluation and use the feedback to inform future planning in PSHE.

# RESOURCE SHEET 4.2

**Factfile on forced marriages**

| Factfile: Forced marriage |
|---|
| **What is it?**<br>Forced marriage is a marriage in which one or both of the people is married without his or her consent or against his or her will. A forced marriage is not the same as an arranged marriage in which both people agree to the assistance of their parents or a third party (such as a matchmaker).<br><br>Everyone in Britain, whatever their religion or belief, has the right to choose whether to get married and who they want to marry. But in some cases people are forced into marriage; it might be to someone they don't like or have never even met. They may be too young to legally get married or don't feel ready to marry at all or it might be that they are lesbian or gay and do not want to marry someone of the opposite sex. |
| **Who does it affect?**<br>All sorts of people could be affected and it is worth remembering that the practice of forced marriage was very common amongst Europeans in the past. It is still practised in some families with links to South Asia, East Asia, the Middle East and Africa. Forced marriages in Western Europe and North America in the twenty-first century generally happen within these migrant communities.<br><br>In most but not all forced marriages, it is the female who is the involuntary spouse – but it can also happen that the male is the forced partner. |
| **Why don't those who are affected do something about it?**<br>Young people often feel unable to speak out against their parents. They may share a sense of 'family honour' and not wish to do anything that they are told brings shame on the family. Sometimes they are told it is a religious practice – it isn't, it's a cultural one.<br><br>Sometimes young people find that they are 'taken on holiday' out of the country – and then it turns out that a marriage has been set up for them and they have no choice in the matter. As this usually happens abroad the young person may not understand what is going on and may not know who to turn to. |
| **What does the law say?**<br>Since 2008 the Forced Marriage Act allows flexibility for each individual case. It works in a way that protects anyone forced into a marriage without criminalising family members.<br><br>The law gives the control and decision about whether or not to revoke the 'forced marriage' back to the individual concerned. |
| **Who can help?**<br>■ The Forced Marriage Unit of the Foreign & Commonwealth Office (FCO)<br>■ Police |

# Topic: Where to turn for help and support

| | |
|---|---|
| **Notes** | The PSHE Education programme of study encourages young people to find and evaluate information for themselves. This topic is particularly focused on information about advice and support and uses the general area of domestic violence as one for investigation.<br><br>Particular care needs to be taken to determine whether or not students in the group may have been affected by domestic violence. Pastoral staff should be consulted as they may be aware of past or present issues affecting the students.<br><br>The activity works on the resilience model – young people will be more empowered when they are encouraged to do things for themselves rather than simply reading about it.<br><br>It uses the basic principle of stories about others and invites students to research a range of helping agencies and find solutions for the characters. |
| **Learning outcomes** | **In this topic students will learn about:**<br>■ exploitation in relationships<br>■ agencies that offer help and support.<br><br>**They will explore:**<br>■ ways of recognising harm and risk in relationships<br>■ ways to present information about helping agencies. |
| **Links to Personal Well-being PoS** | **2.2 Decision-making and managing risk**<br>**b** Students should be able to find and evaluate information, advice and support from a variety of sources and be able to support others in doing so.<br>**c** Students should be able to assess and manage risk in personal choices and situations, minimise harm in risky situations and demonstrate how to help others do so.<br><br>**3 Range and content**<br>**f** The study of personal well-being should include characteristics of positive relationships, and awareness of exploitation in relationships and of statutory and voluntary organisations that support relationships in crisis. |
| **Links to SEAL outcomes** | **Social skills**<br>Students can communicate effectively with others, listening to what others say as well as expressing their own thoughts and feelings. |
| **Links to ECM outcomes** | Stay safe ■ Make a positive contribution |
| **Assessment opportunity** | Activity 2: Who can they speak to? (see page 98)<br>**End of Key Stage Statement – healthy lifestyles**<br>Learners are able to:<br>■ demonstrate confidence in finding professional health advice and help others to do so. |
| **Resources** | ■ Student's Book (pages 60–61)<br>■ Appendix (see the CD): Active Learning Methodologies:<br>  □ Brainstorming (page 3)  □ Research and presentation (page 9) |

# BEFORE RUNNING THE LESSON

The following link is to a video clip that could be played at the beginning of the lesson to place all of the scenarios in the widest context – that of domestic violence: www.thehideout.org.uk/over10/default.aspa. **Only use the listed clip** as other material on this website forms part of one of the subsequent research activities.

# BACKGROUND INFORMATION

General principles when trying to help someone include the following advice.

---

*If you're being hurt*
*If you've been physically or mentally harmed by a relative or someone you're in a relationship with, remember that you are not to blame. Many victims of domestic violence believe that they have created or caused the problems that led to the violence but this isn't the case. The only person to blame is the one who is committing the violent acts.*

*If you feel confident enough, you should call the police. They take crimes like this very seriously and will be able to act quickly. If you don't want to call the police, talk to a friend or a teacher that you can trust about your feelings. The worst thing you can do is stay quiet and allow it to continue.*

---

*If someone you know is being hurt*
*If you're worried that one of your friends, parents or carers is a victim of violence in their own home, tell them about your concerns. It's best to help them talk through the situation and support them if they decide to report the matter themselves.*

*www.direct.gov.uk/en/YoungPeople/CrimeAndJustice/TypesOfCrime*

---

# STARTER ACTIVITY

**ACTIVITY: WHO'S OUT THERE? (Student's Book, page 60)**

> 1. **Apart from the regular emergency services of police, ambulance and fire brigade, what other helping agencies do you know of?**

Run this as a brainstorm. See Appendix (on the CD): Active Learning Methodologies: Brainstorming (page 3).

# MAIN ACTIVITIES

**ACTIVITY: WHO CAN THEY SPEAK TO? (Student's Book, page 61)**

> 2. **Read Sources 1–5. Each of the five people needs help and support. Choose one and research the helping agency listed for them. Plan a presentation about the agency. The presentation should include the following:**
>    - **name of the agency**
>    - **who it's run by and for**
>    - **how it can be accessed**
>    - **example(s) of how they've helped others.**

> **Make your presentation as practical and helpful as possible. Include (if there are any) drawbacks or restrictions to using the agency in question. Your overall aim is that other students will be able to take away:**
>
> - **an awareness of exploitation in relationships**
> - **an ability to recognise harm in risky situations and know where to turn for help and support.**

Run this as a research and presentation activity: See Appendix (on the CD): Active Learning Methodologies: Research and presentation (page 9).

The students should work in groups of five. Each group has one story/agency allocated.

The agency/website for each character is:

- **Sharon:** www.thesurvivorstrust.org
- **Grace:** www.youth2youth.co.uk
- **Simon:** www.mensadviceline.org.uk
- **Jamila:** www.fco.gov.uk/en/travel-and-living-abroad/when-things-go-wrong/forced-marriage
- **Irina:** www.thehideout.org.uk/over10/adults.

---

### End of Key Stage Statement – healthy lifestyles

Learners are able to:

- demonstrate confidence in finding professional health advice and help others to do so.

### Assessment activity
Having undertaken the task 'Who can they speak to?', ask students to work in pairs to produce display material (poster, leaflet, etc.) for their agency. Imagine this would be placed on a PSHE notice board in school.

### Assessment method – display material
Students need to consider the following when planning their work:

- Keep the language clear and simple – think about literacy levels of the readers.
- How will they capture the interest and attention of a passer-by?
- Does it clearly and logically show the basic information (see the task above)?
- The display material should ideally be A3 in size.

Creative responses in PSHE (poems, artwork, etc.) need to be structured so that young people understand a clear objective for the piece of work and are given guidelines to support its structure.

Teachers need to be careful not to be sidetracked into assessing the quality of the artwork/presentation – feedback on this is helpful but ultimately it is the content and its message that is being assessed.

## REVIEW AND REFLECTION

### ACTIVITY: NEW TO ME (Student's Book, page 61)

> **3. Which agency/agencies didn't you know about until today?**

Invite volunteers to share their new information.

# 5 Diversity

## Topic: Shared identity – shared experiences

| | |
|---|---|
| **Notes** | The activity used to start this topic is slightly more demanding than those used elsewhere in the book. It encourages students to reflect on an often overlooked truth – that human experience goes much deeper than skin colour, age, gender, etc.<br><br>The topic goes on to focus on the concept of 'Britishness' as a unifying similarity – whatever our background. This then introduces the idea that citizenship is an activity rather than just a word on a document.<br><br>Students are given an opportunity to explore shared experiences that bring people together in positive ways by looking at a national youth service scheme for young people. They are asked to contrast this with more negative forms of 'belonging'; e.g. gang culture.<br><br>The review and reflection activity takes students back to the key concepts of positive characteristics that can unite people and bring them together as citizens of their country and indeed as human beings living together. |
| **Learning outcomes** | **In this topic students will learn about:**<br>■ factors that can unite people who come from different backgrounds<br>■ examples of community service and citizenship schemes.<br>**They will explore:**<br>■ ideas of what it means to be British<br>■ how shared experiences might bring people together in positive ways. |
| **Links to Personal Well-being POS** | **1.4 Relationships**<br>**b** Understanding that people have multiple roles and responsibilities in society and that making positive relationships and contributing to groups, teams and communities is important.<br><br>**1.5 Diversity**<br>**a** Appreciating that, in our communities, there are similarities as well as differences between people of different race, religion, culture, ability or disability, gender, age or sexual orientation. |
| **Links to SEAL outcomes** | **Empathy**<br>Students can show respect for people from diverse cultures and backgrounds. |
| **Links to ECM outcomes** | Make a positive contribution ■ Enjoy and achieve |
| **Assessment opportunity** | See Topic: Challenging discrimination; Activity 3: Children with HIV & Activity 4: Point of view (pages 108–109) |
| **Resources** | ■ Student's Book (pages 62–63)<br>■ Appendix (see the CD): Active Learning Methodologies:<br>  □ Pairs work (pages 6–7)  □ Small group work (pages 6–7) |

# STARTER ACTIVITY

**ACTIVITY: BEING HUMAN (Student's Book, page 62)**

> 1. Imagine the quote in Source 1 with the word '*black*' replaced by any one of a series of words: *disabled, Jewish, old person*, etc. Does the shared experience of being human outweigh all the differences that can separate us?

Get students to answer this question in pairs. See Appendix (on the CD): Active Learning Methodologies: Pairs work (pages 6–7). When taking feedback the following points may contribute to the discussion.

- Differences do shape who we are – e.g. a woman's experience of life will be different from a man's; a disabled person faces challenges on a day-to-day basis that able-bodied people would never face.
- A person may initially appear to be different from us (e.g. skin colour, gender, body size, etc.) but we may still have had same or similar experiences (e.g. success or failure at school, a loving home situation, the same job).
- Making initial judgements about people based on what they look like or where they come from can disadvantage both you and them (e.g. you may fail to make a friendship that could have been important in your life; your horizons are not broadened by hearing about other people's experiences).
- In summing up, draw attention to the Maya Angelou quote again – every human being faces challenges to '… endure, dream, fail at, and still survive'.

# MAIN ACTIVITIES

**ACTIVITY: WHAT IS BRITISH? (Student's Book, page 62)**

> 2. Read Source 2 and discuss/answer the following questions:
>    a) Which seem good characteristics of being British?
>    b) Which seem negative?
>    c) Do you think of these words when you think of 'Britishness'?
>    d) What else would you add to the list?

Join pairs from Activity 1 together to form groups of four.
  The following may help in guiding discussion and feedback:

> a) Which seem good characteristics of being British?

Many people would suggest the following:

- tolerance
- respect
- fair play
- politeness
- stoicism
- work ethic
- democracy
- queuing
- meritocracy
- rule of law
- sense of humour.

### b) Which seem negative?

- island mentality – this could be interpreted as small-mindedness
- snobbery – is Britain still too hung up on titles, class and the way people speak/their accent?
- being reserved – this could be interpreted as being shy or not interested – or even being 'above it'
- Christian morality – this can become associated with being judgemental, although its original intention was positive and has influenced British culture; e.g. treat others as you would like to be treated.
- xenophobia – this means a fear of things that are 'foreign' and therefore perceived of as strange.

### c) Do you think of these words when you think of 'Britishness'?

Encourage students to explain their thinking. They may have other ideas which will lead on to the discussion for part d).

### d) What else would you add to the list?

Other possibilities here may include:

- the Queen – royalists
- pomp and ceremony (e.g. trooping the colour)
- heavy drinkers
- lovers of the countryside
- fond of animals
- influential fashion and pop music, etc.
- cricket players
- football hooligans
- the BBC.

It is important to encourage the students to talk about their own perceptions. These will differ according to age, location, social group, etc. The key idea is to get them to explore the concept of 'Britishness'.

**ACTIVITY: NATIONAL YOUTH SERVICE (Student's Book, page 63)**

3. Read the article in Source 3 and discuss the following questions. Remember to give reasons to explain your point of view.
   a) Do you think the scheme would be popular amongst young people?
   b) What would be the advantages of bringing different types of people together through a shared experience?
   c) What are the positive things that young people might gain?
   d) Would this scheme provide a 'sense of belonging' for young people that discourages them from negative encounters; for example, gangs and gang violence?

Use small group work. See Appendix (on the CD): Active Learning Methodologies: Small group work (pages 6–7).

In taking feedback the following may help discussion:

**a) Do you think the scheme would it be popular amongst young people?**

- Would its popularity depend on whether it was compulsory or not?
- Should it be compulsory – i.e. something everyone experiences?

**b) What would be the advantages of bringing different types of people together through a shared experience?**

- getting to learn more about people who you might not otherwise meet
- by sharing things together you realise differences are not as pronounced as you may have thought or feared.

**c) What are the positive things that young people might gain?**

- a sense of satisfaction from helping others
- a sense of belonging from being part of a positive initiative
- new skills and confidence
- broadened horizons.

**d) Would this scheme provide a 'sense of belonging' for young people that discourages them from negative encounters; for example, gangs and gang violence?**

- Research shows that gangs provide young people with a sense of belonging and identity – but this often comes at a cost; e.g. safety issues, crime, drug use, alienation from others.
- It is important to encourage the students to talk about their own perceptions. These will differ according to age, location, social group, etc. The key idea is to get them to explore the concept of 'belonging'.

# REVIEW AND REFLECTION

**ACTIVITY: CELEBRATING CITIZENSHIP (Student's Book, page 63)**

**4. Source 4 shows a photograph of new citizens celebrating. After taking part in the National Youth Service *all* young people could be offered a special recognition that they are now active citizens of their country. Draft some key words/ideas for the opening speech that the leader of the citizenship ceremony could make. The speech should outline what unites people and brings them together as citizens.**

In introducing this task you may wish to draw comparisons between Britain where formal statements and events about citizenship are very low key and the United States where public allegiance to the country and the American flag is a daily occurrence in many schools. Compared with the Americans we don't talk very much about what it means to be a citizen of our country.

Allow an appropriate time for students to work on this and then take feedback from volunteers. If students are struggling to find words and ideas to include in the speech then return to the word list in Source 2 for some ideas.

# Topic: Challenging discrimination

| | |
|---|---|
| **Notes** | This chapter is about diversity and appreciating the similarities and differences between human beings. It asks students to consider several different types of discrimination and uses examples for each.<br><br>They are encouraged to think about how to take the initiative in challenging these and other forms of discrimination.<br><br>Activities such as writing letters or looking at policies might seem unimportant – but they are examples of first steps in beginning to challenge discrimination. The opening activity makes clear that first steps can lead to significant change.<br><br>One of the activities uses a technique which is a cross between role play and a guided visualisation – it has been simplified so that students can sit in their usual classroom formation. This method has been chosen as a powerful and empathetic tool.<br><br>In a later activity it will be useful to have a copy of your school's equal opportunities policy. |
| **Learning outcomes** | **In this topic students will learn about:**<br>■ the different forms that prejudice can take<br>■ examples of people who have challenged discrimination.<br>**They will explore:**<br>■ ways to build empathy and understanding<br>■ how to take the initiative in challenging and combating discrimination and prejudice. |
| **Links to Personal Well-being PoS** | **1.5 Diversity**<br>**b** Understanding that all forms of prejudice and discrimination must be challenged at every level in our lives.<br><br>**2.3 Developing relationships and working with others**<br>**d** Students should be able to demonstrate respect for and acceptance of the differences between people, and challenge offensive behaviour, prejudice and discrimination assertively and safely.<br><br>**3 Range and content**<br>**j** The study of personal well-being should include the diversity of ethnic and cultural groups, the power of prejudice, bullying, discrimination and racism, and the need to take the initiative in challenging this and other offensive behaviours and in giving support to victims of abuse. |
| **Links to SEAL outcomes** | **Empathy**<br>Students understand the impact of bullying, prejudice and discrimination on all those involved ... and can use appropriate strategies to support them. |
| **Links to ECM outcomes** | Make a positive contribution |
| **Assessment opportunity** | Activity 3: Children with HIV & Activity 4: Point of view (pages 108–109)<br><br>**End of Key Stage Statement – diversity**<br>Learners are able to:<br>■ take the initiative in challenging or giving support in connection with offensive or abusive behaviour. |
| **Resources** | ■ Student's Book (pages 64–67)<br>■ Appendix (see the CD): Active Learning Methodologies:<br>□ Brainstorming (page 3)  □ Role play (page 10) |

# STARTER ACTIVITY

**ACTIVITY: WHAT CAN PEOPLE DO? (Student's Book, page 64)**

> 1. 'Rosa sat so Martin could walk so Barack could run.' Who are these people and what do you think this quotation means?

Run as a class brainstorm/discussion. See Appendix (on the CD): Active Learning Methodologies: Brainstorming (page 3).

The quotation in the starter activity comes from a song written by Amy Dixon-Kolar in 2008 (see the YouTube clip www.youtube.com/watch?v=I-0NvkuPHZI). It traces the growth of civil rights for black Americans from the frustratingly ignored early protests through to the election of a black president. It draws out the idea that from simple, peaceful protests there grew a movement for change that eventually achieved equality for black Americans in the highest office in the USA.

# BACKGROUND INFORMATION

*Rosa Parks: born 1913–died 2005*
*Civil rights activist who refused to give up her seat for a white man (at this time transport was racially segregated). She was arrested, charged and convicted of civil disobedience. Rosa had a knack for protesting effectively but quietly and was known for her saying, 'Do what is right'.*

*Martin Luther King Jnr: born 1929–died 1968 (assassinated)*
*King was an American clergyman and one of the principal leaders of the United States civil rights movement. He participated in the enormous civil rights march on Washington in August 1963, and delivered his famous 'I have a dream' speech, predicting a day when the promise of freedom and equality for all would become a reality in America. In 1964, he was awarded the Nobel Peace Prize. In 1965, he led a successful campaign to register blacks to vote.*

*Barack Obama: born 1961*
*At High School as one of only three black students Obama became conscious of racism and what it meant to be African-American. After law school, Obama practised as a civil rights lawyer. He was elected as a State Senator in 1996. On 20 January 2009, Obama became the 44th president of the United States – and the first African-American to hold this office.*

# MAIN ACTIVITIES

Use the information in the Student's Book to explain the context for the rest of the activities, i.e. looking at different forms of discrimination and how they can be challenged.

## ACTIVITY: HAVING TO LEAVE (Student's Book, page 65)

2. **Read Source 1. Refugees and asylum seekers generally receive very little empathy and understanding over their situation. This activity is about exploring how people feel when they are forced to make difficult decisions to become a stranger in a new country – and not by choice.**
   a) **When you get home there is a note on the kitchen table saying you must leave in half an hour. You do not know where you are going or how long for, or if you will ever see your home again. You can only take a small rucksack. List the 10 items that you want to take with you.**
   b) **Also on the kitchen table are three tickets. These have been incredibly difficult to obtain because they are rationed. Decide which two people out of all your family and friends will come with you.**

See Appendix (on the CD): Active Learning Methodologies: Role play (page 10).

This has the potential to be a powerful activity about refugees and asylum seekers because it explores how people feel when they are a stranger in a country – and not by choice. Depending on the background of your students some may be upset by this so make sure you've taken into account any traumas or bereavements. You have the option to set up the classroom with the lights dimmed and sad music playing – although this is not essential.

- Work through the activity in the following order, telling the students:
   - 'When you get home there is a note on the kitchen table saying you must leave in half an hour. You do not know where you are going or how long for, or if you will ever see your home again. What is your initial reaction? Write down three words to describe how you are feeling'.
   - 'You can only take a small rucksack. List the 10 items that you want to take with you. You've only got two minutes to do this.' (Time this at two minutes exactly to create the sense of rush and urgency.)
   - 'You also find on the kitchen table three tickets. These have been incredibly difficult to obtain because they are rationed. Decide which two people out of all your family and friends will come with you.' (Again limit time, this time to one minute.)
   - 'You now find out that you will have to share the rucksack with the others who are travelling with you so can only take three items, not 10. Cross off seven items from your list.' (Allow only one minute for this.)
   - 'There is more bad news. One of the tickets is obviously a forgery. You need to leave one of your two people behind. Who is it and how do you feel?'
- Now ask the group to close their eyes and tap one student on the shoulder (choose someone who you feel won't be too upset and will be able to manage this) to read out their responses. They may need a bit of encouragement, but it's important not to force them to read it out.
- Next students should work in small groups to compare their responses with each other and to discuss how it felt to undertake the activity.
- Questions to support processing the activity:
   - How did it feel to have to make such important decisions so quickly?
   - Did you find that group members had similar answers; e.g. taking the same things in their rucksacks?
   - How did you feel knowing you could not have everyone you cared about come with you?
   - Did this activity throw any new light on your understanding of what it must be like to be a refugee?
   - Do you think some of the prejudice experienced by refugees and asylum seekers comes from people's lack of understanding about the situations they may have faced?

- Finally, discuss with your students some of the issues that have arisen for them around asylum seekers, refugees and economic migrants. Use Source 1 in the Student's Book as a way of clarifying definitions and actual numbers of refugees and asylum seekers.
- An interesting article linking asylum seekers and the world of education (about asylum seeker teachers), 'Educators in Exile', appeared in the *TES magazine* on 6 August 2010 – this may provide further useful context for a discussion: www.tes.co.uk/article.aspx?storycode=6053540.

**ACTIVITY: CHILDREN WITH HIV (Student's Book, page 67)**

> 3. **Read Source 2 and discuss the following questions:**
>    a) **Do you understand how HIV is transmitted? In the light of factual information about HIV, did the schools have anything to worry about?**

# BACKGROUND INFORMATION TO HELP THE DISCUSSION

| | |
|---|---|
| *Human* | *only affects people* |
| *Immunodeficiency* | *stops the immune system working properly* |
| *Virus* | *a living cell that can transmit infections* |
| | |
| *Acquired* | *does not occur naturally – got from someone or somewhere else* |
| *Immune* | *the body system that fights illness and infections* |
| *Deficiency* | *not fully functioning or working* |
| *Syndrome* | *a collection of illnesses or conditions* |

*HIV is found in:*

- *blood and blood products*
- *semen, vaginal and cervical secretions*
- *amniotic fluid and breast milk.*

*There is no evidence that the virus is transmitted in:*

- *sweat*
- *saliva*
- *tears*
- *urine/faeces.*

*It is a difficult virus to transmit because you need a clear route into another person's body. You also need a sufficient quantity of the virus.*

*The most common transmission routes are:*

- *sexual activity between any two people of any gender that enables an exchange of semen, vaginal fluids or blood*
- *needles and syringes used to inject when someone who is infected has already used them*
- *from a mother to baby during vaginal birth and when breastfeeding – steps can be taken to reduce the chance of transmission.*

Situations where there is **no** risk of HIV being transmitted:

- blood spilling on to the unbroken skin of another person
- coughing and sneezing
- sharing toilet facilities
- spitting and vomiting
- using public swimming pools
- hugging, touching, kissing
- during dental treatment
- general social contact.

There is **no** known case of HIV infection having been transmitted in childcare settings or schools anywhere in the UK.

A number of websites give more information:

- www.avert.org
- www.cwac.org
- www.worldaidsday.org
- www.tht.org.uk.

**b) What do you think your school would say if it was asked to provide facilities for a Chiva summer camp?**

Encourage students to be realistic and even-handed. Would everyone feel the same? Would there be a range of opinions? What would you want your school to do?

**c) Look at your school's equal opportunities policy to find out if discrimination against people with HIV is covered.**

There is no obligation for young people who are HIV positive to inform their schools. The most recent available statistics, from 2009, showed that in the UK there are at least 1161 young people who are HIV positive. Schools need to address the issues whether they are aware or not of students with HIV in their school.

**d) Are there other school policies that ensure people with HIV won't suffer from discrimination?**

You may find references to HIV/AIDS in the school's pastoral policy/medical guidance/PSHE policy. Check whether policies list a range of things which should not be used to discriminate against people. If HIV status is omitted should the policies be revised? Is this a task for the School Council to raise to ensure equal opportunities include everyone?

**ACTIVITY: POINT OF VIEW (Student's Book, page 67)**

**4. Read Source 3.**
   **a) What do you think of the different attitudes expressed in it?**

Not everyone will have the same experiences of people with disabilities, so sensitivity should be used when taking feedback.

> **b) How do you feel about the fact that most of the people we see on TV are able-bodied, attractive, slender, under 45 years old, etc?**
> **c) Write a letter to the BBC explaining your point of view and expressing your opinions as a future television licence payer.**

This activity can be undertaken by individuals or pairs. Allow adequate time to draft letters before inviting volunteers to read out their responses.

The following may help guide discussion:

- Did students think people should be chosen for their ability to do the job and not for what they look like?
- Did anyone think it was important to ensure that people on TV represent a wide range; e.g. disabled and able-bodied, a wide variety of races, older and younger people, women and men, etc? We are talking here about positive discrimination, i.e. actively making choices to ensure that viewers see the fullest possible range.

## End of Key Stage Statement – diversity

Learners are able to:

- take the initiative in challenging or giving support in connection with offensive or abusive behaviour.

**Assessment activity**

Before undertaking either or both of the activities 'Children with HIV' and 'Point of view', tell students to ensure that they note viewpoints expressed in the discussions. Explain to them that they will be using these as a basis for the extended activity.

Being sensitive to the individuals in your class, allocate students in groups of three and give them one of the two scenarios as follows:

Children with HIV
There is a meeting at the school to try and resolve the disagreement and re-instate the booking made by Chiva.

Characters:

- a school governor who does not want Chiva using the premises
- a representative from Chiva
- a senior member of staff from the school who is chairing the meeting, and sees both sides.

Based on Source 2, play out the meeting, allowing each character to bring out their points of view.

Point of view
A breakfast-time television interview in the studio.

Characters:

- a parent who thinks people with disabilities should not be appearing on children's programmes
- a parent who thinks people with disabilities should be as much a part of children's programmes as anyone else
- the TV presenter – stays neutral in the discussion but tries to ask important questions.

Based on Source 3, play out the interview, allowing each character to bring out their points of view.

**Assessment method – role play or scripting**

The role plays can be planned and performed or alternatively each group can produce a written script. No group should be made to perform ad lib; however, they could read out their script.

The following may be helpful in setting up and running the assessment task:

- Remind students to consider the discussion and the various attitudes they will illustrate in their respective roles.
- Ensure everyone understands the purpose of the role play.
- Allocate group membership and roles carefully.
- Agree a signal that the teacher can use to intervene.
- Keep to a time frame. Suggest a five-minute absolute maximum for the role play.
- Have a clear end to the role play or a cut-off point/time.
- Set criteria for the observers to look or listen for; e.g:
  - What main arguments were used by the opposing characters?
  - What words or actions were used to make their points?
  - Were any of the words/actions used disparaging or insensitive?
  - By the end of the role play did you as an observer agree with one character more than another? Why was this?

After all the groups have performed or read, ensure students can leave characters and feelings behind. This can be done simply by asking every participant to stand up and say 'My real name is … and I live at …' or some other similar reality-check.

In the plenary, draw out key learning points – use feedback from both participants and observers: What was learned? What strategies or decisions were made by the characters? Did each role play cover a wide range of arguments? Did anyone find themselves changing opinion based on what they heard?

# REVIEW AND REFLECTION

**ACTIVITY: COMBATING PREJUDICE (Student's Book, page 67)**

> 5. 'It is harder to crack a prejudice than an atom.' (Albert Einstein)
>    What is it about prejudice that makes it so difficult to combat?

Allow students a few moments to consider their responses before inviting feedback. Some points that could be covered in the discussion:

- Fighting to overturn prejudice and discrimination isn't easy because often it is 'gut reactions' and entrenched views that need to be challenged.
- Discrimination can exercise a very negative power over people's lives so it is important that people feel empowered and supported to challenge its damaging effects.

NB Einstein (who was Jewish) was the victim of anti-Semitism during the Nazi era.

# Topic: Discrimination through invisibility

| | |
|---|---|
| **Notes** | An overlooked element of prejudice and discrimination is the issue of invisibility or silence. The example used to start this is sexual orientation. This has been chosen because many of the other elements of diversity listed in the KS4 Programmes of Study have been incorporated in other topics in this book – but sexual orientation has not been addressed elsewhere. One of the activities (only in the Teacher's Resource Book) is not strictly about invisibility but is about the use of negative language towards lesbian, gay and bisexual (LGB) people. Teachers often tell us that this is something they would like to address in class. Very specific instructions are given to undertake this activity and teachers are encouraged to explore it. Research has shown that LGB people are an example of an invisible minority group who are under-represented on television. Using statistical information, students are provided with an opportunity to investigate this further. This topic then moves students forward to explore how other minority groups are portrayed on TV. It asks them to undertake a short survey that covers people with a physical disability and/or a learning disability, fat people, senior citizens and people with mental health problems. |
| **Learning outcomes** | **In this topic students will learn about:**<br>■ the prejudice of invisibility<br>■ how and where LGB people are portrayed on TV.<br><br>**They will explore:**<br>■ an example of how prejudicial language can cause harm<br>■ how people from minority groups are portrayed on TV. |
| **Links to Personal Well-being PoS** | **1.5 Diversity**<br>a Appreciating that, in our communities, there are similarities as well as differences between people of different race, religion, culture, ability or disability, gender, age or sexual orientation.<br>b Understanding that all forms of prejudice and discrimination must be challenged at every level in our lives.<br><br>**2.1 Critical reflection**<br>e Students should be able to develop self-awareness by reflecting critically on their behaviour and its impact on others.<br><br>**3 Range and content**<br>j The study of personal well-being should include the diversity of ethnic and cultural groups, the power of prejudice, bullying, discrimination and racism, and the need to take the initiative in challenging this and other offensive behaviours and in giving support to victims of abuse. |
| **Links to SEAL outcomes** | **Empathy**<br>Students understand the impact of bullying, prejudice and discrimination on all those involved ... and can use appropriate strategies to support them. |
| **Links to ECM outcomes** | Be healthy ■ Make a positive contribution |
| **Assessment opportunity** | See Topic: Challenging discrimination; Activity 3: Children with HIV & Activity 4: Point of view (pages 108–109) |
| **Resources** | ■ Student's Book (pages 68–69)<br>■ Appendix (see the CD): Active Learning Methodologies:<br>  □ Brainstorming (page 3)   □ Small group work (pages 6–7)   □ Pairs work (pages 6–7) |

*PSHE Education for Key Stage 4 Teacher's Resource Book © Hodder Education*

# STARTER ACTIVITY

## ACTIVITY: WHO CAN YOU NAME? (Student's Book, page 68)

> **1. Can you name five national or international figures who are LGB?**

Run as a pairs work brainstorm. See Appendix (on the CD): Active Learning Methodologies: Brainstorming (page 3) and Pairs work (pages 6–7).
   Examples may include:

### Sport

- Gareth Thomas – Welsh rugby international
- Martina Navratilova – American tennis player
- John Amaechi – UK-born basketball player, now in USA
- Matthew Mitcham – Australian Olympic diver.

### Actors and presenters

- Sir Ian McKellan – Gandalf in *Lord of the Rings*, amongst other roles
- Russell Tovey – *Him & Her*, *Being Human*, *The History Boys*, amongst other roles
- John Barrowman – actor, singer and presenter
- Simon Amstell – comedian and TV presenter
- Ellen Degeneres – comedian and TV host
- Clare Balding – sports commentator.

### Musicians

- Sir Elton John – singer/composer
- Joe McElderry – *X Factor* winner
- k. d. lang – singer
- Stephen Sondheim – librettist for *West Side Story*, and many other shows.

### Writers and academics

- Simon Schama – historian and presenter of *A History of Britain*
- Stephen Fry – writer, broadcaster, comedian and national treasure
- Jeanette Winterson – author of *Oranges Are Not the Only Fruit* amongst other books
- David Starkey – TV presenter, historian and academic.

The following may help to extend the discussion:

- Why are some people happy to disclose their sexual orientation whilst others are not? For example, Stephen Fry has always been open about his sexuality. On the other hand, the Lib Dem politician David Laws only went public about his sexuality when forced to do so.

> **2. Does it make a difference to how we think of a public figure if they reveal that they are LGB?**

Remind students that opinions need to be expressed in such a way that no one is offended, upset or put down.

# MAIN ACTIVITIES

### ACTIVITY: IN OTHER WORDS (additional activity not in Student's Book)

> Sometimes the effects of prejudice can be hidden and unappreciated by those who cause them. If, for example, it's name-calling or using abusive language, it can have a lasting effect. In this activity you will explore possible effects of using negative language.

**The context for this activity:**
The intention of this activity is to help students understand that put-downs and abusive language can cause unintended harm. Explain to the class that this activity is not about changing deep-set beliefs or individual points of view (to which everyone is entitled) – but it is not acceptable to be prejudiced or discriminatory.

A class discussion about the word 'gay' might be useful at some point in this topic – perhaps best placed **after** the activity. At one level the word is descriptive – but many young people (particularly young men) use the word in a derogatory way. The intention in using it isn't incidental, it's important. The gay Welsh rugby player Gareth Thomas spoke about what it felt like to hear that word being used as an insult during the many long years when he was secretive about his own sexuality. He described each time he heard it as nothing more than a small scar on the inside. But as time went on he felt those scars building up, creating a deeper emotion of unhappiness and depression in hearing himself described in negative ways.

As a link between this and the next activity it may be important to note that seven in ten secondary school teachers polled by YouGov in 2009 said that anti-gay language in the broadcast media affects the levels of homophobic bullying in schools.

**Materials:**
Enough flipchart paper and thick felt-tip pens for each small group.

Enough prepared sheets of flipchart paper for one per group of five, each with a heading, such as:

- lesbian
- gay
- bisexual.

(In practice this means you will probably require two sheets for each of the above headings.)

1. You will need to remind the class of the group agreement and specifically address the issue of embarrassment, put-down and offence before beginning.

2. Explain that for this activity alone they are going to be asked to list words which in other circumstances would be unacceptable in the classroom.

3. Divide into groups of five. Give each group one of the prepared pieces of flipchart paper and at least one marker pen per group.

4. Explain that they should brainstorm any words they know that mean the same as the word at the top of their sheet – and write them on the sheet of paper. Emphasise that for this activity only, all words are permissible.

5. Whoever has the pen first has to ensure each member of the group contributes at least one word before the free-for-all brainstorm starts.

6. Allow one minute for this, then circulate the sheets to the next group. Have them read what is on the sheet and invite them to add any more words they can think of.

7. Continue to circulate sheets until they have returned to where they started. Allow groups time to look at the words that have been added to their list.

8. Pin up the sheets where everyone can see them. Discuss briefly:

   - What do you notice about the words?
     (Look for feedback on issues of offence and insult to LGB people.)
   - Why do you think this is?
     (Look for feedback on 'it's only teasing' or 'it's just a joke, it doesn't mean anything'.)
   - Why do some people think it is OK to use insulting and offensive language towards someone who is different from them?
   - Is there a difference between how men and women use this kind of language?
   - What do you notice about what the words are referring to?
     (Here expect responses such as 'It's about what they do'. The words are usually linked to sexual practice. Look for feedback that may include what (gay) men do sexually as being dirty or unnatural. It will also probably include stereotyped (mythological) behaviours.)

9. Then move the discussion on by asking:

   - 'What if this was the only language you ever heard around your own sexual identity? How would this leave you feeling?'
     (Feedback might include: isolation; can't be honest about your feelings; hurt but can't say anything; inferior; low self-esteem.)

10. Ask students to return to groups and ask groups to use reverse of their flipchart paper. Their task is to think about in the context of this activity:
    'If this is what I hear and this is what I feel, how might I behave?'

11. Allow a minute for the group to list possible behaviours and then take feedback. Examples might include: depression, self-harm, self-limiting – and, in extreme cases, suicide.

# BACKGROUND STATISTICS

*Half of those who have experienced homophobic bullying have skipped school because of it and one in five has skipped school more than six times. A third of gay pupils who have been bullied are likely to miss school in the future.*
*Stonewall, The School Report, 2007*

- *50 per cent of LGB adults who had been bullied at school contemplated self-harm or suicide.*
- *40 per cent had made at least one attempt to self-harm.*
- *53 per cent had contemplated self-harm as a result of being bullied.*
- *40 per cent had attempted suicide on at least one occasion.*
- *30 per cent had attempted on more than one occasion.*
*Rivers, I. 2000*

*Seventy-five per cent of young gay people in faith schools experience homophobic bullying and are less likely than pupils in other schools to report it. Of those who have been bullied, 92 per cent have experienced verbal homophobic bullying, 41 per cent physical bullying and 17 per cent death threats.*
*Stonewall, The School Report, 2007*

12. Close the activity by asking:

'Is there anything new that you have learned around using this type of negative language?'

13. An optional closing question for reflection but not necessarily for answering in class:

'Is there anything in your behaviour you might change as a result of this activity?'

**ACTIVITY: UNSEEN ON TV (Student's Book, page 68)**

> **3. Read Source 1 and discuss and answer the following questions:**
> **a) Do the results of the survey surprise you? Why?**
> **b) Looking back over the last few months, can you identify a positive and negative example of LGB people/characters on TV?**
> **c) LGB people are not the only group that can end up being invisible:**
>
> - **Do a short comparison survey looking at these examples: people with a physical disability and/or a learning disability; fat people; senior citizens; people with mental health problems.**
> - **In which programmes have you seen them and how were they portrayed?**

It will be helpful to ensure that students have read and understood Source 1 before proceeding to use this activity. If setting up a small survey it may be easier to give pairs or individuals only one type of person to focus on. Suggest to students that they agree together before starting which TV programme they would like to watch for the survey – try to get a wide spread of programmes and channels.

Use small group work. See Appendix (on the CD): Active Learning Methodologies: Small group work (pages 6–7).

# REVIEW AND REFLECTION

**ACTIVITY: WHAT DO WE DO WITH A VARIATION? (Student's Book, page 69)**

> **4. Read Source 2. What do you think is the message of this poem?**

Read the poem aloud to the students or use a competent and willing volunteer from the class. Ask students to work in pairs and allow a few minutes before inviting feedback from those who wish to share it.

# BACKGROUND INFORMATION

*The poem is by James Berry (b. 1924) who spent his childhood in a village in Jamaica, before working in the United States, and finally settling in Britain in 1948 where he has remained ever since. One of the first black writers in Britain to achieve wider recognition, Berry rose to prominence in 1981 when he won the National Poetry Competition.*

# 6 Values

## Topic: Individual, family and community values

| | |
|---|---|
| **Notes** | This topic begins by asking students to consider what 'values' means to them. It goes on to encourage individual reflection on the values that matter to us and where they come from. |
| | Students listen to each other and reflect on a range of twelve values. They then have to negotiate and collaborate to prioritise the importance of these values within their group. |
| | The concept of a pluralistic society is introduced. Through a series of issue-based scenarios students are asked to consider which shared key values influence our responses to moral questions. |
| **Learning outcomes** | **In this topic students will learn about:**<br>■ different values<br>■ ways of describing society.<br><br>**They will explore:**<br>■ their own and other people's values<br>■ the effect of different or conflicting values. |
| **Links to Personal Well-being PoS** | **2.3 Developing relationships and working with others**<br>c Students should be able to work individually, together and in teams for specific purposes, making use of the social skills of communication, negotiation, assertiveness and collaboration.<br>d Students should be able to demonstrate respect for and acceptance of the differences between people, and challenge offensive behaviour, prejudice and discrimination assertively and safely.<br><br>**3 Range and content**<br>a The study of personal well-being should include the effect of diverse and conflicting values on individuals, families and communities and ways of responding to them. |
| **Links to SEAL outcomes** | **Self-awareness**<br>Students know that they are unique individuals, and can think about themselves on many different levels.<br><br>**Social skills**<br>Students can work well in groups, taking on different roles, co-operating with each other to achieve a joint outcome. |
| **Links to ECM outcomes** | Enjoy and achieve ■ Make a positive contribution |
| **Assessment opportunity** | See Topic: Diverse and conflicting values; Activity 4: Different values (pages 122–123) |
| **Resources** | ■ Student's Book (pages 70–71)<br>■ Appendix (see the CD): Active Learning Methodologies:<br>　□ Brainstorming (page 3)　□ Small group work (pages 6–7)<br>■ Resource sheet 6.1 (page 119) |

# STARTER ACTIVITY

### ACTIVITY: WHAT DO YOU TAKE WITH YOU? (Student's Book, page 70)

> **1. When people are faced with a crisis (e.g. fire, flood, etc.) and have to flee their home, they can only take what they can carry. Assuming you'd take your money, jewellery, laptop and pets, what else would you take?**

Run as a Brainstorm activity. See Appendix (on the CD): Active Learning Methodologies: Brainstorming (page 3).

In taking examples, highlight those not of monetary value but of sentimental or personal value; for example, family photos, teddy bear, particular objects that have meaning (such as a child's first shoe or a piece of artwork done in the early years at school).

Some items are irreplaceable because of the value and meaning they have, rather than their intrinsic worth. Explain that this topic will focus on 'value' in terms other than that linked with money.

# MAIN ACTIVITIES

### ACTIVITY: ME AND MY VALUES (Student's Book, page 70)

> **2. How would you answer the following questions for yourself:**
>    - **What do I value?**
>    - **Why do I value it?**
>    - **Where have our values developed from?**
>
> **Be honest. Remember for the purposes of this activity that your values will not be marked or judged and it is OK to think and act differently from others.**

Use small group work. See Appendix (on the CD): Active Learning Methodologies: Small group work (pages 6–7).

The initial discussion in groups should prepare students to reflect on and make individual notes on their own answers. When taking feedback, try to highlight a range of responses and draw out the different ways students feel about values.

Note the following to support discussions:

- What do I value?
- Why do I value it?

For the two questions above try to draw out the meaning of values to the students – the **why** is as important as the **what**.

Also to support discussions:

- Where have our values developed from?

Some possible influences are:

- views of parents/carers – living day to day with them
- the law – there are penalties for not following it
- religious teachings – where religion is important to an individual it plays a major role in shaping how they see things
- newspapers/television/the internet and the view 'if it's in the news it must be true' – we are constantly surrounded by media messages

- national traditions – they can create a shared sense of pride and belonging
- discussions with friends – friends are likely to share similar experiences, views and opinions, and we like to be like our friends
- experiences – going through an experience can have a major impact on us
- what schools teach – they are trusted to provide reliable sources of information, and the national curriculum is shared by all state sector schools.

## ACTIVITY: EXPLAINING OUR VALUES (Student's Book, page 71)

> 3. We often take the 'big' values listed in Source 1 for granted, and don't make time to talk about what they mean for us. What personal meaning do they hold for you?
>    a) Decide which:
>
>    - has some importance
>    - is important
>    - is very important
>    - is the most important.
>
>    b) Now rank them in order of importance for you.

Run this activity in the same small groups of four as for Activity 2.

1. Use the photocopiable sheet of values cards and the scale cards on Resource sheet 6.1 (page 119).

2. Prepare one set of values cards and scale cards per group of four students.

3. Students should set out the scale cards.

4. The values cards should be shuffled and placed upside down and within reach of all group members.

5. The person who elects to 'go' first should pick up the top card from the pile – they should take some time to consider it and then explain to the rest of the group how they value it and why.

6. As each person takes their turn with the same card everyone else in the group should listen. There is not to be any discussion until everyone has had an opportunity to voice their opinion on the card.

7. They should then discuss where their group feels it is best placed on the scale.

8. The next person in the group now picks a new card and the procedure is repeated.

9. After allowing an appropriate amount of time the teacher processes the activity by asking questions; e.g:

   - How did it feel to talk about issues like this (without interruption)?
   - Was it easy to reach agreement?
   - How did it feel when different members of the group put a different importance on something you valued?

**ACTIVITY: ISSUES AND VALUES (Student's Book, page 71)**

> 4. In groups, choose two of the issues from Source 2.
>    a) Using the values listed in Source 1 decide which could be relevant to each of your two issues. The values you choose may come from different viewpoints. Give examples for each value chosen; for example, tolerance could be one of the values associated with issue 1 – Sadie might think families have the right to bring up children as they choose.
>    b) Discuss the values you have decided on for each issue:
>
>       ■ Which value do you think is the most important in terms of how the community should respond?
>       ■ Which value would most likely help everyone to reach a consensus?
>
>    c) Now answer the following questions:
>
>       ■ Was it easy to see the issue from more than one point of view?
>       ■ How tolerant are we of other people's views when they differ from our own?
>       ■ Were there two or three key values that trumped all the others?

Change the composition of the small groups and create new groups of 4–6 students. Allocate each small group one or two of the issues scenarios. Ask them to discuss the issues and make a note of which values they used to determine how a community should respond.

It may help to give them an example:

**Issue 1**
Sadie is worried that the small child next door is being abused. She has not reported it. Factors to consider:

■ Responsibility – does Sadie have a responsibility to report this?
■ Kindness – isn't it kinder to the child to take action and tell someone?
■ Tolerance – should Sadie put up with this because she thinks families can bring up children however they choose?

Scenarios based on an activity from *Beliefs, Values and Attitudes* (Me-and-Us Ltd, 2009)

# REVIEW AND REFLECTION

**ACTIVITY: AFFIRMATION (Student's Book, page 71)**

> 5. If your school yearbook celebrated you for one of the twelve values listed in Source 1, which would you hope it would be and why?

Invite volunteers to share their responses with the class.

# RESOURCE SHEET 6.1

**SCALE CARDS**

| | | | |
|---|---|---|---|
| HAS SOME IMPORTANCE | IMPORTANT | VERY IMPORTANT | THE MOST IMPORTANT |

**VALUES CARDS**

| | | |
|---|---|---|
| CHOICE | EQUALITY | FREEDOM OF SPEECH |
| FRIENDSHIP | HONESTY | JUSTICE |
| KINDNESS | RESPECT | RESPONSIBILITY |
| RIGHTS | SELF-CONTROL | TOLERANCE |

# Topic: Diverse and conflicting values

| | |
|---|---|
| **Notes** | This topic draws out the idea that every person's individual values can sometimes conflict with the values of those around them.<br><br>It encourages students to think about the factors that influence them when making decisions. This includes how those factors will vary according to the decision to be made. The aim here is to give an example of an enabling strategy to help resist unwanted pressures and influences.<br><br>The main activity is devoted to a free-flowing discussion that allows differences of opinion, attitude and belief to be voiced and accepted. It is important to encourage students to think about the values they hold before responding to difficult questions. The intention behind this is to encourage a creative and wide-thinking approach and to recognise that it is alright to change one's mind as a result of reflection. |
| **Learning outcomes** | **In this topic students will learn about:**<br>■ different ways of making a decision<br>■ examples of current issues on which people hold different values.<br><br>**They will explore:**<br>■ strategies for making decisions<br>■ responses to diverse and conflicting values. |
| **Links to Personal Well-being PoS** | **2.2 Decision-making and managing risk**<br>**d** Students should be able to use strategies for resisting unhelpful peer influence and pressure, assessing when to use them and when and how to get help.<br><br>**2.3 Developing relationships and working with others**<br>**d** Students should be able to demonstrate respect for and acceptance of the differences between people, and challenge offensive behaviour, prejudice and discrimination assertively and safely.<br><br>**3 Range and content**<br>**a** The study of personal well-being should include the effect of diverse and conflicting values on individuals, families and communities and ways of responding to them. |
| **Links to SEAL outcomes** | **Empathy**<br>Students can show respect for people from diverse cultures and backgrounds.<br>Pupils understand the impact of bullying, prejudice and discrimination on those involved.<br><br>**Social skills**<br>Students can achieve an appropriate level of independence from others, charting and following their own course while maintaining positive relationships with others. |
| **Links to ECM outcomes** | Make a positive contribution |
| **Assessment opportunity** | Activity 4: Different values (see pages 122–123)<br><br>**End of Key Stage Statement – diversity**<br>Learners are able to:<br>■ explain how differing cultures, faiths and beliefs may influence lifestyle choices, and demonstrate respect for these differences. |
| **Resources** | ■ Student's Book (pages 72–73)<br>■ Appendix (see the CD): Active Learning Methodologies:<br> □ Pairs work (pages 6–7)  □ Diamond nine (page 6) |

# STARTER ACTIVITY

### ACTIVITY: VALUES AND ACTIONS (Student's Book, page 72)

1. We live in a very busy society where adults seem to have less time to give to family life. What do you think of the values of the parent in Source 1?
2. What value or values do you hold that make you act in a certain way?

Use pairs work. See Appendix (on the CD): Active Learning Methodologies: Pairs work (pages 6–7).

Take feedback, drawing out where possible the links between values and actions and how one influences the other. Some may remember this example:

'I value planet Earth and have concerns about global warming – so I do my best to support organisations that stop the destruction of the rainforests; for example, I only use recycled paper.'

# MAIN ACTIVITIES

### ACTIVITY: DECIDING HOW TO ACT (Student's Book, page 72)

3. Look at Source 2.
   a) How important would each of these approaches be in helping you arrive at a decision? Prioritise the different ways by putting them into a diamond nine as below.

$$
\begin{array}{ccccc}
 & & 1 & & \\
 & 2 & & 3 & \\
4 & & 5 & & 6 \\
 & 7 & & 8 & \\
 & & 9 & &
\end{array}
$$

   b) Now discuss the following questions:
   - Which are the most thoughtful decision-making options?
   - Is it right to go along with others even if you don't support what they plan to do?
   - Should you let others make decisions for you?

Use the diamond nine method: See Appendix (on the CD): Active Learning Methodologies: Diamond nine (page 6).

In this example students can work in pairs and instead of using cards can simply note the numbers from the statements in the text in a diamond pattern on a piece of paper.

In the discussion draw out the realisation that different situations are likely to elicit different responses; in other words, we don't always use the same ways of making a decision – a lot will depend on the situation, who else is involved, the enormity of the decision, etc.

### ACTIVITY: DIFFERENT VALUES (Student's Book, page 73)

4. Look at Sources 3–5. What do you think about these news stories?

Allow some time to reflect individually on the stories, then get students to work in pairs.

Students should think critically and creatively about one of the three news stories. They can choose a story or the teacher may decide to allocate stories, one story to a pair of students.

Pairs discuss their allocated story and devise one or two points which they would like to raise in discussion. These could be:

- a point of view
- a reflection on what they would do
- a question which would need to be answered before they could make their final decision; e.g. 'I would need to know … before I could make a decision about whether I agree or not'.

Take one news story at a time and ask pairs to share their discussion points with the rest of the class, then open up the discussion to other class members.

After hearing the feedback on all three stories, allow pairs time to reflect on what they have heard and to come up with a final comment expressing their opinion on the article.

---

## End of Key Stage Statement – diversity

Learners are able to:

- explain how differing cultures, faiths and beliefs may influence lifestyle choices, and demonstrate respect for these differences.

### Assessment activity

The activity can be extended by using the Sources on page 73 of the Student's Book and the Values cards on Resource sheet 6.1 on page 119 of this book.

The aim of the activity is to encourage students to discuss a range of values and to see how these might influence different standpoints on current social issues.

### Assessment method – small group work

Allocate one of Sources 3 to 5 to each small group and a copy of the Values cards on Resource sheet 6.1 (page 119).

Each group reads their story and then considers two points of view – one in support of the news story and one which disagrees with it:

- Source 3:
  - parents in New Zealand wanting the right to smack their children
  - parents wanting smacking to remain banned.

- Source 4:
  - members of the public who want capital punishment (in the UK, this means hanging) reinstated
  - members of the public who want the ban on capital punishment to remain.

- Source 5:
  - those who want to keep the law banning the wearing of religious symbols in French state schools
  - those who want to repeal the law and allow symbols to be worn in schools.

Groups read the list of values (Resource Sheet 6.1, page 119) and discuss which values they feel motivate and support the different points of view.

Each group reports back on the values that they felt motivated people. The teacher makes a display list of these.

Once all groups have reported back the display list can be reviewed – it is likely that the same values have underpinned different points of view.

---

Draw out the understanding that the same values may motivate people on opposite sides of an argument. Does this fact make it easier to accept and respect a very different point of view from your own?

In the final feedback, use some of the examples given by students to credit clear thinking, a sense of balance and respect for differing views.

# REVIEW AND REFLECTION

## ACTIVITY: CORE VALUES (Student's Book, page 73)

> **5. Is there a particular value that you would hold to, whatever the changing circumstances in your life?**

Allow sufficient time for students to reflect on this. Invite volunteers to share their responses with the class. It is as important to enable them to reflect on the 'if' element as the 'what' element, i.e. is there something of such value in their lives they cannot imagine it changing?

# 7 Consumerism

## Topic: Responsible consumerism

| | |
|---|---|
| **Notes** | This chapter focuses on the theme of consumerism and starts with a session which looks at an everyday essential – food. Students are invited to consider typical 'special offers' and to critically review them. The topic acknowledges that we live in an acquisitive society where often little thought is given to purchasing goods.<br><br>There are two main activities. The first asks students to view their consumption in terms of wants and needs. The second asks them to investigate their role as consumers in challenging supermarkets to reduce wastage and trade responsibly. |
| **Learning outcomes** | **In this topic students will learn about:**<br>■ advertising techniques that encourage spending<br>■ food wastage in the UK.<br>**They will explore:**<br>■ the real value of retail 'offers'<br>■ actions that retailers can take towards responsible food use. |
| **Links to Personal Well-being PoS** | **2.1 Critical reflection**<br>**e** Students should be able to develop self-awareness by reflecting critically on their behaviour and its impact on others. |
| **Links to Economic Well-being PoS** | **1.2 Capability**<br>**d** Becoming critical consumers of goods and services.<br><br>**3 Range and content**<br>**k** The study of economic well-being and financial capability should include social and moral dilemmas about the use of money. |
| **Links to SEAL outcomes** | **Self-awareness**<br>Students can reflect on their actions and identify lessons to be learned from them. |
| **Links to ECM outcomes** | Achieve economic well-being ■ Make a positive contribution |
| **Assessment opportunity** | See Topic: Ethical consumerism; Activity 4: What else do you want to know? (pages 130–131) |
| **Resources** | ■ Student's Book (pages 74–77)<br>■ Appendix (see the CD): Active Learning Methodologies:<br>  □ Brainstorming (page 3)  □ Small group work (pages 6–7) |

# STARTER ACTIVITY

**ACTIVITY: SPECIAL OFFERS? (Student's Book, page 74)**

> **1. Look at the photos and information in Source 1. What special offers are shown and described? Can you think of any others?**

The photos in Source 1 show:

- a 'buy-one-get-one-free' (BOGOF) offer – these are very common in supermarkets and sometimes in other stores. The real value depends on the unit price – has it increased just before this offer is made? If the product is perishable (food) it may be that the use-by date is very close and the food might have to be thrown away before it can be eaten
- tickets purchased via a ticketing agency – special deals are offered for early booking; sometimes there are extra costs added to the face value of the ticket.

Run as a whole-class brainstorm. See Appendix (on the CD): Active Learning Methodologies: Brainstorming (page 3).
  Other 'special offers' may include:

- buy one get one half price
- buy one item get another item free/reduced
- three for the price of two
- buy two tee-shirts get a third free
- but a shirt and get a free tie to go with it
- today is 15 per cent off day on all blue ticketed items, etc.

> **2. a) Have you ever:**
>
>    - **bought an item of clothing from a 'sale' and then not worn it**
>    - **thrown away food from a two-for-one offer because it went off before it could be used**
>    - **ended up realising it wasn't such a 'good deal' after all the extras were added?**
>
> **b) Do you think you have ever been 'taken in' by any of these?**

- These examples rely on motivating the buyer to make compulsive rather than thought-through purchases.
- They often lure people into believing they need something and the bargain seems too good to pass up. However, if you weren't going to buy this in the first place, is it really a bargain?
- People on limited incomes or tight budgets may be particularly affected by these types of offers if they are unable to make a realistic assessment about whether the offer is good value or not.
- These offers create a 'want-it' rather than 'need-it' mentality.

# MAIN ACTIVITIES

**ACTIVITY: RESPONSIBLE CONSUMERISM (Student's Book, page 75)**

> 3. **We would all like to think of ourselves as responsible consumers but inevitably most of us get drawn into buying things. One way to look at our own spending habits is to think of our 'wants versus needs'.**
>    a) **Make a list of everything you can remember buying (or that was bought for you) in the last six months. Categorise them into 'wants' or 'needs'.**
>    b) **Work with another person to compare your lists. Did you find they had the same views on what constituted 'needs'?**

Students should work individually to come up with their own list. Now explain that each student needs to divide their list into two: 'wants' and 'needs'.

WANTS are any items that are not essential and that one could live without.

NEEDS are any items that are essential and necessary to everyday living.

Students should now work with another person to compare their new lists. Did they find they had the same views on what constituted 'needs'?

> 4. **How easy is it to be socially responsible and selective in the face of sophisticated and persuasive advertising?**

It may be increasingly difficult to exercise responsible consumerism in our 'throw-away' society. Some people are able to be clear and plan what they intend to buy based on what they need. However, the large amounts spent on marketing (advertising) create a false 'need' which many consumers do not feel able to resist; for example:

- having the most up-to-date/off-the-catwalk clothing trend
- being seen to use the latest mobile phone technology
- always having the most recent 'designer' trainers
- ensuring that home entertainments systems are totally up-to-date, etc.

Introduce the concept of built-in obsolescence: A method of stimulating consumer demand by designing products that wear out or become outmoded after limited use.
  If you visit a council refuse site it is clear that many items are being disposed of whilst they still work. Charity shops are now dealing in electrical items (that work) as their useable life extends well beyond current trends – it is only desire and demand for newer versions that have made them obsolete. Not all consumers are responsible enough to donate or recycle – some simply dump unwanted goods.

**ACTIVITY: RESPONSIBLE FOOD USE (Student's Book, page 77)**

> 5. **Some supermarkets are already working towards using leftover food to help those in need (see Student's Book, page 77). Research the policies about not throwing out useable food of other supermarket chains that are not mentioned.**

The following supermarket chains were not listed – and there may be more local to your area:

- Morrisons
- Asda
- Lidl
- Netto
- Aldi
- Costcutter
- M&S
- Spar.

Students could write to (or email) the Head Office of these to identify what their policy is on throwing out food.

Alternatively the following websites could be used for research to further extend this activity:

- WRAP: household food waste (www.wrap.org.uk)
- Love Food Hate Waste campaign (www.lovefoodhatewaste.com)
- Wikipedia: search 'food waste in the United Kingdom' (en.wikipedia.org)
- FareShare: Community Food Network (www.fareshare.org.uk).

# REVIEW AND REFLECTION

**ACTIVITY: ONE PERSONAL STEP (Student's Book, page 77)**

> **6. Responsible consumerism needs each individual to make changes. What one personal step could you take to ensure you become a more responsible consumer?**

Allow a few moments for reflection then invite volunteers to share their response with the rest of the class.

**OPTIONAL DISCUSSION ACTIVITY**

This activity should be undertaken as small group work – See Appendix (on the CD): Active Learning Methodologies: Small group work (pages 6–7). When taking feedback if the following are not addressed raise them in the discussion.

> **a) What information should supermarkets provide so that responsible consumers can make informed choices?**

- where the product comes from
- how local it is
- a clear list of all ingredients; e.g. printed in clear type that's easy to read
- what the nutritional percentage (%) values of food are
- what their food wastage policy is
- ethical policies; e.g. selling and using only free-range egg/chicken products
- environmental policies; e.g. not sourcing meat from farms created on former rainforest land and using bio-degradable materials such as paper rather than plastic/polythene bags
- social responsibility policies; e.g. not selling alcohol at loss-leader prices.

> **b) What can consumers do to let supermarkets know that change is needed?**

- ask for really locally produced goods
- buy more goods (e.g. fruit and vegetables) that are weighed in the shop rather than pre-packaged products
- remove unnecessary packaging and leave it at the check-out counter
- ask for products that are in reusable and/or refillable containers
- be selective over purchases and explain (to a member of staff or on a customer comment card) why certain brands or products should not be stocked
- if improvements are noticed acknowledge them – and if not, choose to shop elsewhere and let the company know why.

# Topic: Ethical consumerism

| | |
|---|---|
| **Notes** | The last topic on responsible consumerism is now extended by focusing particularly on ethical issues. The example chosen is the clothing industry and a series of activities explore the positive and negative impacts of the industry on producers in the developing world.<br><br>Students are then invited to think about their own attitudes towards paying more for ethically produced and traded goods. The topic ends by extending questions about ethical consumerism to other goods and services. There is potential here to undertake research to answer the questions posed by the students in the last activity. |
| **Learning outcomes** | **In this topic students will learn about:**<br>■ what can make consumerism unethical<br>■ the human cost of manufacturing in developing countries.<br><br>**They will explore:**<br>■ ethical and unethical factors in goods production<br>■ different attitudes towards the concept of 'fair pricing'. |
| **Links to Personal Well-being PoS** | **2.1 Critical reflection**<br>**e** Students should be able to develop self-awareness by reflecting critically on their behaviour and its impact on others. |
| **Links to Economic Well-being PoS** | **1.2 Capability**<br>**d** Becoming critical consumers of goods and services.<br><br>**3 Range and content**<br>**k** The study of economic well-being and financial capability should include social and moral dilemmas about the use of money. |
| **Links to SEAL outcomes** | **Self-awareness**<br>Students can reflect on their actions and identify lessons to be learned from them.<br><br>**Empathy**<br>Students can see the world from other people's points of view. |
| **Links to ECM outcomes** | Achieve economic well-being ■ Make a positive contribution |
| **Assessment opportunity** | Activity 4: What else do you want to know? (pages 130–131)<br><br>**End of Key Stage Statement – Financial capability**<br>Learners are able to:<br>■ critically evaluate a wide range of goods and services from the consumer's point of view. |
| **Resources** | ■ Student's Book (pages 78–79)<br>■ Appendix (see the CD): Active Learning Methodologies:<br>   □ Whole-class work (page 7)   □ Small group work (pages 6–7) |

# STARTER ACTIVITY

**ACTIVITY: ETHICAL CONSUMERISM (Student's Book, page 78)**

> **1. What does 'ethical consumerism' mean to you?**

Run this as a whole-class discussion. See Appendix (on the CD): Active Learning Methodologies: Whole class work (page 7).

Ask students to think about the products they buy and companies they buy from. How aware are they of:

- working conditions for staff (including not exploiting child labour)
- fair pay
- environmental sustainability of materials used; e.g. recyclable, energy efficiency
- animal welfare issues
- ethical profit sharing; e.g. Fair Trade
- ethical investment policies; e.g. not working with arms dealers.

# MAIN ACTIVITIES

**ACTIVITY: IS LOW PRICE ALWAYS FAIR PRICE? (Student's Book, page 79)**

> **2. Look at the labels of the shirt/blouse, trousers/skirt, shoes/sandals that you are wearing. Where were they made? Chances are they were made in a developing or newly industrialised country such as China, Sri Lanka, Bangladesh or India.**
>
> **3. One way to produce low-price goods is to produce them in situations where the workers do not have employment rights and where wages are low (see Source 1). What do you think the five people listed in Source 1 say in response to this question:**
> **Do consumers need to pay fairer prices (which sometimes may be more than they pay now) to ensure goods are ethically produced?**

Put students into groups of four. See Appendix (on the CD): Active Learning Methodologies: Small group work (pages 6–7). Allocate each group ONE of the five people and ask them to write a statement expressing what they think that person's point of view would be.

Having allowed sufficient time, take feedback from each group in turn. The following points may help extend the discussion:

- Current prices of goods for consumers are likely to be cheaper because goods are produced cheaply. Consumers have a wide choice because they can buy goods from a variety of sources (some of these are likely to be unethically produced).
- Would consumers be prepared to pay more if they knew for certain the producers (including the farmers, factory workers, etc.) were getting a fair wage and price?
- Would consumers be prepared to pay more if they knew that people involved in producing the goods were fairly treated?
- Would you or your family buy fairly traded goods?
- Fair Trade principles include:

    ☐  paying workers a fair price
    ☐  plantations having good wages, housing and health standards
    ☐  environment having to be sustainable
    ☐  no child labour or forced labour allowed
    ☐  farmers and workers able to join co-operatives and unions
    ☐  contracts for long-term planning.

# REVIEW AND REFLECTION

### ACTIVITY: WHAT ELSE DO YOU WANT TO KNOW? (Student's Book, page 78)

> **4.  Read Source 2, which gives examples of the sorts of questions ethical consumers have asked in the past. What questions would you like to see answered to help you become a more ethical consumer?**

Allow students time to formulate their questions. Ask volunteers to share their questions with the rest of the class.

The following examples may start discussion if the students find the activity difficult:

- Are wind-farms an efficient way of harnessing power?
- How can I trace whether a clothing brand uses child labour?
- Apart from Fair Trade, what other ethical labelling or symbols should I be looking for?

---

### End of Key Stage Statement – Financial capability

Learners are able to:

- critically evaluate a wide range of goods and services from the consumer's point of view.

#### Assessment activity

The activity can be extended by asking students to work in pairs. Each pair should be given one of the following areas (or any others you wish to choose) to identify further questions:

- energy utilities; e.g. gas, electricity
- recycling and refuse collection
- fresh produce; e.g. food
- clothing
- electrical products including IT goods
- banking services.

Try to have even numbers of pairs working on any one topic so that they can later join up to form a small group of four.

#### Assessment method – questionnaire design

Students should take time to decide which questions they would need to ask of suppliers to be better informed and to make more ethical choices.

They should have between three and five key questions that could potentially be answered by email or in a telephone conversation.

---

Pairs working on the same topic area should now join up to compare questionnaires. They should agree one questionnaire between them based on the best questions from each original pair. The new questionnaire should still have only a maximum of three to five questions.

Groups should be invited to present their questionnaire to the rest of the class, explaining why they felt these final questions were the most important to ask in order to help them be more ethical consumers.

Other groups can feed back on the list – especially if they can identify other crucial questions that might be asked.

# Topic: Consumerism and giving

| | |
|---|---|
| **Notes** | Although the topic area has some similarities to elements of Citizenship, the focus here is more on personal ethical and moral responses to situations involving money.<br><br>It starts with the everyday personal scenario of street begging and moves consideration on to other ways financial support can be offered to disadvantaged people.<br><br>Students are invited to discuss the way charities raise and use funds and how they might decide to make the best use of their financial donation.<br><br>Ethical issues are raised and considered so that students are aware of the wider implications of their spending and investment. |
| **Learning outcomes** | **In this topic students will learn about:**<br>■ charities and the methods they use to raise funds<br>■ charitable giving and ethical banking.<br>**They will explore:**<br>■ their personal attitudes towards charitable giving<br>■ ethical values that affect investments. |
| **Links to Personal Well-being PoS** | **2.1 Critical reflection**<br>**a** Students should be able to reflect critically on their own and others' values and change their behaviour accordingly. |
| **Links to Economic Well-being PoS** | **1.4 Economic understanding**<br>**a** Understanding the economic and business environment.<br><br>**2.4 Financial capability**<br>**a** Students should be able to manage their money.<br><br>**3 Range and content**<br>**k** The study of economic well-being and financial capability should include social and moral dilemmas about the use of money. |
| **Links to SEAL outcomes** | **Self-awareness**<br>Students can reflect on their actions and identify lessons to be learned from them. |
| **Links to ECM outcomes** | Achieve economic well-being ■ Make a positive contribution |
| **Assessment opportunity** | See Topic: Ethical consumerism; Activity 4: What else do you want to know?<br>(pages 130–131) |
| **Resources** | ■ Student's Book (pages 80–81)<br>■ Appendix (see the CD): Active Learning Methodologies:<br>  □ Pairs work (pages 6–7)  □ Small group work (pages 6–7)  □ Continuum (page 4)<br>■ Resource sheet 7.1 (page 136) |

*PSHE Education for Key Stage 4 Teacher's Resource Book © Hodder Education*

# STARTER ACTIVITY

**ACTIVITY: WHAT WOULD YOU DO? (Student's Book, page 80)**

> 1. You are walking through the town centre. Someone who looks homeless holds out a cup and asks you for some change. What do you do?

Use pairs work. See Appendix (on the CD): Active Learning Methodologies: Pairs work (pages 6–7).
   In taking feedback raise the following points in discussion:

- Does giving money this way encourage begging?
- If you give change to the person begging do you know that they will use it wisely?
- Before handing your money over should you think about whether change will be spent on alcohol or illegal drugs?
- Would it be more supportive to the person begging if you offered to take them and share a cup of tea instead of giving money? That way you are providing something warming and re-hydrating and also giving them your time.
- If you walk by do you give any thought at all to the person begging when you can no longer see them?
- If you want to give money to help disadvantaged people, are there better and more useful ways of making a donation?
- Draw attention to the information in the Student's Book and discuss some of these other ways charities look for funds – are some ways better than others?

# MAIN ACTIVITIES

**ACTIVITY: WHAT'S THE PRIORITY FOR YOUR MONEY? (Student's Book, page 81)**

> 2. If you decided to donate to charity, would you give for emergency aid or development work? Start by thinking about what each can provide and then decide what your priority would be.

Use small group work. See Appendix (on the CD): Active Learning Methodologies: Small group work (pages 6–7).

Emergency aid can provide:

- shelter and medicines
- food and blankets
- specialist rescue services.

Development work can provide:

- literacy, numeracy and ICT training
- employment and voluntary experience
- long-term economic development; e.g. agriculture, businesses, schools, hospitals.

Further points to raise in discussion:

- Remind students that it does not have to be a choice between one or the other of these charitable areas – many people give to both.
- When a disaster strikes emergency aid will always be needed – in some countries this is more easily accessed than others.

- Development work is designed to raise the general standard of living and eradicate disadvantage of the community affected. It does this by enabling people to become self-supporting.
- A lot of people do not give charitably – should we think more or less of them?

## ACTIVITY: WAYS TO DONATE (Student's Book, page 81)

**3.  Find out more about ways that people can give to charity.**

Ways of giving to charity include:

**Payroll:**
If you pay tax through PAYE (Pay As You Earn), Payroll Giving offers a simple way to reduce the cost to you of making regular gifts to charities. If your employer or company/personal pension provider runs a Payroll Giving Scheme, you simply authorise them to make the donation from your wages or pension before deducting any tax.

**Standing Orders:**
Standing orders are customers' instructions to their bank to pay a set amount, to a named charity, at regular intervals (say on the 1st of the month) – either for a specific period of time or until cancelled. At set times, the customer's bank just sends the money to the charity's bank and only the customer can alter the payments.

**Legacies:**
A legacy is an instruction in a person's will to leave money as a gift to a charity. It's a common myth that only the rich and famous leave money to charity when they die. This couldn't be any further from the truth. The reality is without the gifts left in wills from the general public, many of the charities we know and support today wouldn't even exist. Legacies are the foundation for many of the charities in the UK and are vital in making sure that all the good work they do can continue.

## ACTIVITY: HOW WOULD YOU CHOOSE? (Student's Book, page 81)

**4.  What important factors do you think people should consider before investing their money?**

Make sure students understand the background information provided in the Student's Book.

One way to explore the ethical issues is via a continuum. See Appendix (on the CD): Active Learning Methodologies: Continuum (page 4).

Use 'IMPORTANT' and 'UNIMPORTANT' cards at either end of the spectrum (see Resource sheet 7.1, page 136).

Offer each of the following statements with the prefix 'HOW IMPORTANT IS IT TO YOU THAT YOUR MONEY …':

- … does not support companies that provide tanks, guns, ammunition, etc.
- … is invested in companies that search for fuel only in an environmentally responsible way
- … supports companies that do not exploit their workers
- … does not support tobacco manufacturers
- … supports companies that have environmental policies; e.g. recycling, energy efficiency, etc.
- … does not support production of violent and/or pornographic materials?

These statements are also given on Resource sheet 7.1 (page 136), if you want to cut them out for the students to use in groups.

# REVIEW AND REFLECTION

**ACTIVITY: WHO DO I GIVE TO? (Student's Book, page 81)**

> **5. You've won £1000 to divide equally between one national/local charity and one international charity. Which charities would you choose and why?**

Invite volunteers to share their examples. If a number of students suggest the same charity advise them to make a case to the school council that this particular charity could be the focus of annual fundraising in the school.

# RESOURCE SHEET 7.1

**STATEMENTS**

HOW IMPORTANT IS IT TO YOU THAT YOUR MONEY …

… does not support companies that provide tanks, guns, ammunition, etc?

HOW IMPORTANT IS IT TO YOU THAT YOUR MONEY …

… is invested in companies that search for fuel only in an environmentally responsible way?

HOW IMPORTANT IS IT TO YOU THAT YOUR MONEY …

… supports companies that do not exploit their workers?

HOW IMPORTANT IS IT TO YOU THAT YOUR MONEY …

… does not support tobacco manufacturers?

HOW IMPORTANT IS IT TO YOU THAT YOUR MONEY …

… supports companies that have environmental policies; e.g. recycling, energy efficiency, etc?

HOW IMPORTANT IS IT TO YOU THAT YOUR MONEY …

… does not support production of violent and/or pornographic materials?

**CONTINUUM CARDS**

IMPORTANT

UNIMPORTANT

# 8 Personal Finance

## Topic: Budgeting

| | |
|---|---|
| **Notes** | With more and more people getting into debt and struggling to pay back what they have borrowed, it is important that young people have an understanding of how to manage their personal finances. In this topic, students will learn about the reasons why we pay tax on our earnings and why budgeting is important if we are to manage our personal finances effectively. Students will investigate the real cost of living and also the options that are available to them to save for the future. |
| **Learning outcomes** | **In this topic students will learn about:**<br>■ tax: how and why we pay it<br>■ budgeting for a new home<br>■ planning for a secure financial future.<br><br>**They will explore:**<br>■ different tax rates and the services that taxes provide<br>■ the cost of living when moving into a new home – needs and wants<br>■ current and savings accounts and pension schemes. |
| **Links to Economic Well-being PoS** | **1.2 Capability**<br>**b** Learning how to manage money and personal finance.<br><br>**1.3 Risk**<br>**b** Understanding the need to manage risk in the context of financial and career choices.<br><br>**1.4 Economic understanding**<br>**b** Understanding the functions and uses of money.<br><br>**2.1 Self-development**<br>**a** Students should be able to … envisage a positive future for themselves at work.<br><br>**2.4 Financial capability**<br>**a** Students should be able to manage their money.<br><br>**3 Range and content**<br>**h** The study of economic well-being and financial capability should include personal budgeting and ... a range of financial products and services.<br>**i** The study of economic well-being and financial capability should include risk and reward, and how money can make money through savings, investment and trade. |
| **Links to SEAL outcomes** | **Motivation**<br>Students can set goals and challenges for themselves.<br>Students can take responsibility for their lives ... and make wise choices. |
| **Links to ECM outcomes** | Enjoy and achieve ■ Make a positive contribution ■ Achieve economic well-being |
| **Assessment opportunity** | Activity 5: The dream retirement (see page 141)<br><br>**End of Key Stage Statement – financial capability**<br>Learners are able to:<br>■ explain some of the financial products and services that will help them manage their current and future personal finances, identify a range of post-16 options … and support networks that they can use to plan and negotiate their career pathways. |
| **Resources** | ■ Student's Book (pages 82–85)<br>■ Appendix (see the CD): Active Learning Methodologies:<br>  □ Brainstorming (page 3)   □ Pairs work (pages 6–7) |

# STARTER ACTIVITY

**ACTIVITY: WHY DO WE NEED TO PAY TAX? (Student's Book, page 83)**

> 1.  What would happen to society if we didn't pay tax? Discuss all the problems we would face; for example, those who couldn't afford to pay for their own healthcare would have to go without treatment.

Run this activity as a brainstorm. See Appendix (on the CD): Active Learning Methodologies: Brainstorming (page 3).
   Possible answers could include:

- shortage of/no emergency services
- healthcare for only wealthy through insurance, like in the USA
- no financial support for people with disabilities, illness, unemployment, etc.
- end of free education
- no refuse collection
- transport system wouldn't be updated.

The list could potentially be quite lengthy, but it is important for students to clearly understand why we pay tax and its importance.

> 2.  Look at Source 2. Do you think it is fair that different people pay different tax rates depending on how much they earn? Explain your answer.

Possible comments could include:

**Fair:**

- The more you earn, the more you should pay.
- Those who earn more need to help support those on lower incomes as without lower income jobs (e.g. cleaners) things wouldn't function properly.
- Some people are paid far too much so should contribute more to society.

**Not fair:**

- People work hard to get into a position where they have high earnings; why should they be penalised?
- Some people are lazy and don't make an effort to work; why should they get others' hard-earned money?
- Other countries pay less tax than us; why shouldn't we pay less?

# MAIN ACTIVITIES

**ACTIVITY: HOW WELL COULD I BUDGET? (Student's Book, page 83)**

> 3.  a) Make a list of the different things you would have to pay for on a monthly basis if you moved into a one-bedroom flat; for example, mortgage or rent, water rates, council tax, etc. Include essentials such as food, but also other things that you would like to have in your home.
>     b) Try and put a monthly monetary value on each of the things on your list. Your teacher will be able to give you some ideas about costs or you could research them on the internet. When you have the monetary values, add them together to get a total.

Some typical monthly values:

- mortgage/rent: £600
- electricity and gas: £70
- water rates: £20
- credit/store card: £50
- Sky: £30
- mobile phone: £20
- car insurance: £50

- life insurance (mortgage only): £25
- buildings insurance: £30
- contents insurance: £30
- bank loan (optional): £100
- car running costs: £60
- food: £250
- toiletries: £10.

Encourage students to include a budget for clothes, going out, games, music, etc.

Students could use the internet to research any values they aren't sure about. The higher the total the more effective it will be when students realise that some of the items will need to be cut back in the next activity.

> **c) Go back through your list and highlight things that are essential in one colour and things that are desirable in another; for example, if you have included satellite or cable TV you need to think whether this is really necessary.**

Encourage students to discuss their ideas in pairs. See Appendix: Active Learning Methodologies: Pairs work (pages 6–7). They should really consider which items on their list they need to keep, and which they could get rid of or reduce; for example, Sky TV. Could they also do without a car? Is public transport adequate?

> **d) Work out you new monthly expenditure based solely on the essential things. Now times this value by twelve (for each month of the year).**

This activity will give students some idea about the amount they will need to earn if they are to meet all their payments on the list. Remind students however that their list may not necessarily include holidays, savings, etc. Tax and National Insurance would also be deducted, and therefore how much they need to earn to pay for their list of items needs to be on average 20 per cent more than their total to break even.

Encourage students to feed back about how difficult they think it would be to pay for all their items. Lead the discussion to consider the types of jobs students would need to do in order to pay for everything. They will have the opportunity to research jobs in Chapter 10.

**ACTIVITY: WHICH ACCOUNT SHOULD I CHOOSE? (Student's Book, page 84)**

> **4. a) Research and select one bank account you think would be most suitable for you to have your wages paid into each month and one savings account that would be best to save into. Some of the comparison websites such as www.moneysupermarket.com are particularly useful for researching this as they give you a quick overview of each account. You will need to find out the following things about each type of account:**

| Current account | Savings account |
| --- | --- |
| Which bank it is with | Which bank it is with |
| Cost of banking (often free) | Minimum monthly payments needed |

| Current account | Savings account |
|---|---|
| Overdraft facility | Interest rates |
| Card provided (Visa, etc.) | How quickly you can access funds |
| Interest given on money in account | Other incentives |
| Overdraft facility & cost | |
| Amount needed to open account | |
| Other incentives | |

**Once you have selected the most appropriate account for you, write down the details.**

Students can complete this activity by using the internet, and/or using leaflets that have been collected from a range of local banks and/or by having a talk from local bank representatives or similar. The price comparison websites are particularly useful as they give an overview and quick links into specific bank details.

Students will simply need to type 'savings accounts' or 'bank account price comparison' into a search engine and the first few links will take them to the relevant websites. It is worth pointing out that these banks and building societies will pay to be on the price comparison website, so there will be other options which will require further investigation. This could be done by brainstorming other banks that students are aware of and then looking at each individually. Most of the bank websites are easy to navigate and have tabs that link directly to the appropriate information.

**b) In small groups, explain to each other why you have chosen your particular current and savings account:**

- **What were the advantages and disadvantages of each account?**
- **What was the most and the least important factor when deciding?**

Encourage students to discuss their findings with each other so that they can identify whether or not they selected similar accounts and the reasons for their choices.

### ACTIVITY: THE DREAM RETIREMENT (Student's Book, page 85)

**5. a) Describe the type of lifestyle you would like to have when you retire.**
**b) Consider all the things you will need to do as from now to achieve this, and make a plan. In your plan show the different stages of your life and what you will need to do at each stage to achieve your retirement lifestyle. You could include the stages 16, 18, 24, 40, 50, 60 and 70+. You will need to include details about education, career choices, mortgages, savings and lifestyles.**

This activity could be a brief or detailed overview depending on time constraints. Encourage students to consider the things they have learned in today's topic as well as other relevant information from past lessons. Encourage students to share their ideas with others in the class. Students could present their work as a timeline or chart with information about each stage in their life.

## End of Key Stage Statement – financial capability

Learners are able to:

- explain some of the financial products and services that will help them manage their current and future personal finances, identify a range of post-16 options and careers advice and support networks that they can use to plan and negotiate their career pathways.

### Assessment activity

The activity is ideal as an assessment task as it allows students to demonstrate their understanding of a range of personal financing issues and apply them to their own lives. Students could produce a book/project in the manner of *This is Your Life*, but called *This is My Future* in which they cover future stages of their lives. Students could include photos, certificates, leaflets, cut outs, surveys, etc. They could include and plan some of the following events:

- GSCE predictions, possible A-level college courses
- places they would like to travel to
- wedding plans, considering all aspects including venue, reception, transport, honeymoon, how they will pay
- children – how many, names, nursery costs, baby items, etc.
- career – how much they would earn, training, job, etc.
- type of house, cost, mortgage, etc.
- lifestyle – car, shopping, going out
- retirement – at what age, savings, whether they will move house, hobbies.

You could brainstorm with the students the different things they would like to include before they begin work.

### Assessment method – peer or teacher assessment

Students leave their work on the desk whilst other students are given the opportunity to move around the room and look at each other's work. A sheet of paper should be left next to the work so that students can comment on the points listed below. This could also be done by the teacher.

- at least one thing liked about the presentation content
- at least one thing liked about the presentation style
- one thing that could have improved the content
- one thing that could have improved the presentation.

# REVIEW AND REFLECTION

### ACTIVITY: PLANNING FOR MY OWN FUTURE (Student's Book, page 85)

**6. How important do you think it is to plan for your financial future?**

This activity could be done as a written exercise or as a discussion. There may be a mixed response as planning for a future that seems some time away may not be high on students' list of priorities; however, they are likely to at least understand that having a secure financial future is important. Encourage students to consider the type of house they would like, when they would like to retire, etc.

# Topic: Credit and debt

| | |
|---|---|
| **Notes** | Credit is a term we frequently hear on the news, through adverts and in general conversation. However, as it has become so commonplace, the seriousness of its meaning seems to have been watered down and as a result more and more people are getting themselves into unmanageable debt. <br><br> In this topic students will investigate the problems that can arise by failing to manage personal finances effectively. Students will look at reasons for being given credit and how people can fall into a 'repayment trap' if they only manage to pay minimum payments each month. They will also look at ways in which debt can be managed and how organisations such as the Citizens Advice Bureau can support consumers. |
| **Learning outcomes** | **In this topic students will learn about:** <br> ■ financial risks associated with credit and debt <br> ■ how credit providers make money through interest payments <br> ■ advantages and disadvantages of credit and store cards. <br><br> **They will explore:** <br> ■ how the use of credit cards can lead to a 'debt trap' <br> ■ how debt can lead to bankruptcy and insolvency <br> ■ the different types of credit cards that are available. |
| **Links to Economic Well-being PoS** | **1.2 Capability** <br> **b** Learning how to manage money and personal finances. <br> **d** Becoming critical consumers of goods and services. <br><br> **1.3 Risk** <br> **a** Understanding risk in both positive and negative terms. <br> **b** Understanding the need to manage risk in the context of financial and career choices. <br><br> **2.4 Financial capability** <br> **a** Students should be able to manage their money. <br> **b** Students should be able to understand financial risk and rewards. <br> **c** Students should be able to explain financial terms and products. <br> **d** Students should be able to identify how finance will play an important part in their lives and in achieving their aspirations. <br><br> **3 Range and content** <br> **h** The study of economic well-being and financial capability should include Personal budgeting ... credit, debt and a range of financial products and services. |
| **Links to SEAL outcomes** | **Motivation** <br> Students can take responsibility for their lives ... and make wise choices. |
| **Links to ECM outcomes** | Enjoy and achieve ■ Make a positive contribution ■ Achieve economic well-being. |
| **Assessment opportunity** | See Topic: Budgeting; Activity 5: The dream retirement (page 141) |
| **Resources** | ■ Student's Book (pages 86–89) <br> ■ Appendix (see the CD): Active Learning Methodologies: <br>    □ Brainstorming (page 3) <br> ■ Internet access <br> ■ Visitor from Citizens Advice Bureau (optional) |

# STARTER ACTIVITY

## ACTIVITY: UNDERSTANDING DEBT AND CREDIT (Student's Book, page 86)

> 1. a) In pairs, discuss what you think the terms debt and credit mean.
>       Give examples to show your understanding.
>    b) Where have you heard these terms? Do you hear them frequently?
>    c) Do you associate them with being positive or negative?

Debt: When you owe money to someone or to a business. You are likely to have to pay back more than you borrowed as interest is added.

Credit: Borrowed money that you can use to purchase things you need when you want them and then repay the funds back at an agreed time.

Encourage discussion about debt and credit with students. It is important to make students aware that although it is commonplace and is advertised frequently, it carries with it a huge responsibility and shouldn't be taken lightly.

# MAIN ACTIVITIES

## ACTIVITY: WHY WE NEED CREDIT (Student's Book, page 87)

> 2. Make a list of all the different things for which people might be given credit; for example, a mortgage.

Possible answers could be:

- mortgage – house
- car loan
- store cards
- electrical goods
- home improvement.

> 3. What problems could arise that would affect people's ability to pay back their debts?

Possible answers could include:

- redundancy
- reduced working week
- illness
- accident.

## ACTIVITY: THE IMPACT OF BANKRUPTCY (Student's Book, page 87)

> 4. Source 2 shows the problems that thousands of individuals and businesses are facing. One suggestion to help is for banks to lend more.
>    a) How would this help?
>    b) What potential problems might it result in?

Possible answers could include:

- By lending additional funds, banks help businesses to keep running during difficult times. They can use funding to buy stock or essential equipment or to pay back other debts until things pick up.
- If more money is leant by banks, it puts individuals and businesses into further debt. If the business doesn't pick up or people don't find work, then they have no way of paying back the new debts or the old.

> **5. Do you know any national or local businesses that have closed down? What is likely to be the impact on:**
> **a) the owners?**

Discuss students' ideas as a class. Possible suggestions could be:

- bankruptcy
- loss of property (if loans to set up the business were secured on property, this would result in loss of that property)
- poor credit rating
- reputation
- unemployment.

> **b) the employees and their families?**

Discuss students' ideas as a class. Possible suggestions could be:

- unemployment
- lower income, maybe through benefits
- low morale if no other employment is found
- defaulting on mortgage payments
- fewer luxury items
- less money to spend in local area (ripple effect).

Run a brainstorm for students to come up with businesses that have closed down. See Appendix (on the CD): Active Learning Methodologies: Brainstorming (page 3). Possible examples could include: Woolworths, Zavvi, MFI, MK One, Dolcis, Ethel Austin. Students will probably know of other local stores.

### ACTIVITY: WHICH DEAL IS THE BEST? (Student's Book, page 89)

> **6. a) Using the internet or newspapers, search for different offers that are currently available from credit card companies. Look for details such as those in Source 4 and select one credit card that you think offers the best value. Alternatively, you could use the details in Source 4 for this activity.**
> **b) Imagine you are going on a shopping spree. Make a list of all the different things you would buy and their cost, up to the limit of your chosen card.**
> **c) Now, using the APR and minimum payments rates from the card you have chosen, follow the first four steps in the flow chart in Source 3 to find out:**
> - **how much the minimum payment would be in the first month**
> - **how much of that minimum payment is interest, and how much is paying off the original loan.**
> **d) Now work out or estimate the answers to the following questions (use Source 3 to help you). If you only paid the minimum each month:**
> - **how much would you still owe after twelve months**
> - **how much would you end up paying to clear your debt, and how much of this is interest**
> - **how long would it take you to clear the debt**
> - **how long would it take you to clear the debt if you didn't have to make any interest payments?**

If you have access to the internet this task will be easier, particularly by using price comparison websites. It is important to point out to students that the credit card companies pay to be on price comparison sites and that there will be other offers available if they look for them. Students should follow the step-by-step guidelines as they appear above and in the Student's Book.

It is a good idea to set a limit at a round number, ideally no more than £5000. If students get stuck they can refer back to the example in the Student's Book.

Students may need some support to work out the calculations. They can also refer back to the Student's Book example if they need help.

---

**e) As a class discuss your findings:**
- **Who had the best credit card deal?**
- **What problems could people face if they only pay the minimum amount?**

---

This is a particularly important discussion to have with students. Encourage students to share their views and findings about credit cards, but emphasise the problems that people can get into if they only pay back minimum amounts each month. You could also bring in discussion about the availability of credit and that it is now relatively easy to get compared to 30 years ago.

# BACKGROUND INFORMATION AS OF MAY 2010

---

*Credit card interest rates are one of the major reasons for debt. Credit card borrowing in the UK has reached an all-time high; the total amount in the UK stands at £238 billion, which is increasing daily. Around 24 per cent of credit card users are still paying off credit card debts from the previous year's Christmas. Estimates show that if a person repays only the minimum amount on their credit-card balance it will take 30 years to clear.*

- *debt in the UK increases by £154 million every day*
- *the average household debt in the UK is £59,670*
- *one person in Britain is declared insolvent or bankrupt every 4.8 minutes*
- *in the UK around 124 properties are repossessed every day*
- *the amount of interest paid on debt in the UK has now reached £252 million per day*
- *the amount of people who owe money on credit cards but are unable to pay them has doubled in the last 12 months*
- *debt in Britain grows by around £1 million every nine minutes*
- *the Citizens Advice Bureau deals with 6600 problems concerning debt every day.*

*www.articlesbase.com/debt*

---

**ACTIVITY: PROS AND CONS OF CREDIT CARD USE (Student's Book, page 89)**

---

7. **Sort the statements in Source 5 into advantages and disadvantages of using credit or store cards. Add any others you can think of.**

---

The statements in Source 5 should be divided like this:

**Advantages:**

- Ease of purchase
- Useful in emergencies
- Incentives offers; e.g. air miles or insurance offers
- Protect your purchases
- Help build a good credit history.

**Disadvantages:**

- Encourage people to spend money they haven't got
- High interest rates – minimum payment debt trap
- Credit card fraud.

8. **Make a poster or leaflet informing people about the do's and don'ts of credit card use and strategies for avoiding debt. Research and include information about where people can seek information should they need advice – The Citizens Advice Bureau is a good starting point.**

This activity will get students thinking about what they need to do to manage effectively their finances and any debts they may have in the future. The Citizens Advice Bureau website (www.citizensadvice.org.uk) provides clearly explained instructions about ways to manage finances and where to seek advice, information which can be used by students to produce their leaflets. You could arrange a visitor from Citizens Advice to talk to students and field any questions they might have. You could display posters or leaflets in the classroom or around school. The best could be photocopied and given out to the year group or sixth form.

# REVIEW AND REFLECTION

**ACTIVITY: TEMPTATION (Student's Book, page 89)**

9. **Do you think credit cards provide too much 'temptation' for people?**

Students could complete this as a written exercise or through discussion. Encourage students to consider how easy it is for people to get credit today and how the media and advertising keep people wanting more and more, and offer ways to get what they want without paying for it with money they actually have. They could also consider whether or not there should be restrictions on the advertising of such products and financial services.

# 9 The Future

## Topic: At what age can I ...?

| | |
|---|---|
| **Notes** | Envisaging a positive future for themselves helps students feel confident about developing new roles and responsibilities. It is part of making the transition to becoming an adult member of society. One of the roles that a student needs to reflect upon is the self as a citizen who is now experiencing and acquiring further legal rights and responsibilities. This topic encourages students to think about the different ages people can legally experience certain rights and be held responsible for their actions. It encourages students to consider arguments for and against changing certain age limits. It asks them to consider in a structured way how financial independence can be attained. |
| **Learning outcomes** | **In this topic students will learn something about:**<br>■ the multiple roles and responsibilities that people have in society<br>■ the need to manage risk in a range of personal and social situations<br>■ managing money and personal finances.<br>**They will explore:**<br>■ a way of recognising your rights and responsibilities<br>■ managing change and transition. |
| **Links to Personal Well-being PoS** | **1.3 Risk**<br>**a** Understanding risk in both positive and negative terms and understanding that individuals need to manage ... in a range of personal and social situations.<br>**1.4 Relationships**<br>**b** Understanding that people have multiple roles and responsibilities in society and that making positive relationships and contributing to groups, teams and communities is important.<br>**2.3 Developing relationships and working with others**<br>**b** Students should be able to use the social skill of negotiation within relationships, recognising their rights and responsibilities and that their actions have consequences. |
| **Links to Economic Well-being PoS** | **1.2 Capability**<br>**b** Learning how to manage money and personal finances.<br>**2.3 Enterprise**<br>**d** Students should be able to manage change and transition. |
| **Links to SEAL outcomes** | **Social skills**<br>Students understand their rights and responsibilities as individuals who belong to many different social groups. |
| **Links to ECM outcomes** | Achieve economic well-being ■ Make a positive contribution |
| **Assessment opportunity** | See Topic: Study or employment – what's out there?; Activity 1: What are my options? (page 162) |
| **Resources** | ■ Student's Book (pages 90–91)<br>■ Resource sheet 9.1 (page 152)<br>■ Appendix: Active Learning Methodologies (see the CD):<br>  □ Continuum (page 4)  □ Small group work (pages 6–7)  □ Timeline (page 10) |

# STARTER ACTIVITY

Read aloud with the class the section in the Student's Book explaining at what age students can do things like get a job, buy and drink alcohol, legally have sex, get married or drive different types of vehicles.

Ask them for feedback:

- Did anything surprise them?
- Did anything annoy them about the way the law operates?
- Do they think all these laws are right for everyone?

# MAIN ACTIVITIES

### ACTIVITY: TOO MUCH TOO SOON? (Student's Book, page 91)

> **1. What reasons could you suggest for why a 16-year-old is allowed to pilot a glider but not drive a car?**

Encourage students to explore the concepts of:

- risk: Risk-taking can be positive (new skills and thrills) as well as negative (not considering the consequences). Where 16-year-olds are able to access gliding it will usually be via an organised club or CCF – not an individual pursuit such as driving. There will inevitably be more supervision in the former.
- regulation: Society has created different approaches to regulating different activities. Not all regulation codes correspond exactly to each other – they have been devised at different times and for different circumstances.
- financial implications: The relative costs of the two activities mean there will be far fewer 16-year-olds able to afford gliding.
- competitiveness: See risk-taking above. Peer pressure/influence is less likely to negatively impact on gliding as compared to the informal 'boy racer' mentality sometimes associated with driving.

The following points may also be included:

- Interaction with other users of airspace is very different from the interaction of users on roads. Roads can be extremely overcrowded; pedestrians, cyclists, motorcyclists and motorists have competing needs.
- Reaching the threshold of becoming a glider pilot would involve more hours of compulsory supervised practice.
- Gliding tends to be a recreational/sporting activity – and fewer people do it. Driving a motor vehicle is more likely to be a daily and utilitarian activity undertaken by many.

> **2. The law says at 10 years old a young person can be held responsible for criminal activity and stand trial for the crime they have committed. Is that too young? Give reasons for your answer.**

### 10 IS NOT TOO YOUNG

- By the age of 10 a child should be able to recognise the difference between right and wrong and behave accordingly.

*PSHE Education for Key Stage 4 Teacher's Resource Book © Hodder Education*

- The age of 10 does not necessarily mean that a child will be prosecuted in court for every crime.
- Criminalising children is necessary to show that their actions were wrong. Children who commit crimes have often grown up in communities without a structure of control. They may see drug-taking, domestic violence and criminal activity in their homes, and they have often skipped school. Because this may be their regular experience, they may not know that their actions are wrong unless they are criminalised for them.

## 10 IS TOO YOUNG

- Not all 10-year-olds are exactly the same. They may be at different stages in their development.
- Even if they know right from wrong, children do not have the emotional maturity to be responsible in law for their actions.
- Children cannot have a fair trial. A 10-year-old may struggle to understand the trial process. Children are unlikely to have the concentration to follow the evidence properly and may not be able to give clear and consistent instructions to their lawyers.

# BACKGROUND INFORMATION

*Age of criminal responsibility:*

- Age 8 – Scotland (the principle in Scotland is that even though it has one of the lowest ages of criminal responsibility it takes pride in its system for dealing with children; only the most serious crimes, such as murder, eventually lead to prosecution in the courts)
- *Age 10 – England*
- *Age 13 – Netherlands, Canada, France*
- *Age 14 – Russia, Japan, Germany, Italy*
- *Age 15 – Finland, Denmark, Norway, Sweden*
- *Age 16 – Spain and Portugal*
- *Age 18 – Belgium, Brazil, Peru.*

*In the US it is 10 for federal crimes but as low as 6 in some states.*

3. **Look at the different ages at which young people are legally allowed to do certain things – is there any specific activity for which you would either raise or lower the age limit? Why?**

You could carry this out as a continuum activity. See Appendix: Active Learning Methodologies: Continuum (page 4). The discussion question could be enhanced by using the series of statements based on the information on Resource sheet 9.1.

4. **Look at Source 1. What are the arguments for and against raising the age at which people can marry/have a civil partnership?**

Put students into groups to carry out small group discussions. See Appendix (on the CD): Active Learning Methodologies: Small group work (pages 6–7).

# BACKGROUND INFORMATION

> *Birth, marriage and death are the standard trio of key events in most people's lives. But only one – marriage – is a matter of choice. The right to exercise that choice was recognised as a principle of law even in Roman times and has long been established in international human rights documentation. Yet many girls, and a smaller number of boys, enter marriage without any chance of exercising their right to choose. Some are forced into marriage at a very early age. Others are simply too young to make an informed decision about their marriage partner or about the implications of marriage itself. They may have given what passes for 'consent' in the eyes of custom or the law, but in reality, consent to their binding union has been made by others on their behalf.*
> INNOCENTI DIGEST, *No. 7, March 2001, UNICEF, Innocenti Research Centre*

### ACTIVITY: MONEY MATTERS (Student's Book, page 91)

> **5. You may open a bank account when you're 7 – but is a 7-year-old really capable of managing their own money? Discuss your answer.**

Most students will probably say no to this. Encourage them to think why the age is so low. Point out that:

- the average age for beginning to receive pocket money is 7 (Personal Finance Education Group [PFEG])
- children may often save up pocket money in order to buy gifts; e.g. for Mother's Day, family birthdays, etc.
- over 75 per cent of 7–11-year-olds are already saving for the future (PFEG)
- is it about encouraging good financial habits (e.g. saving to earn interest) in younger children?

> **6. Starting with age 7, draw a timeline of when a person, in law, gets other rights associated with financial independence. Use the information on Student's Book pages 90–91 to help you.**

See Appendix (on the CD): Active Learning Methodologies: Timeline (page 10).

**Answer:**
At 13 years of age you may:

- get a part-time job – with some restrictions.

At 16 years of age you may:

- buy a lottery ticket
- get a National Insurance Number
- live independently, subject to certain conditions being met.

At 17 years of age you may:

- hold a licence to drive most vehicles
- leave school.

At 18 years of age you are:

- legally seen as an adult in the eyes of the law
- allowed to leave home without parental consent
- allowed to get married/have a civil partnership without parental consent
- allowed to open a bank account in your name without a parent or carer's signature
- allowed to make a will
- allowed to place a bet.

> 7. With financial independence comes the responsibility to manage money wisely. List two responsibilities you think are needed for this. Share these with a partner and then with a group.

Possible answers might include:

- Take on the responsibility for paying your own bills.
- Put money aside (save) for the future and/or unforeseen events.
- Prioritise what you spend your money on; e.g. pay rent, pay off bills and debts before spending on luxuries.
- Not getting into debt (especially when this may harm other people); e.g. taking out loans you can't repay.
- Pay bills and debts within agreed time limits.

# REVIEW AND REFLECTION

## ACTIVITY: YOUR OPINION (Student's Book, page 91)

> 8. How do you think that the lawmakers who decide these ages should be taking account of young people's opinions? What one piece of advice would you give them?

Consultation could happen by:

- local youth parliament bodies providing ideas via their local MPs
- working with UK Youth Parliament representatives
- schools holding their own referenda and feed back to their MP.

Invite students to offer their individual advice to the lawmakers.

# RESOURCE SHEET 9.1

**STATEMENTS**

| | |
|---|---|
| You should not have to get your parents' consent if you want to marry or have a civil partnership at 16. | The age at which a person can buy alcohol should be lowered to 16. |
| The age at which people can buy a lottery ticket should be raised to 18. | Driving certain types of cars, e.g. fast sport cars, should be restricted to people over 25. |
| Part-time jobs, e.g. paper rounds/Saturday jobs, should be available to people aged 11 upwards. | The age at which a person can leave school should be lowered to 14. |

**CONTINUUM CARDS**

| |
|---|
| AGREE |
| UNSURE |
| DISAGREE |

*PSHE Education for Key Stage 4 Teacher's Resource Book © Hodder Education*

# Topic: Moving on

| | |
|---|---|
| **Notes** | This topic invites students to reflect on a change which each of them will be facing in the next few years: the transition to further education or work.<br><br>It begins by inviting them to think back to primary school experiences and whether these have shaped where they are now. It then moves to the present by using a personal development audit. The aim of this is to build their self-esteem by identifying personal skills and qualities over and above the more formal and academic qualifications they may be achieving.<br><br>Finally they are asked to look to the future and plan for this next significant transition. This is done by visualising a positive future for themselves in the form of a reflective letter and their contribution to a 'wall of ambition'. |
| **Learning outcomes** | **In this topic students will learn about:**<br>■ auditing their personal development.<br><br>**They will explore:**<br>■ progress in personal skills and qualities<br>■ hopes and aspirations for the next five years. |
| **Links to Personal Well-being PoS** | **1.1 Personal identities**<br>**b** Recognising that the way in which personal qualities, attitudes, skills and achievements are evaluated affects confidence and self-esteem. |
| **Links to Economic Well-being PoS** | **1.2 Capability**<br>**c** Understanding how to make creative and realistic plans for transition.<br><br>**2.1 Self-development**<br>**a** Students should be able to develop and maintain their self-esteem and envisage a positive future for themselves in work.<br><br>**3 Range and content**<br>**e** The study of economic well-being and financial capability should include the personal review and planning process. |
| **Links to SEAL outcomes** | **Self-awareness**<br>Students can identify their strengths and feel positive about them.<br><br>**Motivation**<br>Students can monitor and evaluate their own performance. |
| **Links to ECM outcomes** | Enjoy and achieve ■ Achieve economic well-being |
| **Assessment opportunity** | See Topic: Study or employment – what's out there?; Activity 1: What are my options? (page 162) |
| **Resources** | ■ Student's Book (pages 92–93)<br>■ Resource sheet 9.2 (page 157)<br>■ Appendix (see the CD): Active Learning Methodologies:<br>  □ Graffiti (page 7)<br>■ Sticky notes |

# STARTER ACTIVITY

## ACTIVITY: LOOKING BACK (Student's Book, page 92)

> 1.  The last time you faced a change as big as the one you're facing now (taking public exams and deciding what comes next) you were in primary school. Read Source 1. Think of something that was said about you in primary school that has turned out to be completely right or completely wrong.

Allow students a few minutes to recall an example of a comment from primary school. Invite members of the group to share examples with the whole class.

- Did anybody feel stuck with a 'label' about themselves as a result of a comment?
- If so, did anyone feel the label influenced their behaviour from that point onwards?
- Is labelling someone positively or negatively a self-fulfilling prophecy?

Was anyone surprised by the comments about the 'celebrities' listed in Source1? If so, why?

# MAIN ACTIVITIES

**Note**

There is likely to be insufficient time for both of the two activities that follow ('Taking stock' and 'Looking forward') to be undertaken in a PSHE session in class. You could do either one or the other of the activities or alternatively set one as a homework task.

## ACTIVITY: TAKING STOCK (Student's Book, page 93)

> 2.  Provide examples to evidence your progress in the areas outlined in Source 2. The example below should help.
>
> | Your active participation in learning and school life | |
> | --- | --- |
> | | EXAMPLES |
> | Developing and defending a point of view | Participating in a class debate on the causes of global warming |

Either allow sufficient time for students to complete this in class, or alternatively to undertake it as homework.

- Give students a copy of the audit form on Resource sheet 9.2 (page 157).
- Remind them that this should focus on skills and qualities which may prove equally as valuable as qualifications when taking part in future interviews for career or education. Being able to talk about an example of some of these skills and qualities at an interview will help demonstrate that they have reflected on their progress and are able to recognise and explain their personal worth.

Students may struggle initially to think of examples to evidence their progress. The following examples may help:

| Your active participation in learning and school life | |
| --- | --- |
| Developing and defending a point of view | ■ Participating in a class debate on the causes of global warming<br>■ Arguing the case for choosing a particular charity to be supported by the form or school |

| Your ability to make informed and responsible choices | |
| --- | --- |
| Negotiation and assertiveness skills | ■ Being an effective member of a small group when undertaking activities in class<br>■ Challenging unhelpful behaviour by other members of the youth club who were smoking on the premises |

| Your self-awareness and self-management | |
| --- | --- |
| Positive values and attitudes | ■ Not letting one poor mark deter working hard to regain a good module grade<br>■ Demonstrating good teamwork skills in the local five-a-side tournament |

| Your contribution to community life | |
| --- | --- |
| Combating prejudice and discrimination | ■ Getting involved to prevent a younger pupil from being bullied<br>■ Campaigning for the removal of 'street furniture' that hampers access for people with disabilities |

■ Now ask students to work in pairs to interview each other in turn, one taking the role of interviewer, one of interviewee. The questions to be asked should be formulated along the lines of:
'Give me an example of a time when you … (e.g. contributed to your local community)'
■ After each student has had a turn at being interviewed, bring the whole group back together and consider the following questions:
  □ How does it feel to talk about yourself in a positive way?
  □ It may feel strange to 'sell yourself' – but why is it important that you are able to do this in a way which sounds positive but not boastful?
  □ How will you ensure you look after this audit form and use it in the future?

**ACTIVITY: LOOKING FORWARD (Student's Book, page 93)**

> 3. One way of managing your life as things are changing is to visualise a positive future for yourself. Write a letter to yourself about what you are hoping for and where you want to be in five years' time. Here are some questions to consider:
>
>    - Do I have an idea of a career or job I want to do?
>    - Do I want to continue in full/part-time study?
>    - How will I finance the things I want; for example, clothes, holidays, entertainment?
>    - Can I combine both studying and working?
>    - Your friends or you may be leaving school soon – how will that affect you?
>    - When will it be the right time to leave home and move out (see Source 3)?

Either allow sufficient time for students to complete this in class, or alternatively to undertake it as homework.

- Tell students to work on their own and undertake the activity as a personal reflection.
- When the whole group has reconvened, use the following questions to encourage students to reflect further on the activity and how it might affect their future planning:
  - How easy was it to visualise yourself in five years' time?
  - What seemed to be the biggest 'unknowns' in thinking about the future?
  - Did you find that answering some of the questions raised new questions?
  - How will you begin to research the careers/education information you need?
  - Identify a trusted adult, at school or at home, with whom you can discuss your letter. What help do you need from them?

# REVIEW AND REFLECTION

**ACTIVITY: MOVING ON (Student's Book, page 93)**

> 4. If you could do or be anything you wanted to, where would your ambition lead?

You will need to have prepared for this activity by having sticky notes available in sufficient quantity to allow one per student.

Explain to the students that together they are going to create a graffiti 'Wall of Ambition' in the classroom.

Give each student a sticky note and tell them to write their answer to the question on it. Remind them this could be a career (doctor), a place (Canada), a goal (Ferrari), an achievement (being a good parent). When the students have had time to complete their 'brick' for the wall ask them to come forward in groups to place their bricks on the wall.

For other ways to use the 'graffiti' method see Appendix (on the CD): Active Learning Methodologies: Graffiti (page 7).

# RESOURCE SHEET 9.2

**AUDIT FORM – PERSONAL DEVELOPMENT: YOUR SKILLS AND QUALITIES**

When looking for examples remember to consider:

- subjects and courses
- homework assignments and projects
- tutor time, assemblies
- school trips and outings
- voluntary clubs, school council
- sports teams, music/drama performances, enterprise activities
- discussions with parents/carers
- use of free time in and out of school; e.g. community events and clubs
- work experience
- one-off events and activities.

| Your active participation in learning and school life | |
|---|---|
| Developing and defending a point of view | |
| Researching information from a variety of sources | |
| Working positively with others | |

| Your ability to make informed and responsible choices | |
|---|---|
| Accessing and using formal and informal sources of help | |
| Lifestyle choices; e.g. health and well-being | |

| **Your ability to make informed and responsible choices** |
|---|

| Negotiation and assertiveness skills | _____ |

| **Your self-awareness and self-management** |
|---|

| Positive values and attitudes | _____ |
| Qualities and skills you are developing towards your working life | _____ |
| Ability to self-manage | _____ |

| **Your contribution to community life** |
|---|

| Member and/or leader of groups | _____ |
| Projects and initiatives that benefit the school and/or wider community | _____ |
| Combating prejudice and discrimination | _____ |

# Topic: Study or employment – what's out there?

| | |
|---|---|
| **Notes** | With an expectation that students will stay in education or training beyond 16, it is important for students to know the pathways that are available, the risks associated with them and where they can get the information they need. For young people today there is likely to be increased competition for places in both education and employment, so having an idea of potential pathways is essential. In this topic students will look at learning pathways that will be available to them when they have completed their GCSEs, the advantages and disadvantages of each and where they can obtain the information needed to make informed decisions. |
| **Learning outcomes** | **In this topic students will learn about:**<br>■ the different pathways that are available at the end of Year 11<br>■ where they can find information about future pathway options<br>■ risks associated with the different pathways.<br><br>**They will explore:**<br>■ questions they need to consider when thinking about future options<br>■ advantages and disadvantages of different pathways. |
| **Links to Personal Well-being PoS** | **1.1 Personal identities**<br>**a** Understanding that identity is affected by a range of factors, including a positive sense of self. |
| **Links to Economic Well-being PoS** | **1.2 Capability**<br>**c** Understanding the qualities, attitudes and skills needed for employability.<br><br>**1.3 Risk**<br>**b** Understanding the need to manage risk in the context of financial and career choices.<br><br>**2.1 Self-development**<br>**a** Students should be able to develop and maintain their self-esteem …<br>**d** Students should be able to assess the importance of their … achievements …<br><br>**2.2 Exploration**<br>**a** Students should be able to identify, select and use a range of information sources to research, clarify and review options and choices in career and financial contexts … |
| **Links to SEAL outcomes** | **Motivation**<br>Students can look to long-term not short-term benefits and can delay gratification. |
| **Links to ECM outcomes** | Enjoy and achieve ■ Make a positive contribution ■ Achieve economic well-being |
| **Assessment opportunity** | Activity 1: What are my options? (see page 162)<br><br>**End of Key Stage Statement – economic well-being and financial capability**<br>Learners are able to:<br>■ identify a range of post-16 options and careers advice and support networks that they can use to plan and negotiate their career pathways, relate their abilities, attributes and achievements to career plans, setting personal targets and evaluating choices. |
| **Resources** | ■ Student's Book (pages 94–95)<br>■ Appendix (see the CD): Active Learning Methodologies:<br> ☐ Small group work (pages 6–7) ☐ Pairs work (pages 6–7)<br>■ Internet access (optional)<br>■ Visits from Connexions/careers advisors (optional) |

# STARTER ACTIVITY

Ask students to think about the jobs that their parents, grandparents or family friends do. Ask them to discuss the comments people make about their work; some may be positive, some may be negative. Ask them to think about what they would like to be saying about their employment or work in the future. The comments will hopefully be positive, at which point they should consider what they will need to do in order to get to this position in their future. This is then an appropriate time to introduce the aim of today's session.

# MAIN ACTIVITIES

### ACTIVITY: WHAT ARE MY OPTIONS? (Student's Book, page 95)

**1. a) Using the information in Source 1, draw your own flow diagram that shows the pathway you might follow. Include as much detail as you can; for example, you could include the name of a college, specific subjects you would like to study or types of voluntary work. Your teachers will be able to provide further information, as will careers advisors and school and college websites. An example of a flow diagram is given below.**

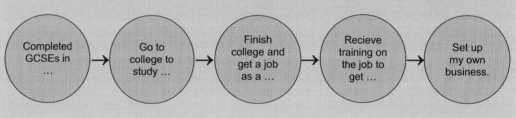

This task works better if students can have access to the internet and the school careers library.

Discuss with students:

■ the fact that they will soon have to make choices about the direction their life will take when they have finished their GCSEs
■ the four pathways that are displayed in the Student's Book on page 94 as options when they have finished their GCSEs.

Explain to students that they are going to make a flow diagram charting what could happen to them in the future. An example is given above and in the Student's Book.

Using the information from the Student's Book, the internet and the school careers library, students should complete their flow diagrams including as much detail as possible. If you are able to organise visits from organisations such as Connexions or the head of the sixth form, this would be a good opportunity to introduce them to the students.

Encourage some students to share their plans with the class. Those listening could offer feedback or other ideas that may not have been considered.

**b) You may find that some sections of your flow diagram are more difficult than others to complete as you don't yet have the information you need. Make a list of all the questions you need answers to in order to add further detail to your flow diagram; for example: What courses are available at my local college? How would I be expected to travel there? If I went into an apprenticeship, how much would I earn?**

*PSHE Education for Key Stage 4 Teacher's Resource Book © Hodder Education*

Without access to the right information or knowing where to get the information, completing a career flow diagram can be difficult. Discuss with the students the information that was missing from the work in part a) of the activity. Encourage students to generate questions that they think they still need to answer in order to make an informed choice about what to do when they finish their GCSEs; for example:

- If I don't stay at this school to do A levels, which college could I go to?
- What A level courses does the college offer?
- What entry requirements does the college have?
- How would I get to college each day?
- How is college different from sixth form?

**c) In groups, discuss your questions with each other to see if anyone has similar questions, or if anyone is able to help you answer the questions you have.**

Ask students to share the questions they have generated with others in their class. See Appendix (on the CD): Active Learning Methodologies: Small group work (pages 6–7). This is important as many of the questions generated will apply to some if not all of the students in the class.

Having generated the questions students could now try and answer them and add further detail to their flow diagram. Alternatively you could combine parts a) and b) of the activity and generate questions prior to students beginning their flow diagram. This will depend on how independent your students are and how much structure they need.

**d) As a class, make a list of the questions that still remain unanswered. Discuss who or which organisations would be able to provide the information needed.**

There are likely to be some questions students have that remain unanswered. Lead a discussion and display those questions and ask students to make a note of them. If the students are unable to answer the questions they need to know where they can get the answers from and how to access the information.

**e) From your list of questions, select three that are of interest to you. Make a note of these and over the next week see if you can find the answers to them. Feed back in your next lesson what you have found.**

Using the Student's Book for basic ideas, students could make a list or spider diagram of the different ways they can seek information about their future. They should include sources of information they have used in today's lesson, but also think of others; for example, the school guidance counsellor, teachers, parents, Connexions (and other local organisations), sixth form and college open days/evenings, work experience, internet (for example, www.fasttomato.com).

**End of Key Stage Statement – economic well-being and financial capability**

Learners are able to:

- identify a range of post-16 options and careers advice and support networks that they can use to plan and negotiate their career pathways, relate their abilities, attributes and achievements to career plans, setting personal targets and evaluating choices.

**Assessment activity**

This activity can be extended to paired or small group work in which students work together to produce a role play in which one person is the student and the other a school guidance counsellor, and up to two other students could be parents. The students need to produce a script in which the student is given advice about their future options and asks relevant questions. The pair or group will need to think carefully about the information they will need to provide, the questions and the answers. Students should then perform their role plays to the rest of the group.

**Assessment method – peer assessment**

Each group presents to the whole class. Following the presentation, peers are asked to stay in their working groups and identify:

- at least one thing they liked about the presentation content
- at least one thing they liked about the presentation style
- one thing they think could have improved the presentation content
- one thing they think could have improved the presentation style
- whether the information provided was enough to help the student make an appropriate decision.

**ACTIVITY: WHAT ARE THE RISKS? (Student's Book, page 95)**

2. Make a copy of the table below. Using the information in Source 2, fill in the table to show the advantages and disadvantages of each pathway option (some of the advantages and disadvantages could relate to more than one option). Add any others you can think of.

|  | Full-time education | Work-related training | Full-time employment | Time out |
|---|---|---|---|---|
| Advantages |  |  |  |  |
| Disadvantages |  |  |  |  |

Answers:

|  | Full-time education | Work-related training | Full-time employment | Time out |
|---|---|---|---|---|
| **Advantages** | Higher qualifications to put on CV<br><br>Likely to lead to a higher-paid job<br><br>Opens more employment options<br><br>Nationally recognised qualifications | Earn straight away<br><br>Leads to a skilled trade/ profession<br><br>Likely to lead to a higher-paid job<br><br>Nationally recognised qualifications | Earn straight away | Keep options open<br><br>Valuable experience, e.g. travelling |
| **Disadvantages** | Could lead to a large debt<br><br>Increased competition as more students apply | Lower pay until qualified | Less chance for promotion<br><br>Lower earnings | Could lead to a large debt<br><br>Low/no income<br><br>Most friends follow a different pathway |

Lead a discussion with students about which pathway would give them the most opportunities. This is likely to be full-time education, although it is important to add that there is no right or wrong answer, as everyone has different aspirations and expectations.

# REVIEW AND REFLECTION

**ACTIVITY: WHERE WILL YOU BE? (additional activity not in Student's Book)**

Working in pairs, talk to your partner about the flow chart you completed in Activity 1. For each stage of your chart, think of the challenges you may face. Offer advice to each other about how these challenges could be overcome. Do you face the same challenges?

Encourage discussion in pairs looking forward to when they are age 20/21. See Appendix (on the CD): Active Learning Methodologies: Pairs work (pages 6–7).

Students should draw on the information they have gained in this topic. If students are comfortable to do so, ask them to share their ideas with the rest of the class.

# 10 Employability

## Topic: Types of employment and employment trends

| | |
|---|---|
| **Notes** | The types of work available to young people are constantly changing. The most popular jobs in the future may not yet exist. It is important for young people to know the types of employment opportunities they will have in the future and how they can be financially supported to achieve their aspirations. They also need to be aware of how employment patterns can change over time so that they can be ready in the future.<br><br>In this topic students will learn about the differences between employed, self-employed and voluntary work and some of the advantages and disadvantages associated with them. They will also look at how students can receive finance to stay in education and how employment trends are expected to change in the future. |
| **Learning outcomes** | **In this topic students will learn about:**<br>■ different types of employment opportunities that are available<br>■ how financial issues will influence their choice of future employment<br>■ how employment patterns and trends are changing.<br><br>**They will explore:**<br>■ the advantages and disadvantages of different types of employment<br>■ how external factors could affect your employment decisions. |
| **Links to Personal Well-being PoS** | **1.1 Personal identities**<br>**b** Recognising that the way in which personal qualities, attitudes, skills and achievements are evaluated affects confidence and self-esteem. |
| **Links to Economic Well-being PoS** | **2.2 Exploration**<br>**c** Students should be able to investigate the main trends in employment and relate these to their career plans.<br><br>**3 Range and content**<br>**a** The study of economic well-being and financial capability should include different types of work, including employment, self-employment and voluntary work. |
| **Links to ECM outcomes** | Enjoy and achieve ■ Make a positive contribution ■ Achieve economic well-being |
| **Assessment opportunity** | See Topic: Creating a Curriculum Vitæ; Activities 2 & 3: My CV (page 171) |
| **Resources** | ■ Student's Book (pages 96–99)<br>■ Appendix (see the CD): Active Learning Methodologies:<br>  □ Pairs work (pages 6–7)   □ Whole-class work (page 7)<br>■ Internet access |

# STARTER ACTIVITY

**ACTIVITY: TYPES OF EMPLOYMENT (Student's Book, page 96)**

> **1. a) Under the headings 'Employed', 'Self-employed' and 'Voluntary', put the jobs shown in Source 1 into the correct category (some could fall in more than one – explain why, when this is the case). Add to your lists so that for each category you have eight different jobs.**

Possible answers could be:

**Employed:**

- solicitor
- accountant
- lifeguard
- farmer
- firefighter
- television producer
- dressmaker
- removal person
- software engineer
- plumber
- environmental worker.

**Self-employed:**

- solicitor
- accountant
- lifeguard
- farmer
- television producer
- dressmaker
- removal person
- software engineer
- plumber.

**Voluntary:**

- environmental worker
- working in a soup kitchen
- working in a charity shop
- collecting for charity
- pet fostering
- working with the elderly or disabled
- school governor
- magistrate.

> **b) Look through your lists and highlight the jobs in each list that you would most like to do if you had to choose.**

Students simply highlight jobs that would interest them in readiness for part c) of the activity.

> **c) Now work with a partner and explain to them the reasons why you highlighted your particular jobs. Were you partner's reasons for choosing their jobs the same as yours?**

Encourage students to discuss their answers with their partners. See Appendix (on the CD): Active Learning Methodologies: Pairs work (pages 6–7). Hopefully they will realise that whilst much of what people want from their work is different, there will also be common factors such as regular hours, good pay, etc.

# MAIN ACTIVITIES

**ACTIVITY: PROS AND CONS (Student's Book, page 97)**

2. Make a copy of the table below. Look at the advantages and disadvantages in Source 2 and put them where you think they should go in your table. Some could be used more than once.

|  | Employed | Self-employed | Voluntary |
|---|---|---|---|
| **Advantages** |  |  |  |
| **Disadvantages** |  |  |  |

Answers to the table:

|  | Employed | Self-employed | Voluntary |
|---|---|---|---|
| **Advantages** | e) Guaranteed income <br> m) Paid holiday <br> n) Pension paid <br> r) Workers' rights | c) Decide own pay <br> d) Flexible working hours <br> f) Hours to suit <br> g) Job satisfaction <br> l) Own boss | a) Can lead to a paid job <br> g) Job satisfaction |
| **Disadvantages** | b) Childcare costs <br> i) Monitored performance | h) Lack of appreciation <br> k) No sick pay <br> o) Set-up costs <br> q) Unpaid holiday | j) No income <br> p) Time-consuming |

**ACTIVITY: EMPLOYMENT TRENDS (Student's Book, page 99)**

3. Select four of the boxes about employment trends in Source 4 and for each one think of a reason/reasons why this trend is likely to happen.

*PSHE Education for Key Stage 4 Teacher's Resource Book © Hodder Education*

Possible answers could include:

a) In the next ten years (from 2010) the government predicts that employee jobs will grow steadily and that self-employment will increase rapidly.

During the recession unemployment rose very quickly; as the economy begins to recover new jobs will be created but not enough to cater for all those made unemployed. As a result, it is expected that more and more people will use what could be considered a bad thing to set up their own businesses and become self-employed. Some will use redundancy money to help with set-up costs whilst banks have been encouraged by the government to support new fledgling business.

b) It is estimated that around two-thirds of the new jobs will go to women and that around two-thirds of all the new jobs will be part-time.

Part-time work often suits women better, particularly if they have children. Part-time work is also cheaper for companies as they come out of recession.

c) It is estimated that nearly three million new jobs will be created in the services sector (both private and public), some in well-paid professional jobs but also a great many in lower-paid service-sector jobs.

Manufacturing in the UK is in decline, so more and more people provide services of some sort or another. Unless manufacturing increases dramatically, which is unlikely, we will have well-paid service-sector jobs as well as lots of lower-paid service-sector jobs such as cleaners.

d) Most workers will have between 20 and 25 jobs in their working lives.

Loyalty isn't really considered to be important in today's employment market; people no longer have a job for life. If people want promotion and better pay they are likely to need to move elsewhere.

e) One in four employees will stay with their employer for less than a year, whilst one in two will stay for less than five years.

Once people have gained skills they may want to move on for promotion; also many people will be employed on temporary contracts which means once their work is complete they are no longer needed so will have to find work elsewhere.

f) The top ten jobs in 2015 don't yet exist, as new industries and problems will see the creation of new jobs.

Technology and ideas are changing so quickly that many new types of jobs are being created every day. It will be more important to have the skills which allow you to adapt quickly to new job types, rather than just a set of skills for a specific job.

## ACTIVITY: FUNDING FOR THE FUTURE (Student's Book, page 99)

4. Students may or may not be aware that the government announced in their spending cuts that the Educational Maintenance Allowance (EMA) would be cut. You could show students the following web link www.bbc.co.uk/news/education-12216285 which highlights this issue. Lead a discussion or debate about whether or not students think this was the right thing to do. Encourage students to be mature about the issue and consider the present financial situation of the country and their own future.

There is no right or wrong answer to this question, but it does raise an interesting issue for discussion. Possible answers are:

**For keeping the EMA:**

- some families simply can't afford to keep children in education even if they want to, therefore they should be given financial help
- job opportunities are limited at present; it's better to keep children in education
- it helps students step out of the poverty trap/cycle
- it reinforces the importance the government has put on education.

**Against keeping the EMA:**

- students should learn because they want to, not for financial gain
- morally it is wrong to pay to keep people in education
- too many students are staying in education; some need to begin apprenticeships, etc.
- money could be better spent on something else.

If the discussion is slow, you could use some of the arguments above to stimulate discussion further.

# REVIEW AND REFLECTION

**ACTIVITY: YOUR FUTURE (Student's Book, page 99)**

> 5. **Using the information you have learned in this topic, write a paragraph explaining how your own future could be affected. You need to consider the following factors:**
>
> - **the type of employment you may enter into**
> - **how your education could influence this**
> - **the cost of your education and who pays**
> - **unemployment rates**
> - **future employment trends.**

Encourage students to consider their own future and how this may be affected if the predicted trends do happen. Ask some students to read their work to the rest of the class.

You could also develop the written work into a discussion by using the following questions as prompts.

- How could the different factors/trends affect you?
- Will they affect others in the same way?
- Is it something you are worried about?
- What do you need to do to overcome any problems if there are any?

See Appendix (on the CD): Active Learning Methodologies: Whole-class work (page 7).

# Topic: Creating a Curriculum Vitæ (CV)

| | |
|---|---|
| **Notes** | This topic encourages students to reflect on their existing skills, experiences and achievements. It helps them to identify what they have already accomplished and use this to market themselves now and in the future.<br><br>It focuses on helping students consider the possibilities for presenting themselves in the best light on a CV.<br><br>The final activity does not follow the usual pattern of a summative example or review and reflection task with which most of these topics are completed – instead it asks students to enquire more widely about options for designing a CV. |
| **Learning outcomes** | **In this topic students will learn about:**<br>■ effective ways to present personal information<br>■ the essentials for creating their own Curriculum Vitæ (CV).<br><br>**They will explore:**<br>■ how to compile their own CV<br>■ how to compare their CV with those of other people. |
| **Links to Personal Well-being PoS** | **2.1. Critical reflection**<br>**b** Students should be able to reflect on their own and others' strengths and achievements, give and receive constructive praise and criticism, and learn from success and failure. |
| **Links to Economic Well-being PoS** | **1.2 Capability**<br>**c** Understanding how to make creative and realistic plans for transition.<br><br>**2.3 Enterprise**<br>**c** Students should be able to take action to improve their chances in their career. |
| **Links to SEAL outcomes** | **Self-awareness**<br>Students can identify their strengths and feel positive about them.<br><br>**Social skills**<br>Students can give and receive feedback and use it to improve their and other people's achievements. |
| **Links to ECM outcomes** | Achieve economic well-being ■ Make a positive contribution |
| **Assessment opportunity** | Activities 2 & 3: My CV (see page 171)<br><br>**End of Key Stage Statement – career**<br>Learners are able to:<br>■ complete application procedures, including CVs and personal statements, and prepare for interviews. |
| **Resources** | ■ Student's Book (pages 100–102)<br>■ Appendix (see the CD): Active Learning Methodologies:<br>  □ Brainstorming (page 3)  □ Pairs work (pages 6–7)<br>■ Resource sheet 10.1 (page 172) |

# STARTER ACTIVITY

**ACTIVITY: THE BEST OF ME (Student's Book, page 101)**

> **1. a) Look at Source 1. Why do you think an employer might be more favourable to the third example?**

Employers may feel that the type of person described in the third example will settle in more quickly to a new situation. It may appear that she will work more easily with new colleagues if she is an outgoing person who interacts well with others.

> **b) What's the best way to describe your interests? First brainstorm a list of words to identify your interests, then work in pairs to write a bullet list that outlines your hobbies and activities in an interesting and useful way – remember you want to make a prospective employer interview you.**

Initially undertake an individual brainstorm, with each student identifying a list of words. See Appendix (on the CD): Active Learning Methodologies: Brainstorming (page 3).

Students could then work in pairs assisting each other to build up the word list into a series of bullets which outline their hobbies and activities in an interesting and useful way. See Appendix (on the CD): Active Learning Methodologies: Pairs work (pages 6–7).

Take feedback encouraging students to share their examples, highlighting examples that are particularly successful.

# MAIN ACTIVITIES

**ACTIVITY: MY CV (Student's Book, page 101)**

> **2. Compile your own CV. Look at Source 2 on page 102 of the Student's Book and try and follow the good advice for setting out your skills and experience. Use the interests you identified in Activity 1b) in your CV.**
> **3. Work with someone else and look at each other's CV. Identify areas for improvement in light of the advice given in Source 2 on page 102 of the Student's Book and make suggestions to help the other person.**

Read through Source 2 in the Student's Book – it may help if different group members each read aloud a different part of the document.

Pay particular attention to the learning points in the comment balloons.

Use the template provided on page 172 (Resource sheet 10.1) and give students time to begin to build their own CVs.

Students may find it helpful to work in pairs, providing support and coaching to each other in order to achieve the best possible results. See Appendix (on the CD): Active Learning Methodologies: Pairs work (pages 6–7).

# End of Key Stage Statement – career

Learners are able to:

- complete application procedures, including CVs and personal statements, and prepare for interviews.

**Assessment activity**

First the students compile their CVs as in the original task – see above.

Then in pairs they identify areas for improvement, and next others in the class are invited to give feedback.

Each student then prepares a version of their CV without any identifying details (for example, names, addresses, etc. are removed).

**Assessment method – peer review/peer critique**

The teacher collects in the anonymous CVs and redistributes them across the class.

Individual students are given the task of reviewing the CV with the aim of making a series of constructive comments. They should be encouraged to use Source 2 (Nick Alexander's CV) to remind themselves of areas to comment on. These can include:

- improvements to spelling, punctuation, grammar and layout
- which parts of the CV 'sell' the writer well
- which parts of the CV could be improved – students should make suggestions for how this might happen.

The reviewer makes clear notes on the CV copy as in Source 2. If working electronically, they could use a 'track changes' or 'comments' feature.

Any student who feels they have read an outstandingly well-written and presented CV can share what made it so with the rest of the class.

**ACTIVITY: FURTHER RESEARCH (Student's Book, page 101)**

4. Ask family friends and relatives for copies of their CVs so that you can compare and contrast different ways of setting them out. You could use templates from programs such as Word to practise various layouts.

This activity is designed as a follow-up (take home) activity. If students are unable to access support or IT outside school, suggest that they access the school's IT facilities and use the following website to help them work further on a personal CV: www.connexions-direct.com/index.cfm?pid=75&catalogueContentID=117.

# RESOURCE SHEET 10.1

**CV TEMPLATE**

| CURRICULUM VITÆ | |
|---|---|
| **Name** <br><br> **Address** <br><br><br><br> **Phone** <br><br> **Email** <br><br> **Nationality** <br><br> **Age** | |
| **Achievements and Interests** | ■ <br><br> ■ <br><br> ■ |
| **Work Experience/ Employment** | ■ <br><br> ■ <br><br> ■ |
| **Education and Qualifications** | ■ <br><br> ■ <br><br> ■ |
| **Reference 1** | |
| **Reference 2** | |

*PSHE Education for Key Stage 4 Teacher's Resource Book © Hodder Education*

# Topic: Skills and qualities needed for employment

| | |
|---|---|
| **Notes** | It's worth recognising that whilst there are platitudes to offer students (see the starter activity), some of them won't find things easy so they will need to think through the range of skills, qualities and qualifications they may need to face the world. The rest of this topic offers more ideas to explore this. This topic encourages students to reflect on the important but sometimes overlooked fact that we can all learn skills but many of our personal qualities are innate. Some skills and qualities may have to be developed – whatever the case we have to capitalise on these. There is an activity that enables students to reflect on their own personal qualities and give and receive constructive feedback from their peers. Website information is provided which could enable students to move into more detailed examination of skills/qualifications that will be required as they enter the world of work. In planning these activities it will be important to identify what resources are available in school for careers education. |
| **Learning outcomes** | **In this topic students will learn about:**<br>■ the importance of qualifications and qualities<br>■ the personal qualities that contribute to employability.<br>**They will explore:**<br>■ their own qualities, and receive feedback from others<br>■ the skills and qualifications needed for future employment. |
| **Links to Personal Well-being PoS** | **2.1. Critical reflection**<br>**b** Students should be able to reflect on their own and others' strengths and achievements, give and receive constructive praise and criticism, and learn from success and failure. |
| **Links to Economic Well-being PoS** | **1.1 Career**<br>**a** Understanding that everyone has a 'career'.<br>**b** Developing a sense of personal identity for career progression.<br>**2.1 Self-development**<br>**c** Students should be able to assess their needs, interests, values, skills, abilities and attitudes in relation to options in learning, work and enterprise.<br>**d** Students should be able to assess the importance of their experiences and achievements in relation to their future plans.<br>**2.2 Exploration**<br>**a** Students should be able to identify, select and use a range of information sources to research, clarify and review options and choices in career and financial contexts relevant to their needs.<br>**3 Range and content**<br>**e** The study of economic well-being and financial capability should include the personal review and planning process.<br>**f** The study of economic well-being and financial capability should include skills and qualities in relation to employers' needs. |
| **Links to SEAL outcomes** | **Self-awareness**<br>Students can identify their strengths and feel positive about them.<br>**Social skills**<br>Students can give and receive feedback and use it to improve their and other people's achievements. |
| **Links to ECM outcomes** | Achieve economic well-being ■ Make a positive contribution |
| **Assessment opportunity** | See Topic: Creating a Curriculum Vitæ; Activities 2 & 3: My CV (page 171) |
| **Resources** | ■ Student's Book (pages 103–105)<br>■ Appendix (see the CD): Active Learning Methodologies<br>   □ Small group work (pages 6–7)  □ Pairs work (pages 6–7)<br>■ Internet access |

# STARTER ACTIVITY

## ACTIVITY: THE WORLD IS YOUR OYSTER (Student's Book, page 103)

> **1.  What do you think the saying 'the world is your oyster' means?**

Ask the class what they understand by this.
  Draw out some of the following nuanced meanings:

- The world is yours to grab – you have to seize the opportunity.
- It's worth making the effort to achieve the prize (i.e. breaking an oyster open isn't easy – but it can be worth it when a pearl lies at the centre).
- What seems like an enormous, complicated or difficult undertaking can be overcome when you find the right technique.

# MAIN ACTIVITIES

## ACTIVITY: STRIKING A BALANCE (Student's Book, page 103)

> **2.  Arjun's outline shows a balance between qualifications, skills and qualities. Can you identify one of these for Arjun in each case?**

Arjun's qualifications include:

- studying for A levels in Physics, Maths and Systems & Control, and an AS level in Further Maths.

Arjun's skills include:

- running a computer-repair business from home.

Arjun's qualities include:

- level-headedness  ■ likeability  ■ diplomacy.

## ACTIVITY: WHAT'S THE DIFFERENCE? (Student's Book, page 104)

> **3.  a)  What's the difference between a qualification, a skill and a quality?**

**Qualifications are:** achievements that are recognised by the awarding of a certificate/diploma/degree, etc.

**Skills are:** abilities that enable us to do certain things; for example, run a business, repair/fix things, make things, make decisions and prioritise, etc.

**Qualities are:** personal characteristics such as determination, loyalty, honesty, etc.

> **b)  A vet will have to have particular qualifications (see Student's Book, page 104). But what qualities would it be good for a vet to have?**

Use small group work. See Appendix (on the CD): Active Learning Methodologies: Small group work (pages 6–7). When taking feedback draw out the following:
Qualities you would hope to find in a vet could be:

- kindness and gentleness – towards owners and animals
- good communication skills – to explain treatment choices and options
- empathy – appreciating that the animal may be very important to the owner
- honest and genuine – having the animal's best interests at heart (it's not all about the money!).

You might wish to contrast the qualities with qualifications/skills:

- good diagnostic/clinical skills
- surgical skills
- business skills
- management skills.

Most jobs will need people to have both qualifications and qualities.
If necessary, remind students that 'skills' are sometimes recognised by qualifications/certificates/competencies. Skills can be learned but qualities are usually innate.

### ACTIVITY: PERSONAL QUALITIES (Student's Book, page 104)

> 4. Look at Source 2 and score yourself against the list: A score of 5 means that you are strong in the quality. A score of 1 means you do not have much of this quality in you.

This activity starts with personal reflection and then moves on to pairs work. See Appendix (on the CD): Active Learning Methodologies: Pairs work (pages 6–7).
After an appropriate time for personal reflection and scoring, invite students to share their scores with a member of the class they feel knows them reasonably well. Students give each other feedback to ascertain whether they agree with the scoring:

- Has their partner been too hard on themselves or not hard enough?
- Has their partner overlooked any good personal qualities?
- Are there any other personal qualities (not on the list) that the partner can identify?

The quality list is derived from www.authentichappiness.sas.upenn.edu. Go to the section called 'VIA Strengths for Children' under 'Questionnaires', which measures 24 strengths in more detail. You will need to register if you want students to take part in the questionnaire.

## BACKGROUND INFORMATION

> 'These questionnaires measure character strengths and aspects of happiness. All are yours to use at no charge. For each one, you'll immediately receive your score and see how it compares to the scores of others who have used this website. We'll keep a record of your scores, so that you can return later and see how far you've progressed. To see your earlier scores, log in and choose the Test Center link.

> *You must complete our free registration form to use the questionnaires. Once you are registered, you may log in whenever you like to use them again or view your scores.*
>
> *Your responses to these questionnaires will be used in research about happiness, but your email address, name and password will not be included with them. We use them only to give you access to your own records and to send information about the website, if you agree to receive our emails.'*
>
> *www.authentichappiness.sas.upenn.edu*

**ACTIVITY: FURTHER WAYS TO SELF-ASSESS (Student's Book, page 105)**

> **5. The websites featured in Source 3 are a starting point when thinking about future careers. Explore these to help you identify the types of skills and qualifications you will need to develop for the career path you would like to follow.**

This activity encourages students to work individually to explore websites that provide support, advice and signposting to a range of careers. You may decide that you would like them to carry out their research outside the lesson and then perhaps bring back their results to share with the whole group.

- The www.direct.gov.uk website offers plenty of help to students to find the career that's right for them. It takes them through a possible range of job profiles and provides action-planning tools.
- The www.connexions-direct.com/jobs4u site provides case studies and a job-search database.

> **6. What are the qualities you need to develop in order to help you achieve what you want to in the future?**

Having researched the skills and qualifications needed for a particular career, students should be encouraged to consider what qualities they need to support their pathway; for example:

- if medicine is the choice, it will require determination, the willingness to make sacrifices with your social life whilst studying, being objective about people
- if the chosen career is in retailing, it will require stamina, resilience and determination to keep going when work is difficult or quiet, approachability.

# REVIEW AND REFLECTION

**ACTIVITY: SELF-REFLECTION (Student's Book, page 105)**

> **7. Complete this sentence: 'One new thing I've learned about myself today is …'.**

Hear feedback from volunteers and encourage reflection on the link between new learning and future planning.

# Topic: Rights and responsibilities at work

| Notes | Young people entering the 'world of work' should understand that both employer and employee have responsibilities to ensure a good relationship ensues. Employees' rights help protect workers, but trade unions can extend this protection by offering specific support.<br><br>In this topic students will learn about the expectations future employers will have of them and their rights as employees. They will consider their responsibility as students and the effects that not being responsible could have in school, and whether or not the effects would be the same at work. Students will learn about the role of trade unions and the support they offer to employees. |
|---|---|
| Learning outcomes | **In this topic students will learn about:**<br>■ relationships between employers and employees<br>■ what trade unions are and how they protect their members.<br>**They will explore:**<br>■ the rights that all employees have at work<br>■ the expectation employers have of their employees<br>■ methods used by trade unions to support their members. |
| Links to Economic Well-being PoS | **2.1 Self-development**<br>**b** Students should be able to identify major life roles and ways of managing the relationships between them.<br><br>**3 Range and content**<br>**c** The study of economic well-being and financial capability should include rights and responsibilities at work and attitudes and values in relation to work and enterprise. |
| Links to SEAL outcomes | **Empathy**<br>Students can see the world from other people's point of view. |
| Links to ECM outcomes | Enjoy and achieve ■ Make a positive contribution ■ Achieve economic well-being |
| Assessment opportunity | See Topic: Creating a Curriculum Vitæ; Activities 2 & 3: My CV (page 171) |
| Resources | ■ Student's Book (pages 106–107)<br>■ Appendix (see the CD): Active Learning Methodologies:<br>    □ Brainstorming (page 3)   □ Whole-class work (page 7) |

# STARTER ACTIVITY

Ask students to look at the list of employer responsibilities in the Student's Book (page 106) and to write down any they think should be added to the list.

The statutory responsibilities are in the Student's Book, so encourage students to think about the less obvious things that employers could provide; for example, crèche facilities for young children, canteen area, etc.

# MAIN ACTIVITIES

### ACTIVITY: RESPONSIBILITIES (Student's Book, page 106)

> **1. a) Make a list of all the different responsibilities you think an employee should have; for example, being punctual.**

Run this as a brainstorm. See Appendix (on the CD): Active Learning Methodologies: Brainstorming (page 3).

Possible answers could be:

- punctual
- appropriate dress
- work hard

- enthusiasm
- politeness
- professionalism

- good communication
- reliable
- honest.

> **b) Go through your list. Highlight which are also appropriate to you at school.**

Most of the answers to part a) should also apply to this part of the activity. Encourage students to think about the reasons why; for example, if you are regularly late you will disrupt lessons as teachers have to stop to add to the register.

> **2. Discuss the following:**
> **a) Are you always as responsible as you should be in school? If not, why not? If yes, why do you think it is important to be responsible?**

Encourage students to be honest and reflect on their own attitudes to school and responsibility. Ask students to share their ideas.

> **b) What happens when someone behaves irresponsibly at school? What is likely to happen if someone behaves irresponsibly at work? Are there any differences?**

Students should hopefully acknowledge a significant difference between the two, i.e. in school students are given numerous chances; they may be given appropriate sanctions, but the school is there to help them, whereas in the world of work if an employee is irresponsible they may be given a warning but will eventually lose their job. This could have an impact when applying for future employment as references may be called.

**ACTIVITY: UNIONS AND STRIKE ACTION (Student's Book, page 107)**

> **3. Why are trade unions important for employees when we already have employment laws that are in place to protect workers?**

Possible answers include:

- Employment laws clearly define the role of the employer and rights of the employee.
- Trade unions are a supportive body for employees that can help if employees' rights aren't being met.
- Trade unions will also champion other causes such as pay rises and large-scale redundancy.
- Trade unions help identify and police employees' rights.

> **4. Read Source 2. What would be the impact of strike action by British Airways cabin crew?**

Possible answers include:

- delays for flights
- passengers stranded abroad
- damaged reputation/credibility/customer relations
- loss of business/income
- damage to employer–employee relations
- inconvenience to holiday-makers, business travellers, etc.

> **5. Most of the teachers in your school will be part of a union. What would be the impact (both short and long-term) if they voted to strike over pay and conditions?**

Possible answers include:

- trust between teachers/students/parents might be damaged
- child care issues for parents, possible need to take day(s) off work
- parents' business/income affected
- impact on education, particularly for students with exams
- students fall behind.

> **6. Can you think of any jobs in which workers might not be allowed to strike? Why would they not be allowed?**

- It is illegal for police to strike, but they could adopt a work to rule, which would have an impact on services.
- Nurses are legally allowed to strike, but are encouraged only to do so if it is not detrimental to patient care.
- Prison officers are legally allowed to strike but have a 'no strike' voluntary agreement in their contract.
- The armed forces are not allowed to strike, although in recent years there has been talk about an armed forces federation which would be similar to a trade union.

> 7. The organisation the National Union of Students (NUS) is a union set up for students. Imagine that you are setting up a student union in your school. Produce a leaflet/poster/manifesto outlining what you stand for, what services you would provide, and the rights and responsibilities students, staff and the school have. The NUS website may help you with some ideas – www.nus.org.uk.

Encourage students to think carefully about the different things they would want to introduce. There may be a temptation from students to consider obvious, less important issues such as 'no school uniform'. A class discussion on some of the issues would be a good way to start. See Appendix (on the CD): Active Learning Methodologies: Whole-class work (page 7).

Possible ideas could include:

- quality of food in canteen and prices
- help to interview new staff
- school environment
- health education
- drop-in sessions.

# REVIEW AND REFLECTION

**ACTIVITY: JUST A MINUTE (Student's Book, page 107)**

> 8. In pairs play a game of 'just a minute'. You must talk for one minute about rights and responsibilities at work without pausing or hesitating. Your partner needs to listen carefully to see if you repeat yourself. Once you have had a go swap with your partner.

This game can be played in pairs, or as an alternative invite five or six students to the front of the class to talk. When one of the students pauses, hesitates or repeats themselves it continues to the next person. When the minute is up the last person to speak is the winner.

# Topic: Employment opportunities

| | |
|---|---|
| **Notes** | Employment opportunities for young people will vary across the country. If they have aspirations to follow a particular career ambition then they may need to be prepared to move to where the work is. This could mean a change in lifestyle and upheaval from their local area.<br><br>In this topic students will investigate employment opportunities at a range of scale: local, national, European and global. Students will also consider the factors that could influence their decisions about moving from their local area and why it can be a difficult choice to make. |
| **Learning outcomes** | **In this topic students will learn about:**<br>■ local, national, European and global employment opportunities<br>■ different ways they can search for work<br>■ the different factors to consider when seeking work abroad.<br><br>**They will explore:**<br>■ types of jobs that are available in different locations<br>■ useful places to search when looking for employment<br>■ the pros and cons of working abroad. |
| **Links to Economic Well-being PoS** | **2.2 Exploration**<br>a Students should be able to identify, select and use a range of information sources to research, clarify and review options and choices in career and financial contexts relevant to their needs.<br><br>**3 Range and content**<br>d The study of personal well-being should include the range of opportunities in learning and work and changing patterns of employment (local, national, European and global). |
| **Links to ECM outcomes** | Enjoy and achieve ■ Make a positive contribution ■ Achieve economic well-being |
| **Assessment opportunity** | See Topic: Creating a Curriculum Vitæ; Activities 2 & 3: My CV (page 171) |
| **Resources** | ■ Student's Book (pages 108–111)<br>■ a range of local newspapers with job sections<br>■ internet access<br>■ atlas<br>■ map of the UK |

# STARTER ACTIVITY

Go to the following web link http://news.bbc.co.uk/1/hi/talking_point/8090086.stm which displays an interactive map featuring stories about children at work around the world. Ask students to select some of the countries and read the stories about what other children do. Now ask students to compare their own lives with the stories. Discuss the similarities and differences. Introduce the concept to students that although they may not be paid they are already at work each day whether at school or at home. This activity could also be done without the web link by simply asking students to make a list of the work they do at home.

# MAIN ACTIVITIES

### ACTIVITY: CATEGORIES OF WORK (Student's Book, page 108)

> 1. a) Using a selection of local newspapers, look through the jobs sections and make a note of how many jobs you find in each of the categories in Source 1.

This activity is to give students an initial idea of the local job market. Students could work in pairs. As they look through, ask students to make a mental note of any interesting features about the jobs. The categories of jobs can be found at the adult careers learning resource guide.

> b) Discuss the following questions.
> - Which category of job was the most and which was the least common?
> - What does this activity tell you about the local labour market?

The answers to these questions will vary depending on the newspapers used, region, etc. Lead a discussion about student's views on these questions and ask them to consider whether or not the jobs are:

- high or low paid
- need low or high qualifications
- new or traditional
- require experience or no experience.

Students may need prompting with some of these points as they may not know what is considered high or low pay (the average Briton earns around £28,000), or what some qualifications are. Students will hopefully find a range of jobs that fit a range of the categories.

> - Which jobs are most likely to be there in the future? Why?
> - Which jobs are most likely to disappear in the future? Why?

These are both difficult questions to answer as students will hear about all sorts of jobs in which people are being made unemployed, and the answers will vary from region to region. More likely however is that manufacturing industries will continue to decline in this country as products can be made cheaper elsewhere, whilst technology and IT-based industries will continue to grow. Building and construction is also likely to recover slowly from recession.

> ■ **Are there any jobs that you have found that are of interest to you? If yes, explain why you are interested in them; if no, explain what type of job you are interested in and why.**

Students could be encouraged to share their ideas with the class and give reasons for their choices.

> ■ **Where else could you get information about local jobs?**

Possible answers include:

- local newspapers
- local job centre
- organisations such as Connexions
- internet
- local store advertising.

## ACTIVITY: LOOKING FOR WORK (Student's Book, page 109)

> 2. a) Go to **www.direct.gov.uk/en/Employment/Jobseekers/LookingForWork/index.htm**. Click on 'Find a job now' and then 'Search for a job'. Simply type in a job that is of interest to you and click 'Search'. You will be presented with a list of jobs from all over the country. Glance through the list and click on any that take your interest.
>
> b) Choose 10 different jobs, and for each one mark their location on a map of the UK. You may need to use an atlas to help you find the different locations. Next to each location write down what the job is, wages and any other key information.

This activity will require the use of the internet so that students can research different jobs in the UK. Once they have found their jobs students need to mark the locations of the jobs on a map of the UK.

Students should realise that if they are unable to find jobs locally, they may need to move to where the work is.

> c) In small groups discuss the locations you have found for your particular job. Would you be prepared to move? Are you likely to find the same job locally? How would you feel if you had to move away from family and friends?

This activity highlights the fact that the friends and family relationships students have whilst at school will change dramatically if they look for work elsewhere and sacrifices may have to be made if students wish to fulfil aspirations. Encourage students to share their views with the rest of the class.

**ACTIVITY: WORKING IN EUROPE (Student's Book, page 110)**

> 3.  **Source 2 shows that the number of British people working in Europe is not evenly distributed. Give reasons why more British people choose to work in Germany, Ireland, Spain, France and the Netherlands than any other European countries.**

Possible answers include:

- some of the countries speak English
- large British communities are already established
- good weather
- close to the UK.

> 4.  **Using the internet, go to www.eurojobs.com. Think back to the jobs you looked at in Activity 2 (Student's Book, page 109) and use the website to search for similar jobs. Are the details similar?**

Students should be able to see that the jobs they are interested in are likely to be available elsewhere in Europe. If they are unable to get a job in the UK, they may choose to move abroad. They may decide that the quality of life would be better and move anyway.

> 5.  **What incentives would you need to pack up, leave Britain and work in a European country? Discuss you reasons in pairs.**

Possible answers include:

- higher pay
- relocation package
- cheaper tax rates
- better quality of life
- better climate
- quick transport links back to the UK if needed.

**ACTIVITY: MIGRATION, MEDIA AND PREJUDICE (Student's Book, page 111)**

> 6.  a) **Why do you think that newspapers and other media sources write such provocative headlines as those in the Student's Book (page 111)?**

Possible answers include:

- sell more newspapers
- increase advertising revenue (the better the story, the more papers sold, the more companies will pay to advertise as more people will see their product)
- political agendas.

> b) **What is the likely impact on the individuals and communities being referred to in such headlines?**

Possible answers include:

- reinforce stereotypes
- increase prejudice/racism/discrimination
- social unrest.

**ACTIVITY: WORKING ACROSS THE WORLD (Student's Book, page 111)**

> 7. Make a list of all the positive and negative factors of moving outside of the EU to work.

Possible answers include:

**Positive:**

- new cultures
- better climate
- better quality of life
- lower tax rates
- new experiences.

**Negative:**

- don't understand culture
- long way from home
- moving cost
- miss family.

Encourage students to consider which column outweighs the other. Which are the most important factors; for example, for many, family bonds will be too great to move.

# REVIEW AND REFLECTION

**ACTIVITY: WHAT ABOUT YOU? (Student's Book, page 111)**

> 8. a) Can you ever see yourself moving away to work? If so, how far do you think you are likely to go – national, European or global?

Encourage students to share their answers and explain why they would or wouldn't be prepared to move abroad. Would this mean that their employment opportunities could be limited?

> b) Do you think your attitude will change with time? Explain your answer.

Encourage students to consider what might happen as they get older; for example, married with children, may want a new start (consider those who move to Australia for a better quality of life). Do they want more adventure? Maybe they will have to move where the work is.

# 11 Business and Enterprise

## Topic: Business structure and organisation

| | |
|---|---|
| **Notes** | As more and more people become self-employed and set up their own businesses, it is useful for students to know how businesses structure and organise themselves, as this may be a pathway they choose to follow.<br><br>This topic gives students an overview of the two main types of business structure and how a business can be organised within these models. Students will look at the strengths and weaknesses of each model and investigate the structures used by well-known companies. They will also look at the structure used in their own school before considering the type of model they would use if they were to set up their own business. |
| **Learning outcomes** | **In this topic students will learn about:**<br>■ different types of business structure<br>■ how well-known businesses are structured<br>■ how business structures can be organised.<br><br>**They will explore:**<br>■ the advantages and disadvantages of tall and flat business structures<br>■ how businesses are structured and organised depending on their product/service<br>■ the structure and organisation of their school. |
| **Links to Economic Well-being PoS** | **1.4 Economic understanding**<br>a Understanding the economic and business environment.<br><br>**3 Range and content**<br>b The study of economic well-being and financial capability should include the organisation of different types of business, and workplace roles and identities. |
| **Links to SEAL outcomes** | **Social skills**<br>Students can communicate effectively with others, listening to what others say as well as expressing their own thoughts and feelings. |
| **Links to ECM outcomes** | Make a positive contribution ■ Achieve economic well-being |
| **Assessment opportunity** | See Topic: The world of business; Activity 5: Marketing a product (pages 193–194) |
| **Resources** | ■ Student's Book (pages 112–114)<br>■ Appendix (see the CD): Active Learning Methodologies:<br>□ Pairs work (pages 6–7)<br>■ Internet access |

# STARTER ACTIVITY

**ACTIVITY: WHAT MAKES A SUCCESSFUL PRODUCT? (Student's Book, page 112)**

> **1. a) Make a list of the latest gadgets you have bought recently or would like to buy.**

Students simply make a list of all the products they have recently bought or would like to buy. The list may be full of expensive and largely electrical gadgets which will make parts b) and c) of the activity easier to complete.

> **b) Choose one from your list and give reasons why you think it has become so successful.**

Possible answers include:

- good advertising
- additional upgrades, new applications, styles that are available; e.g. cases, etc.
- novelty factor
- makes life easier/better
- replaces an existing version and does it better.

> **c) Speak to two other people in your class to find out what product they chose and the reasons they think their product became successful. Were their reasons for the product's success the same as yours?**

Encourage students to discuss their ideas. Hopefully they will find that their reasons for stating why their product was successful will be similar to others'. This activity could then be taken further by asking students to decide which the most important reason for success is; for example, making life better might be seen as the most important for obvious reasons.

# MAIN ACTIVITIES

**ACTIVITY: WHICH IS THE RIGHT TYPE OF BUSINESS STRUCTURE? (Student's Book, page 113)**

> **2. Using the information from sources 1–4 on Student's Book pages 112–113, produce two spidergrams showing the advantages and disadvantages of the two main types of business structure.**

Students should use the information from pages 112–113 to complete this activity. They should consider for each whether or not the advantages outweigh the disadvantages.

> 3. a) **Choose one of the well-known companies below. Use the internet to research the type of business structure it uses. Before you carry out your research, try and predict the type of business structure you would expect the company to use based on what you know about the company already. Were you right?**
>
>    **NIKE    BP    TESCO    VODAFONE    TOYOTA    McDONALD'S**
>
>    b) **Discuss your findings as a class:**
>
>    - **Is there one business structure that is more common than the others?**
>    - **If so, why do you think this is?**
>    - **Why do you think an appropriate business structure is so important?**

This activity is to help students understand in further detail how well-known companies are structured. Students can simply type terms such as 'Tesco business structure' into a search engine to find relevant information in both text and graphical form. Ask students to print out relevant graphical examples. Encourage students to share their findings with each other to see if there is one particular type of structure that is more favoured than another and the reasons for this. Some of the diagrams that students find may appear tall, but are in fact flat and have a number of layers simply due to the size of the company; for example, Toyota.

NIKE: flat        TESCO: flat        TOYOTA: flat
BP: tall          VODAFONE: flat     McDONALD'S: tall.

Students will find that there is a mixture of business structures in the list because the structure is suited to the product on offer; for example, Nike trust its employees to make decisions within the different departments without having to go back and seek approval. However, McDonald's wants a uniform approach across their business which helps keep costs down, and therefore operates a tall structure.

> 4. **What type of business structure does your school use and why?**

Discuss students' answers as a class. The structure will vary depending on the type of school and size. If a school has a very traditional structure, i.e. a head, two deputies, four assistant heads, heads of subject and heads of years, Key Stage heads, teaching staff, etc, it could be considered to be a tall structure.

Students should use the advantages and disadvantages in the Student's Book to explain why they think this type of structure is most appropriate.

**ACTIVITY: ORGANISING A SCHOOL (Student's Book, page 114)**

> 5. **Although your school isn't a profit-making business, it does provide a service. Using the information about business structures and organisations, produce a business structure for your school. You would obviously start with the head teacher at the top. Before you begin you may wish to work with a partner to make a list of the different roles you know that staff do in your school; for example, deputy heads, assistant heads, heads of year, department heads, etc.**

Ask students to use what they have learned about business organisations to draw out a structure for their school. Depending on how well known staff are, they may need help with staff roles and positions. Encourage students also to include canteen staff and cleaners as they are all part of the organisation. Students may find it easier to work in pairs or small groups for this activity.

> **6. Imagine you are going on *Dragons' Den*. In pairs, think of a product you would want to get funding for. Pitch your product to your partner, explaining the type of business structure you would employ and how you would organise it.**

In pairs, encourage students to think about an existing or new product. See Appendix (on the CD): Active Learning Methodologies: Pairs work (pages 6–7).

Students should pitch their product to their partner but concentrate on the type of business structure and organisation they would use. Students will again need to consider the advantages and disadvantages and factors such as the size of the business and the product being sold; for example, if it is a small company that designs websites, it is likely to be a flat company organised by function as there may only be a handful of people employed.

# REVIEW AND REFLECTION

> **Can you think of other examples in which structures similar to those you have discussed about businesses and your school are needed? Make a list of your ideas.**

Encourage students to share their answers; these may include government, police, church and football clubs. Use this opportunity to remind students about the importance of appropriate structures.

# Topic: The world of business

| Notes | To set up a successful business it is important to understand and use correct economic and business terminology. As more people are encouraged to set up their own business, the successful ones will be those that have considered all the factors and have a clear vision for their organisation.<br><br>In this topic, students will learn about key economic and business terminology and the importance of having a detailed business plan if they are considering their own business. They will also investigate the importance of effective marketing through the use of the 5Ps and how well-established companies use them to great effect. |
|---|---|
| Learning outcomes | **In this topic students will learn about:**<br>■ the importance of a detailed business plan<br>■ key economic and business terminology.<br><br>**They will explore:**<br>■ what is needed for a successful business plan<br>■ definitions of economic and business terminology. |
| Links to Economic Well-being PoS | **1.3 Risk**<br>**a** Understanding risk in both positive and negative terms.<br>**b** Understanding the need to manage risk in the context of financial and career choices. |
| Links to ECM outcomes | Enjoy and achieve ■ Make a positive contribution ■ Achieve economic well-being |
| Assessment opportunity | Activity 5: Marketing a product (see pages 193–194)<br><br>**End of Key Stage Statement – financial capability**<br>Learners are able to:<br>■ demonstrate a range of enterprise skills when working independently and with others, and critically evaluate a wide range of goods and services from the consumer's point of view. |
| Resources | ■ Student's Book (pages 115–117)<br>■ Appendix (see the CD): Active Learning Methodologies:<br>  □ Small group work (pages 6–7)   □ Research and presentation (page 8)<br>■ Internet access |

# STARTER ACTIVITY

**ACTIVITY: EMPLOYED OR SELF-EMPLOYED? (Student's Book, page 115)**

> 1. Discuss why you think more and more people in the UK are setting up their own businesses.

Possible points raised in discussion could include:

- redundancy during the recession has seen more people set up their own business due to the shortage of jobs
- inspiration through TV shows such as *Dragons' Den*
- being your own boss is an attractive idea
- flexible hours
- new idea/gap in the market that people want to exploit.

This idea is developed further in later topics in the chapter.

# MAIN ACTIVITIES

**ACTIVITY: BUSINESS PLANS (Student's Book, page 115)**

> 2. Why are business plans so important when setting up a new business?

Possible answers include:

- clear reasons are established for setting up the business
- clear thought is given to the marketing of the product
- management and staff know their roles and responsibilities
- financial assessments can be made which, if realistic, are more likely to secure funding such as bank loans
- provide a benchmark demonstrating good organisational management
- set out plans for future growth.

**ACTIVITY: THE LANGUAGE OF BUSINESS (Student's Book, page 117)**

> 3. Make a copy of the table below. Put each of the economic and business terms in Source 1 into the correct category.

| Organisation | Money | People | Product | Publicity |
|---|---|---|---|---|
|  |  |  |  |  |

Some of the answers in the following table could fit into more than one category.

| Organisation | Money | People | Product | Publicity |
|---|---|---|---|---|
| ■ Business<br>■ Industry<br>■ Management | ■ Accounting<br>■ Assets<br>■ Cash flow<br>■ Depreciation<br>■ Expense<br>■ Finance<br>■ Fixed cost<br>■ Forecast<br>■ Liabilities<br>■ Net income/<br>profit<br>■ Net worth<br>■ Opportunity cost<br>■ Payback period<br>■ Profit margin<br>■ ROI<br>■ Revenue<br>■ Sales prospect<br>■ Variable cost | ■ B2B<br>■ B2C<br>■ Contract<br>■ Entrepreneur<br>■ Supplier | ■ Product<br>■ SWOT<br>analysis | ■ 5Ps<br>■ Target<br>market |

**4. Is there one category that is more important than any of the others in the successful running of a business? Explain your answer.**

Students should have realised that money/financial terminology is often the most common when referring to business. The reason for this is obvious, as a business is about making money and increasing profits. After students have written their answers, ask some to read them out and get other students to feed back. Although money may be referred to the most in this activity, students need to be aware that to run a successful business all factors are as important as each other. Discuss the reasons why with students; for example:

- If the product/service is no good, reputation will suffer and the business will fail.
- If the product/service is good but the publicity isn't, no one will know about the product and it won't sell.
- If the sale price is too low, no/little profit will be made; if it is too high, fewer will be sold resulting in the same problem.
- If the company is disorganised, decisions about a range of issues may not be made and therefore other problems will follow.

Encourage students to come up with other ideas.

**ACTIVITY: MARKETING A PRODUCT (Student's Book, page 117)**

> 5. Choose a well-known company or brand and explain how it achieves the 5Ps marketing mix. An example for McDonald's can be seen in Source 2.

The 5Ps of marketing a product is a simple tool that clearly highlights the factors that need considering when launching a business, product or service. By ensuring the 5Ps have been considered, business is more likely to be successful than if some are missing; for example, launching a product in the wrong place could mean that people don't have the finances needed, or that they are loyal to a well-established equivalent.

Working in small groups, students can research one of the companies in the Student's Book or select one of their own. Using the internet, students should research the company and note down examples of how their company has used the 5Ps as a marketing tool to increase sales. They could then present their findings to the class. See Appendix (on the CD): Active Learning Methodologies: Small group work (pages 6–7) and Research and presentation (pages 6–7).

**Example: McDonald's 99p saver menu**

- Right product: fast food, on the go – ideal for busy and fast-paced lifestyles
- Right price – 99p: keeping it under a pound encourages more people to buy it and makes the consumer think they are getting a bargain. Profit may not be high on some of the 99p saver menu items
- Right people: Aimed at all, but the advertising is particularly targeting teenagers, who could be out with friends and wanting to grab a quick bite to eat – 99p is affordable for this age group
- Right place: McDonald's restaurants are found everywhere
- Right publicity: adverts are at bus stops and in newspapers and magazines likely to be read by teenagers, and during the commercial breaks of teenage television shows such as *Hollyoaks*.

---

### End of Key Stage Statement – financial capability

Learners are able to:

- demonstrate a range of enterprise skills when working independently and with others, and critically evaluate a wide range of goods and services from the consumer's point of view.

### Assessment activity:

For this assessment activity it is suggested that students work in teams. The object of the task is for students to produce a presentation to the rest of the class showing how they would market a particular product of their choosing. The groups will need to consider the 5Ps of marketing and how each would apply to their product. They will need to consider the following and produce appropriate work to present to the class:

- posters/leaflets to advertise the product
- TV/radio advertising promotions
- surveys finding out people's views and target market
- where and how the product will be sold
- promotional offers that would be included to encourage people to buy the product
- price lists
- the product itself.

---

**Assessment method – peer assessment**

Each group presents to the whole class. Following the presentation, peers are asked to stay in their working groups and identify:

- at least one thing they liked about the presentation content
- at least one thing they liked about the presentation style
- one thing they think could have improved the presentation content
- one thing they think could have improved the presentation style
- whether the presentation would convince them to buy the product.

# REVIEW AND REFLECTION

**ACTIVITY: RISK-TAKER OR NOT? (Student's Book, page 117)**

6. Can you ever see yourself setting up your own business? Do you see yourself as a risk-taker or not? Explain why.

Encourage students to consider the question and then share their answers as a class. Lead the discussion to consider why students would or wouldn't be prepared to take a risk in setting up their own business.

# Topic: The how and why of business financing

| | |
|---|---|
| **Notes** | We need businesses to be successful for all the benefits they bring, particularly in terms of employment opportunities. It is important for businesses to seek finance that is most appropriate to their needs and will lead to sustained growth.<br><br>In this topic, students will look at the different options businesses have with regards to securing funding and why this is important. They will also have the opportunity to apply their knowledge to different scenarios to reinforce their understanding of the funding options. |
| **Learning outcomes** | **In this topic students will learn about:**<br>■ the reasons businesses need financing<br>■ the types of finance available to businesses<br>■ the importance of businesses in society.<br><br>**They will explore:**<br>■ internal and external finance<br>■ the advantages and disadvantages of different types of finance<br>■ which types of finance are most appropriate for which products. |
| **Links to Economic Well-being PoS** | **1.3 Risk**<br>b Understanding the need to manage risk in the context of financial and career choices.<br><br>**1.4 Economic understanding**<br>a Understanding the economic and business environment.<br>b Understanding the functions and uses of money.<br><br>**2.3 Enterprise**<br>i Students should be able to demonstrate and apply understanding of economic ideas.<br><br>**2.4 Financial capability**<br>c Students should be able to explain financial terms and products.<br><br>**3 Range and content**<br>g The study of economic well-being and financial capability should include a range of economic and business terms.<br>j The study of economic well-being and financial capability should include how and why businesses use finance. |
| **Links to SEAL outcomes** | **Social skills**<br>Students can work and learn well in groups, taking on different roles, co-operating with others to achieve a joint outcome. |
| **Links to ECM outcomes** | Enjoy and achieve ■ Make a positive contribution ■ Achieve economic well-being. |
| **Assessment opportunity** | See Topic: The world of business; Activity 5: Marketing a product (pages 193–194) |
| **Resources** | ■ Student's Book (pages 118–119)<br>■ Appendix (see the CD): Active Learning Methodologies:<br>☐ Pairs work (pages 6–7)  ☐ Brainstorming (page 3)<br>☐ Whole-class work (page 7)  ☐ Research and presentation (page 9)<br>■ Internet access |

# STARTER ACTIVITY

### ACTIVITY: WHY BUSINESSES NEED FINANCE (Student's Book, page 118)

> **1. a)** In pairs make a list of all the reasons you can think of why new businesses need finance.

Get students to work in pairs to brainstorm some reasons. See Appendix: Active Learning Methodologies: Pairs work (pages 6–7) and Brainstorming (page 3).
   Possible answers include:

- set-up costs
- buy supplies
- rent or buy a building
- transport
- stock
- advertising.

Students are likely to come up with lots of other ideas. During feedback put their ideas on the board and then ask them to make a copy in preparation for part b) of the activity.

> **b)** Choose a particular type of business of interest to you and number each reason for finance in your list in order of importance for your choice.

Ask students to number their reasons in order of importance. There is likely to be a range of different views about which items are more important for businesses to spend money on. This should help the students understand how difficult it is for businesses in the real world. Explain to students that if a business spends money on one product, then it can't spend it on something else. This is known as 'opportunity cost', which is featured in the previous topic.

> **c) Discuss:**
> - **Was it difficult to number your reasons in order of importance?**

There may be a mixture of answers to this question as students will start at different points, i.e. without set-up costs there would be nothing to advertise; not enough spent on stock could mean the business loses customers; not enough spent on advertising could mean not enough product sold; not enough product sold could mean that loans can't be repaid; too much on new premises or equipment could lead to a shortage of money to buy stock, etc.

> - **If so, what does this suggest about the difficulties businesses have when starting up or allocating finance?**

There has to be a balance when first setting up so that all required items/ expenditures can be financed.

> - **Were there any reasons that had to be financed for the business to work?**

Encourage students to share their ideas as a class about the difficulties businesses face. See Appendix (on the CD): Active Learning Methodologies: Whole-class work (page 7).

# MAIN ACTIVITIES

**ACTIVITY: BUSINESS FINANCING (Student's Book, page 119)**

> 2. **In small groups choose one or two of the different types of business finance in Source 1 (look up any terms you don't understand in the glossary). Use the internet to research:**
>
>    a) **how the finance is given**
>    b) **examples of this type of finance.**
>
>    **Feed back the information you have found to the class.**

Students simply need to grasp the basic concept about how each type of business finance actually works. This knowledge will be used in Activity 3.

# BACKGROUND INFORMATION

*Trade/store credit*
*This is the easiest way that companies obtain funding. Companies buy goods and services and have anywhere from seven days until six months to pay for them; when companies need more credit from suppliers the financial controllers will negotiate longer credit terms or larger credit lines, which means being able to access larger amounts of money, from a number of different suppliers. This can work well because the creditors do not want the customer to go into bankruptcy, taking their money with them.*

*Lease/hire purchase*
*Instead of buying equipment, many companies choose to lease it – this is a form of financing. Cars, computers and heavy equipment can be financed for short periods or indeed longer periods. If it is a short period it is referred to as an operating lease and at the end of the lease the property is still useful and is returned to the finance company. Long-term leases are ways of funding a purchase rather than buying the temporary services of a piece of equipment. These are often referred to as capital leases. For capital leases, the leased assets and the financing liability are recorded on the leasing company's books as though the company had bought the equipment outright.*

*Business mortgage*
*This is best suited for financing the purchase of land/buildings for a business. Mortgages are ideal for a firm with property at the heart of its business. The benefits are that mortgages:*

- *offer tax benefits*
- *mean that businesses are not at the mercy of a landlord*
- *are tailored to suit repayment expectations and budget*
- *limit capital expenditure, freeing up cash for business ventures to get the business underway or put into other investments.*

*Bank loan*
*Approaching a bank for a business loan is a common route to funding a company start-up. Any lender will want to review a detailed business plan before imparting any funds and will expect collateral, in the form of either the firm's assets or a property. Securing a loan against the latter is risky. Benefits are that people tend to feel more comfortable with a loan because they have a greater understanding of it.*

**Factoring**

*Factoring is an efficient way of getting paid more quickly by essentially 'selling' your invoices to a specialist company. It is an up-and-coming form of business finance, usually adopted by many businesses early on in the piece to avert future, often fatal, cash flow crises. Benefits are that it provides near-instant invoice payments, frees up your time (as you're no longer chasing customers for payment) and many factoring companies offer a 'trial' so you can see if it is right for you before you commit.*

**Overdraft**

*An overdraft occurs when withdrawals from a bank account exceed the available balance. In this situation a person is said to be 'overdrawn'. If there is a prior agreement with the account provider for an overdraft protection plan, and the amount overdrawn is within this authorised overdraft limit, then interest is normally charged at the agreed rate. If the balance exceeds the agreed terms, then fees may be charged and higher interest rates might apply.*

**Venture capital**

*Venture capital is the term used when investors buy part of a company. A venture capitalist places money in a company that is high risk and has a high growth. The investment is usually for a period of five to seven years. The investor will expect a return on the money either by the sale of the company or by offering to sell shares in the company to the public.*

**Grant**

*There is a range of government support available to people wanting to start their own businesses, not only through grants and other funding but also through numerous advisory, guidance and information services. Government grants are almost always awarded for a specific purpose or project and are usually for proposed projects only – not for those that have already started. Most require businesses to match the funds they are being awarded. In other words, the grant covers a proportion of the money needed, whilst the business supplies the rest. Depending on the location, type of business and what the business needs the funds for, it may be eligible for a number of grants and support.*

*Adapted from information found on www.ecademy.com*

---

3.  **A business uses finance for a variety of reasons. Make a copy of the table below. Using the information in Source 2, decide which type of finance is most appropriate for each. Add any other examples you can think of.**

| Overdraft/credit | Bank loan | Hire purchase/ lease | Mortgage | Company profits | Investor |
|---|---|---|---|---|---|
|  |  |  |  |  |  |

Possible answers:

| Overdraft/credit | Bank loan | Hire purchase/ lease | Mortgage | Company profits | Investor |
|---|---|---|---|---|---|
| Temporary shortage of funds 'Buying' goods before paying for them | Start-up costs | Equipment Company cars, lorries, etc. Computers New premises (not owned by the business) | Buying property/premises | Advertising New staff Research and development Staff training | Take part ownership (% can be negotiated) of company (useful if company has large debts) New experience/ ideas Start-up costs |

> 4. Read each of the scenarios in Source 3. For each one give advice as to
>    what type of finance is most appropriate and why. You may need to advise
>    using more than one source of finance.

If students have understood how the different types of finance work, they should be
able to work out which type of finance is most appropriate for the scenarios.
Encourage students to justify their choice of finance through discussion with each
other and as a class.

Answers:

- Internet DVD business: bank loan / overdraft / credit
- Gardening business: company profits / bank loan or hire purchase (depending
  on the cost of the lorry)
- Florist business: mortgage / company profits / credit.

# REVIEW AND REFLECTION

**ACTIVITY: THE IMPORTANCE OF BUSINESS (Student's Book, page 119)**

> 5. Why are businesses, whatever their size, so important to our society? What
>    problems would we have if businesses couldn't get finance when they
>    needed it?

Encourage students to share their ideas with the class. Possible answers include:

- businesses create work for people
- trade between businesses sustains jobs
- businesses create new products and services
- without business finance, unemployment would increase.

# Topic: Entrepreneurship and risk

| | |
|---|---|
| **Notes** | Entrepreneurial and enterprising attitudes are the backbone of the business world. It is important for students to understand that despite what they hear on the news about businesses collapsing, new enterprises can succeed if the risks are considered and managed well and the people involved have the qualities needed to be successful.<br><br>In this topic students will look at what it means to be enterprising and how to go about managing the risks associated with setting up businesses. Students also look at the qualities needed to be a successful entrepreneur and how risk can be reduced in business. |
| **Learning outcomes** | **In this topic students will learn about:**<br>■ what it means to be enterprising<br>■ managing risks within business<br>■ the qualities needed to be a successful entrepreneur.<br><br>**They will explore:**<br>■ successful entrepreneurs and the products that have made them successful<br>■ SWOT analyses and how they can be used to reduce risks in business<br>■ the role of teamwork in enterprise. |
| **Links to Economic Well-being PoS** | **1.1 Career**<br>**c** Understanding the qualities, attitudes and skills needed for employability.<br><br>**1.2 Capability**<br>**a** Exploring what it means to be enterprising.<br><br>**1.3 Risk**<br>**a** Understanding risk in both positive and negative terms.<br>**c** Taking risks and learning from mistakes.<br><br>**2.3 Enterprise**<br>**e** Students should be able to show drive and self-reliance when working on work-related tasks.<br>**f** Students should be able to develop approaches to working with others, problem-solving and action planning.<br>**g** Students should be able to understand the key attitudes for enterprise …<br>**h** Students should be able to develop and apply skill and qualities for enterprise. |
| **Links to SEAL outcomes** | **Self-awareness**<br>Students can identify their strengths and feel positive about them.<br><br>**Motivation**<br>Students can view errors as part of the normal learning process.<br><br>**Social skills**<br>Students can work and learn well in groups, taking on different roles, co-operating with others to achieve a joint outcome. |
| **Links to ECM outcomes** | Enjoy and achieve ■ Make a positive contribution ■ Achieve economic well-being |
| **Assessment opportunity** | See Topic: The world of business; Activity 5: Marketing a product (pages 193–194) |
| **Resources** | ■ Student's Book (pages 120–123)<br>■ Appendix (see the CD): Active Learning Methodologies:<br>  □ Brainstorming (page 3)   □ Small group work (pages 6–7)   □ Group work (pages 6–7)<br>■ Internet access |

# STARTER ACTIVITY

**Think about a typical school day, from waking up in the morning to when you go to bed. Now make a list of all the things you have that make your life easier or more comfortable; for example, hot running water, cold milk from the fridge, television, alarm clock, car, bike, etc.**

**Consider for a moment how different you life would be if you didn't have these things; for example, no hot running water because boilers weren't invented. Everything you use every day has been made and when something is made there is an opportunity to make money from it.**

Discuss the concept with students that anyone can be an entrepreneur, but their success may largely depend on the product and the competition, amongst other things. Encourage students to think about how different their lives would be if they didn't have all their 'mod cons'.

# MAIN ACTIVITIES

## ACTIVITY: WHAT MAKES AN ENTREPRENEUR? (Student's Book, page 121)

**1. a) Make a list of any other entrepreneurs you may have heard of. You may need to think of a product or service and then who created it; for example, the Dyson vacuum cleaner was created by Sir James Dyson.**

You could run this activity as a brainstorm. See Appendix (on the CD): Active Learning Methodologies: Brainstorming (page 3).
Possible answers include:

- Sir Alan Sugar
- Sir Richard Branson
- Sir James Dyson
- Peter Jones
- Theo Paphitis
- Karren Brady
- Anita Roddick.

Students are most likely to give the names of those entrepreneurs they have seen on television. Try to encourage all the names listed to be researched in part b) of the activity, along with any others that students think of.

Students may think of some products but not know who invented them. In such cases they could use the internet at the start of part b) of the activity to find out the entrepreneur associated with their product; for example, iPad – Steve Jobs.

**b) Select one of the entrepreneurs from your list and use the internet to research them in greater detail. Produce a case study similar to the one about Duncan Bannatyne in Source 1. Try to find out the following details:**

- **when they were born and other personal details**
- **their first invention/idea**
- **how they got their idea 'up and running'**
- **when they made their first million**
- **any setbacks they had**
- **what they have done since.**

For this activity students should use the internet to research their chosen entrepreneur and find out the information indicated in the activity. Students could also include any other information they think is important, such as charities that the entrepreneurs have set up or work for.

> c) **In small groups, talk about what you found out about your entrepreneur.**
>
> - **What do they all have in common?**
> - **Did they all face the same problems?**
> - **What do they tell you about being successful?**

Put students into groups to discuss their findings. See Appendix (on the CD): Active Learning Methodologies: Small group work (pages 6–7).

By covering a range of entrepreneurs, students should begin to realise that anyone from any background can succeed if they have the right idea/product/service and a positive approach. Students should share their findings with others in their group and discuss the challenges that their entrepreneurs had to overcome, and the qualities they have which has led to their success. Possible ideas for the qualities are enthusiasm, people person, bedside manner, commitment, hard working, exciting, energetic, etc. Ask students to share ideas as a class once they have had time to discuss in small groups.

These ideas will be looked at in more detail in the next section of the Student's Book.

### ACTIVITY: ENTERPRISE QUALITIES (Student's Book, page 122)

> 2. **For each enterprise quality in Source 2 (on page 121 in the Student's Book) explain the problems an entrepreneur would face if they didn't have that quality.**

Possible answers include:

**Persuasion**
If an entrepreneur didn't have skills of persuasion they may not be able to get people to see the potential in their idea and as a result money may not be invested. They may not be able to recruit workers to support them for the same reason.

**Idea**
If the initial idea is no good, they won't get support from anyone as it would be difficult to see the idea/product succeeding.

**Energy**
If the entrepreneur hasn't got the energy and enthusiasm to take their idea forward they won't get support. People won't invest in or work for someone who they think lacks the commitment.

**Risk**
Without taking risks the idea won't 'take off'. This is risk in terms of investing their own money, possibly giving up another job to work on their idea full time; the risks must be calculated, however. The other three factors must already be in place.

> 3. **Rank the qualities in order from the most important to the least and explain your order. Is this possible to do?**

There is no right or wrong answer to this question as it is a matter of personal opinion. It does provide a good discussion point between students and hopefully they should realise that rank ordering the qualities is difficult as all qualities are needed; for example, if you take away a good idea, then you will find it difficult to **persuade** people to take **risks**, etc. Students should work in pairs or groups to complete this activity.

> **4. Why is financial risk such an important issue and a reason why many people are put off? For example, think about what could be lost if the business venture failed.**

Students can work individually, in pairs or in small groups to complete this activity. Possible answers include:

- if money to invest is borrowed against a home, that home could be lost
- bankruptcy
- stress and strain on family
- unemployment for employees
- lack of security and benefits compared to working for a larger company.

> **5. Do you think you have the qualities to be an entrepreneur?**
> **6. Do you think others think you have the qualities to be an entrepreneur?**

Students could initially write an answer and then use this as a discussion point in pairs, small groups or as a class. See Appendix (on the CD): Active Learning Methodologies: Group work (pages 6–7).

Encourage students to be honest and share their ideas about the qualities they have and whether or not they think others would agree with them. This is a good activity as it gets students to consider how they are perceived by others, but needs careful management if personal comments are made that could cause offence.

### ACTIVITY: SWOT (Student's Book, page 122)

> **7. a) Read Source 3. In pairs or small groups, carry out a SWOT analysis on the Apple iPad. Use the internet to research it further if you need more specific detail.**

Answers could include:

**Strengths:**

- well-known brand
- new technology
- is the best merge between a smart phone and a notebook
- it's slim, light-weight, has a great design and is a multi-touch screen device, with a super-fast wi-fi connection
- internet pages launch almost immediately so you can get the ultimate experience in internet browsing
- it comes with various features and a full-size keypad in order to best fit user needs
- the display is very good, user interface is easy to use as it is almost the same as on the iPhone
- high-quality battery, lasting up to 10 hours
- different versions to suit different needs; e.g. with or without 3G, different memory capacities.

**Weaknesses**

- price: expensive for a hybrid between a phone and a notebook
- it still lacks a series of important features:
  - □ no USB, only the iPhone port for everything
  - □ no camera
  - □ no multi-tasking
  - □ a virtual keyboard is not as easy to use as a real keyboard.

**Opportunities**

There is the opportunity to make more money through:

- the sale of apps from the i-Store
- accessories such as covers, external keyboards, stands, etc.
- upgrades.

**Threats**

- high price, which could see customers buy cheaper alternatives
- it may compete with other Apple products, including the iPhone and MacBook
- competitors coming into the market with newer more technically advanced products.

> **b) Work in pairs to make a list of ways in which you can minimise the threats and maximise the opportunities for the iPad; for example, launch a webcam add-on to take pictures and use for video-calling over wi-fi.**

One of the big criticisms of the iPad at its launch was the lack of a camera for internet video-calling or USB ports to add existing webcams. The new version of the iPad is set to include a camera.

# REVIEW AND REFLECTION

**ACTIVITY: A WORLD WITHOUT RISK (Student's Book, page 123)**

> **8.  What would the world be like if we didn't have entrepreneurs who are prepared to be enterprising and take positive risks?**

Possible answers could be:

- fewer new inventions/gadgets, etc.
- most things we have today wouldn't be here
- higher unemployment/fewer jobs
- lower incomes
- lower standard of living
- more physical labour as many of the things that machines do for us today would have to be done by hand.